"This book will inspire, encourage, and lift your spirits! It will help you live life with more passion and power. Read it, and re-read it. You'll be glad you did!"

"Dr. Bev Smallwood has created a vital resource that can offer real help and hope, saving thousands the despair and hopelessness that comes from unforeseen, devastating circumstances."

"You may well find your very own story hidden among the pages of this life-changing book. If you have ever wrestled with the question 'Why me?' or longed for freedom from confusion, bitterness, or anger, you need only open to any chapter in this handbook of hope!"

"Bev Smallwood's total dedication to help people fight to rebuild their broken and shattered lives shines through every page. I have personally stood on the edge of the water screaming, 'This wasn't supposed to happen to me!' I thank God for this beautiful offering. It changed my life as it answered questions, challenged my faith, and brought more hope, healing, and strength. It can do the same for you. Don't wait another day. New life has just begun."

THIS *WASN'T* SUPPOSED TO HAPPEN TO ME

THIS *WASN'T*
SUPPOSED
TO HAPPEN TO
ME

10 MAKE-OR-BREAK CHOICES
WHEN LIFE STEALS YOUR DREAMS AND ROCKS YOUR WORLD

BEV SMALLWOOD, Ph.D.

THOMAS NELSON
Since 1798

NASHVILLE   DALLAS   MEXICO CITY   RIO DE JANEIRO   BEIJING

Published in Nashville, Tennessee by Thomas Nelson. Thomas Nelson is a trademark of Thomas Nelson, Inc.

Published in association with Cythia Zigmund, Literary Services, Inc., P.O. Box 888, Barnegat, NJ, 08005, www.literaryservicesinc.com.

Thomas Nelson, Inc. titles may be purchased in bulk for educational, business, fund-raising, or sales promotional use. For information, please e-mail SpecialMarkets@ThomasNelson.com.

All Scripture quotations, unless otherwise indicated, are taken from The Holy Bible, New International Version®. © 1973, 1978, 1984, International Bible Society. Used by permission of Zondervan Bible Publishing House.

Scripture quotations noted NASB are taken from New American Standard Bible®, © 1960, 1977, 1995 by The Lockman Foundation. Used by permission.

Scripture quotations noted KJV are taken from The Holy Bible, King James Version.

Library of Congress Cataloging-in-Publication Data

Smallwood, Beverly.
    This wasn't supposed to happen to me : ten make-or-break choices when life steals your dreams and rocks your world / Bev Smallwood.
        p. cm.
    Includes bibliographical references.
    ISBN 978-0-7852-2811-0 (hardcover)
    1. Choice (Psychology)—Religious aspects—Christianity. 2. Decision making—Religious aspects—Christianity. 3. Dreams—Religious aspects—Christianity. 4. Life change events—Religious aspects—Christianity. 5. Adjustment (Psychology)—Religious aspects—Christianity. I. Title.
    BV4509.5.S633 2007
    248.8'6—dc22

                                                                    2007032045

Printed in the United States of America

07 08 09 10 11 QWM 9 8 7 6 5 4 3 2 1

**To my mother,
Wilma Joyce Hannaford.**

Widowed at thirty-six, she maintained an unwavering faith in
God, an optimistic attitude, and sacrificial service to others.
My mom didn't let difficult circumstances control her.
No matter what challenges she faced, she never gave up
and kept her sweet spirit to the end.

I first learned the ten choices I've recorded in this book
by watching my beloved mother's life.

Contents

CONTENTS

Acknowledgments

First and foremost, I thank God for giving me the inspiration, strength, and endurance to write this book. Thank You, Lord, for the privilege of being a channel for Your love and healing.

I can't say enough positive things about my literary agent, Cynthia Zigmund of Literary Services, Inc. Without Cindy's vision, her extensive knowledge of the publishing world, her diligent attention to detail, and her patient guidance and support, this book would not be in your hands. I appreciate you so much, Cindy.

It's been such a joy to work with Debbie Wickwire at Thomas Nelson. Beginning with our first conversation, I felt a heart connection with Debbie, as she really understood and shared my sense of purpose about this book. Debbie has superb insight about what it takes to capture the attention of and make a difference to the reader. Thank you for believing in me, Debbie.

Jennifer Day at Thomas Nelson helped me stay on track with the technicalities and legalities of publishing a book. Thanks also to Jennifer Stair, whose keen eye and editing talents helped to polish this manuscript. I also appreciate the many others at Thomas Nelson who made it happen.

I'm thankful for the support of so many others who worked tirelessly behind the scenes to help prepare this book and the book proposal. The excellent coaching of Amanita Rosenbush, Sam Horn, and Susan Page helped me create a compelling book proposal. Rhonda Hogan was a whiz at getting the necessary permissions. Several top-notch assistants helped in tasks like scheduling and transcribing interviews, typing, editing, formatting, and keeping the office flowing while I juggled speaking, counseling, and writing. Thank you, Deana, Linda, Beth, Kathy, Dana, and Kitty.

I want to say a special thank you to the many people who were willing to be interviewed so that their stories could be used to help others. In so doing, my friends, you chose once again to extract good from your own heartbreaking experiences. I admire you for that. I also appreciate the thousands of clients who have trusted me to share their journeys, teaching me more about the ten choices than I ever taught them. With their identities protected by case composites and changes in some of the details of their circumstances, I've drawn on many of their insights in this book.

I'm blessed to have so many friends who have encouraged, listened, shared suggestions, helped me make important contacts, and simply been there for me. You know who you are. I am deeply grateful for the treasure of your friendship.

Finally, I absolutely would not have made it without the love and support of my family. My children, Greg and Amy, consistently demonstrate their love for me through emotional support, prayers, and practical help. My grandchildren, Joseph, Ethan, Scarlett, and Eli, are the lights of my life. So many times in this long and exhausting process, I've been reenergized by an enriching conversation, the exhilarating fun of play, or a warm hug and kiss. I love you all.

Introduction

"Is this the last time we'll see him, Mommy?" I clung to my mother's hand as we stood before my father's open coffin.

She answered gently through her tears. "It's the last time on this earth, Bev, but he'll be waiting for us in heaven."

Somehow, I couldn't find much comfort in that. At barely nine years old, I couldn't make sense of this. Only seven months ago, my thirty-eight-year-old father had been strong and healthy. We played and laughed together on his breaks from the long hours of ministering, studying, and preaching. I would curl up in the recliner and snuggle with him. I was "Daddy's girl."

During the months when the cancer was spreading, he lost ninety pounds. We prayed—everybody did. Surely my father wouldn't die. After all, he had dedicated his life to helping others. He was a man who was so committed to his calling that, too weak to stand without bracing himself, he held on to the pulpit and preached the Sunday before he passed away. Yet despite all the prayers, he did die, and my mom and I had to go on. To make matters worse, my family had been living in a home the church had furnished for the pastor. However, the pastor didn't live there anymore, so my mother and I were forced to move. Not only had I lost my father, I'd lost my home.

I had questions, big questions. I was reeling from a crisis of faith. *Why did this happen?* I kept wondering. It didn't seem fair. I thought God was supposed to protect us from pain like this.

This was the first, but definitely not the last, time I would ask deep, searching questions after my dreams, hopes, and plans were sabotaged by personal trauma. I know firsthand what it's like to be a teenage mother, trying desperately to finish college, struggling to make it in a marriage in which alcohol made life predictably unpredictable. I know what it's like to go through divorce, questioning and berating myself for not being able to fix it. At another time in my life, I lost my best friend to cancer. I've had the experience of receiving a dreaded medical diagnosis: incurable and potentially fatal. My life has been threatened at the business end of a gun. I've walked with someone dear through the anguish, the legal consequences, and, thank God, the recovery process of drug addiction. I lived through seven years of being the sole caretaker for my mother, losing her day by day to Alzheimer's—the thief of memory and self.

I'm not having a pity party here. I just want you to know at the outset that I'm no stranger to the things I write about in this book. True, I haven't experienced exactly what you're going through, but believe me, I've struggled with my own thoughts and emotions. I've been faced with the ten choices we'll discuss, and I can't say that I've always made the right ones at first. However, I can personally testify to the effectiveness of the strategies I'll share with you. I know from experience that sometimes you don't see results immediately. Rather, they come gradually, when you act with persistence and determination.

BUT YOU DON'T UNDERSTAND MY SITUATION!

It's true: I don't know exactly what you've been through. I wish I could sit with you for as long as it takes and hear your story, as I have with literally thousands of others over twenty-five years of practice as a psychologist.

Whether you are reading this book because you survived a weather catastrophe, lost a loved one prematurely, experienced a disabling accident, lost your job, been a victim of crime, watched your home burn, experienced a major health crisis, found out your child did the unthinkable, had your identity stolen, been betrayed by someone you trusted, or experienced any of hundreds of other life events that were just not supposed to happen, this book is for you.

I agree with you that your situation is unique in many ways. Even people who have been through the same traumatic experience bring to their reactions different backgrounds, different thought habits, healthy or unhealthy coping skills, differing levels of optimism and self-confidence, and individual personalities. People are not robots. They are complex, intricately and wonderfully made. As a result, they interpret events differently, attach different meanings, and react in their own unique ways when attempting to recover.

Yet I've discovered that there are significant similarities in the experiences of those whose lives have taken sudden tragic turns. The most important of those similarities is the power of choice on which the quality of their future depends. Catastrophic experiences do alter your life. However, it is up to you what the ultimate nature of that change will be.

In preparing this book, I have analyzed my observations of the successes and failures of thousands of trauma survivors, both in my psychological clinic and in the seminar room. I've provided you with a solid foundation from spiritual wisdom literature and scientific research. Further, I've interviewed nearly a hundred trauma survivors, shared insights from (disguised) clinical clients, and incorporated my own personal experiences with tragedy.

I've simplified my findings by distilling them into ten major choices, turning points on the road to emotional healing. Mind you, *simple* doesn't mean *easy*. However, as you make the journey through your own unfamiliar, frustrating, frightening personal wilderness where all the old road signs don't seem to apply anymore, you need to avoid potholes and keep from getting stuck. That's why it's critical to understand the choices you can make and the actions you can take.

In this book, I will also share with you the amazing comfort of divine strength. I can tell you that God has always been there for me, even when my troubles were of my own making. I have known the comfort of his presence, the kind of peace that doesn't make rational sense, and a calling and sense of purpose that have kept me going when I couldn't see the way.

(One of my favorite scriptures reads, "And we know that in all things God works for the good of those who love him, who have been called according to his purpose."[1] This does not mean that all things *are* good; rather, this verse assures us that if we align our hearts with God's principles, He will bring good out of the most difficult scenarios. I've witnessed this over and over in my own life. No matter what has happened, God has helped me to *grow* through the experience, not just *go* through it. No matter what your religious background or spiritual perspective, know that the principles I will share with you *work*.)

MEET YOUR TRAVELING COMPANIONS

The people you'll read about in this book had at least one thing in common: one day they were on top of the world; the next day the world was on top of them! They were going about their normal, everyday lives when a traumatic event rocked their world. They experienced

> *One day you're on top of the world. The next day the world's on top of you!*

something that was never supposed to happen to them. Reeling from shattered assumptions and broken dreams, they questioned and searched, trying desperately to understand what happened. In this book, you will learn from their struggles and their victories.

Whether you've been in exactly the same situation as these people or not, you've at least "been there." You know all about the shock, the anger, the hurt, the confusion. So do I. I understand.

ENCOURAGING NEWS AT THE OUTSET

You and I are about to walk hand-in-hand through some of the most grueling, puzzling, and painful of life's struggles. As we begin this journey together, I want to emphasize some good news: this storm you are passing through can and will change you. I know, that doesn't sound like good news, but remember, *how* it changes you is up to you. Disaster doesn't have to bury you. It could bring out aspects of your character that will make you stronger, more compassionate, less judgmental, and wiser. You do have a choice in the matter. You cannot always control *whether* you get hit by personal tragedy, but you can always choose how you react to it.

> *I've learned, the hard way, that some poems don't rhyme, and some stories don't have a clear beginning, middle, and end. Life is about not knowing, having to change, taking the moment and making the best of it without knowing what's going to happen next.*
>
> —GILDA RADNER

In *Man's Search for Meaning*, Viktor Frankl describes prisoners in concentration camps who chose to walk through the huts comforting others, giving away their last piece of bread. Frankl noted that everything can be taken away except one thing: the power to choose one's attitude in any given set of circumstances.[2]

An abundance of psychological research demonstrates convincingly that it is neither the amount nor intensity of the stressors in your life that are the strongest predictors of future emotional problems. Rather, the key to adjustment is what you believe about the events in your life and how you respond to them—your thoughts, your attitudes, and your actions.[3] While you can't control many of the troubles that land in your lap, you can successfully work on how your mind processes what happened, how you behave as a result, and whether you embrace a more spiritual point of view. Your own reaction is one aspect of life circumstances over which you can exert influence. Once you understand that, you will be much more likely to demonstrate resilience and exhibit fewer long-term stress-related symptoms. Not only can you survive, but you can also emerge as the butterfly from the darkness of the cocoon, beautiful after the struggle.

Most of us have heard the oft-quoted Serenity Prayer: "Lord, grant me the serenity to accept what I cannot change, the courage to change what I can, and the wisdom to know the difference." Yet after a traumatic event, many people spend their thoughts and efforts trying to do just the opposite. They try to change the unchangeable, making futile attempts to rewrite history, persuade another person be different, or convince the world to change its mind. They want to make things "unhappen." All this does is set them up for failure.

Sometimes people act helpless in the face of what they actually could fix. They come to believe that no matter what they do, it won't make any difference, falling into the inertia commonly known as "learned helplessness." These individuals are destined for stress-related emotional disorders of all kinds: depression, anxiety, Post-Traumatic Stress Disorder, physical stress disorders, and even suicide.

But it doesn't have to be that way! Here's the truth of the matter. Even though adversity creates negative feelings at first, the suffering caused by deep and hurtful losses can also create lasting personal benefits. Not convinced yet? It's hard to believe it in the middle of the pain you're in? Stay with me.

THE TWO SIDES OF ADVERSITY

I remember an old *Hee-Haw* routine. (For younger readers, that was a corny country comedy television show.) Junior Samples and one of the other regulars on the show were discussing a series of events that had transpired:

> "My friend went up for his first ride in a little private airplane."
> "That's good."
> "No, not exactly. He was looking out and got excited and fell out of the dang thing."
> "Ooh, that's bad."
> "Well, not really. There just happened to be a big haystack right where he fell."
> "Wow! That's good!"
> "Not so fast. There was a pitchfork in the haystack."
> "Oh, no. That's bad."
> "But . . . he missed the pitchfork."
> "All right! That's good!"
> "Yeah, but he missed the haystack too."

What happened to you—is it good or is it bad? For a while after adversity hits, you probably won't be lucid enough to ask this question because you'll be so sure that it's bad. Anger, disappointment, and grief are natural emotions resulting from unexpected personal disaster. There's no way around it—you will suffer, and we all know that suffering is "bad," right?

However, as time passes, a powerful paradox begins to emerge. In spite of the pain, you find yourself reaping certain life-changing benefits. In fact, in my seminars on organizational or personal change, I often hear a most interesting observation. I ask participants to consider this question: "What was the worst day of your life?" Then I ask them to identify the best day. Oddly enough, several people have listed exactly the same day for both! Therefore, the worst of circumstances brought out the best in them.

There are two sides to adversity. Troubles can defeat and destroy you, or they can stimulate a rate and depth of personal growth that isn't possible in calmer times.

How will adversity affect you? There's no way around it: when tragedy first hits and sometimes for long afterward, you will suffer. However, this suffering does not have to be your final destination. You can heal.

Unfortunately, some people never heal and grow because they allow bitterness to corrupt their spirits and rob them of the chance to build a happy future. Others stay wounded because they refuse to acknowledge that they have a problem. They carry the burden of hurt all by themselves and don't take advantage of the support of others. Still other people remain trapped in tossing endless questions at fate or at God. They hold on to the "Why me?" victim mentality or the chronic blame game. Putting into practice the strategies in this book will help you avoid all these pitfalls.

Every significant crisis in your life is a turning point. Make the right choices and you will undergo a positive transformation and develop strength. In this book, I'm going to show you how to make the choices that enable you to recover emotional health, rediscover meaning in your life, and formulate a revised plan for your future. You'll gain firsthand knowledge of how adversity can truly be a catalyst for lasting and significant positive personal change.

ADVERSITY'S POWER TO TRANSFORM

I believe God has placed in nature many illustrations of principles we humans need to understand. Let's talk about one of those natural phenomena, the diamond, which will bring into clearer focus the fact that the trouble you are facing can actually bring about a positive transformation.

Diamonds have been a source of fascination for centuries. They are imperishable and the hardest and most brilliant of all precious stones. Interestingly, the word *diamond* comes from the Greek word *adamas,* which means "unconquerable." Indeed, diamonds are formed after millions of years of pressure, pressure, pressure.

Diamonds form when carbon is crystallized by tremendous heat and pressure in the depths of the earth. Then the diamond-bearing ore is brought to the surface through volcanic eruptions. After the volcanic eruptions subside, these precious gems remain encased in solidified magma.

Not all diamonds are found where they first came to the earth's surface. Many are washed away in the topsoil, having traveled far away from their original locations before being discovered.

Do you see some similarities between the diamond's adventures and your own struggles? For starters, I'll bet you can relate to "pressure, pressure, pressure" that seems like it's lasted millions of years. Then, just when you think life might be calming down a little, the volcanoes begin. You're hit with one blow after another, and you wonder just how much you can take. Notice, however, that those very "volcanoes" are bringing up valuable substances within you. Life's volcanoes can help bring to the surface our strength and other positive qualities that have been buried deep within us. The process makes them available to us not only during the current crises, but also for the rest of our lives. Yet when we're in the midst of the chaos, it's hard to realize we're being molded and formed so that we are better human beings.

The diamond's travels after rising to the surface are often replicated in our own lives. Sometimes traumatic experiences cause you to have to go to physical places to which you wouldn't have voluntarily traveled if your life had proceeded normally. For example, would displaced hurricane survivors have chosen to move to their new locations had the storm not hit? Even if you remain in the same physical location after a difficult experience, you're taken to a whole new land emotionally. When this happens, remember that you may have been repositioned for unbelievable discoveries and opportunities you may otherwise have missed.

Like the diamond, you can emerge from your trials without being crushed. It all depends on how you respond to the heat, pressure, and volcanoes of life. Make the right choices, and you'll become stronger at the core, more beautiful, and more valuable to yourself and those around you. Remember—without heat and pressure, there would be no diamonds.

By trying, we can easily learn to endure adversity. Another man's, I mean.

—MARK TWAIN

WHAT IS NORMAL?

In my experience as a psychologist, I've found that people who are recovering from trauma are often relieved to learn that the emotions they are going through are normal. Until then, they

10

cannot quell the secret fear that they are going crazy. You've probably had strange and unfamiliar thoughts and chaotic emotions yourself. Maybe you've even told yourself, "I have really lost it this time!"

As you discover the similarities between your emotional struggles and those of others, you will gain comfort and a sense of control. Yes, these new thoughts and feelings are probably unfamiliar to you. However, they are *normal* reactions to a *very abnormal* situation. You are not alone, your reactions are not crazy, and you *can* get better.

DOES TIME HEAL ALL WOUNDS?

You've probably heard the advice given by well-meaning people: "Just give it time; time heals all wounds." And it's true—time does have a way of deintensifying the pain. But is that the same thing as healing? Should you just let time go by and hope for the best?

Some who have tried the "wait and hope" strategy have ended up in my psychological clinic. It is years after the traumatic event, and they are still trying to sort out the compounded damage to their confidence, relationships, or career. While they have "moved on" after the original trauma, they haven't really moved much at all. They still overreact to real or imagined threats. They are still unable to make rational decisions and maintain healthy relationships. They live with easily triggered hidden anger and grief just beneath the surface. All of this interferes with their most earnest attempts to go on living as if everything were all right. They are stumped and stymied, unable to fulfill their potential and follow courses of action that would give their life the most meaning.

Sometimes it is my clients themselves who offer me the most insight. One woman, whom I'll call Amanda, was trying to deal with the anger and grief that followed when her husband was killed

11

by a drunk driver. She and I had been discussing the hard work she had been doing and the progress she had made. Then the question of, "Does time really heal all wounds?" came up. If people just do nothing and hope everything returns to normal eventually, does that work?

Amanda answered wisely, "They say time heals all wounds. But it's kind of like breaking your arm. Over time, it will heal. But if it's not set properly, it will heal crooked. It will be weak and easily reinjured."

So no, time alone does not heal all wounds. It takes hard work, too. There is no shortcut or detour from the emotional struggle that leads to true recovery. Real recovery extends far beyond the lessening of pain. Its true purpose is to lead to the emergence of a stronger, wiser, more resilient person.

While time and distance can give you some perspective on the tragic events you've been through, they can also allow the wounds to be pushed under the surface and covered up. You might not feel the emotions intensely all the time, but that doesn't mean the wound is genuinely healed. When the wound is still raw and even infected, almost any bump can trigger the pain and remind you of the original trauma. Recovery requires diligence, patience, and difficult emotional work. You can do it though, step by step, and you can use this book as a tool to help you do it.

HOW BEST TO USE THIS BOOK

This Wasn't Supposed to Happen to Me is the result of my lifelong personal and professional search for real answers about how to deal with what I call the "unexpected unthinkable." It is my deepest desire that the principles, strategies, and stories I share in these pages will strengthen, encourage, and equip you to rise above what has happened to you and rebuild a meaningful life.

However, let me give you a heads-up about this book. Life is not easy, and neither is this book necessarily an emotionally easy read. Why? Because the stories I'll share are about real people going through real pain like you. Hearing about their hurts and struggles might initially trigger your own heartache as you feel along with them and remember similar details of the trauma in your own life. Don't run from it, though. You, too, can not only go through it, but you can grow through it.

This is not a book to read and put on the shelf. This is a book that can help you throughout the weeks and months and even years after your difficult experience. It's okay to read the entire book now. However, if right now the pain is fresh and you are too overwhelmed to read the entire book, then just find the chapter that speaks to the struggle you're having right now and read it. Then later, when you're able to think more clearly and see a bit farther down the road, you can come back and read more of the book, stopping to really reflect on chapters that correspond with the choices you face as you continue the process of healing and growth.

> *You may have to fight a battle more than once to win it.*
> —Margaret Thatcher

I encourage you to keep a notebook in which you write about new reflections, insights, and steps of progress. Gradually, you will put together some (not all) of the pieces of the puzzle, recover emotionally, and reestablish a meaningful life.

ARE YOU READY TO WORK?

Though you may be feeling powerless, you still have the power of choice! We're about to explore and take action on ten critical choices—emotional turning points that will make or break the rest of your life. Before I introduce the ten, however, allow me to show you an overall model that describes the experiences of most people reading this book.

You're going about your life *comfortably*, "knowing" where you are and where you're going and how things are going to be. (Or so you believe.) Then, *wham! Catastrophe* hits, in one form or another. At first you are reeling, out of control, powerless to turn back the clock and undo what has happened. Life has disobeyed the rules, and you are in the throes of personal or professional *crisis*. The good news is, you have the power of *choice*, and the choices you make during your crisis and afterward determine your future. Fall prey to the seduction of the ten negative choices, and you're doomed to a life of ongoing *calamity*. But exercise your God-given ability to make ten wise choices, and you'll have greater strength of *character* and a stronger sense of purpose.

When you truly consider the outcomes—calamity or character—it gets easier to make the right choices. Together we'll work on all ten:

1. Denial or Reality

2. Victimhood or Responsibility

3. Why or How

4. Doubt or Faith

5. Bitterness or Forgiveness

6. Guilt or Self-Forgiveness

7. Isolation or Connection

8. Depression or Grief

9. Avoidance or Courage

10. Powerlessness or Purpose

At each fork in this road, if you take the first option and head backward, you compound the losses of your trauma. However, take the right, "the road less traveled," and you will gradually and surely emerge a stronger and wiser person.

At the end of each chapter, you will have the opportunity to make a commitment to the wise choice. Read it, reread it, post it, memorize it if you like—but in any case, use it as a reference to guide your thoughts and actions as you move forward.

This is not a one-time choice after which you can say, "Phew! Glad that's done!" Yes, you make a firm, initial choice to pursue each of the ten positive courses of action, and then you must continue to affirm that decision each time you confront a situation that tempts you to stray back into negative territory. As you persist, those positive choices accumulate and become strong habits that will serve you well the rest of your life.

William A. Ward wisely said, "Adversity causes some to break, others to break records."[4] Which will it be for you? As you make these ten life-restoring choices and courageously act on your decisions, you will reclaim a life worth living.

Are you ready to take the first step?

1

"I'm Fine . . . Really!"

CHOICE #1: DENIAL OR REALITY

"I can't believe this is happening!" Linda shared with me. "That's what I said to myself over and over in those first few days after my husband of forty-one years was in the accident, and we were waiting endless hour upon hour in the ICU waiting room. When I would open my eyes in the morning after the little bit of restless sleep I'd gotten, it would hit me all over again. I really just couldn't believe it. I kept wondering, when will I wake up from this nightmare?"

Linda was describing the experience of denial, the kind that often occurs right after an unbelievable, shocking loss. As we'll see in a moment, this type of denial can actually be an adaptive protective shield that allows you time to assimilate the facts and keeps you from totally buckling emotionally at the enormity of what you are facing. You just can't take it in all at once. It would be too much.

However, denial can become pathological. A little later, we'll discuss the conditions under which this defense mechanism crosses that line, actually threatening your mental and physical health rather than protecting it. First, let's explore further what denial is and how it works.

DENIAL AS A DEFENSE MECHANISM

In general, defense mechanisms are psychological strategies used by an individual (and sometimes by a group) to cope with reality and to maintain self-image. Usually operating subconsciously, defenses serve to protect us from uncomfortable or unacceptable awareness of our circumstances or of certain aspects of ourselves. These mechanisms exist to relieve stress, usually by distorting reality in some way.

Even mentally healthy people use many of the various defenses throughout life. Used at the right time and in appropriate measures, they add to their sense of well-being through the reduction of harmful or painful emotions, enabling them to keep functioning in times of stress.

In general, denial is one of the most primitive, even childlike, of the defense mechanisms. The underlying premise of denial is, if you just "shut your eyes tightly," you can protect yourself, and others can't "see you." When I think about this, I'm reminded of something that happened on one of the gazillion trips I've made to McDonald's with my grandchildren.

Eli, my youngest grandchild, had been feeling the oats typical of a "terrible two" and had clearly disobeyed (again!) one of the safety rules in the McDonald's play area. The scolding tone in my voice made it plain that this was it; he was in trouble. Eli disappeared into the colorful tubes, and I awaited his emergence. However, I became distracted by a call on my cell phone, allowing him to sneak out of the playscape without my noticing him.

Did he find himself a great hiding place? No. I looked up and he was sitting in plain view on the floor against the wall, his little hands cupped over his eyes. He was confident that he had become invisible and that the ominous storm would pass him by. (Yes, he was really cute and it did tug at my heartstrings, but I managed to follow through.)

That day, Eli provided a vivid demonstration of the underlying fantasy about denial—just don't look at it or explain it, and it will go away.

Denial is a rejection of external reality that feels too threatening. Unconsciously, semiconsciously, or consciously, you refuse to perceive disturbing facts in order to ward off the anxiety they stimulate. But is this always a bad thing?

HAS DENIAL BEEN UNJUSTLY DEMONIZED?

If you ask me, denial has acquired an undeservedly bad reputation. In some therapeutic circles, the mere word is spoken with criticism attached. True enough, when denial is taken so far that it prevents your being able to cope with a real threat or obscures your ability to perceive the facts needed for problem solving, denial works against you. More about that momentarily. But often denial actually works for you.

You might think of the helpful type of denial as an "emotional circuit breaker." Think about the circuit breaker in your home electrical system. What's its purpose? To protect the system from shorting out in case of an overload of voltage. Your emotional circuit breaker acts in a similar way to prevent you from breaking down when you experience an unbelievable overload of emotion that, in the normal course of things, your own "system" is ill equipped to handle.

Now let's explore a couple of real-life examples of how denial can help you cope effectively with adversity. The first story demonstrates how denial helps work for you in the early stages of tragedy when you've just been hit with terrifying, life-changing information.

The doctor had just come into the family room at the ER to deliver quietly the deafening news: seventeen-month-old Jacob was dead. The autopsy would later reveal he had died of asymptomatic viral pneumonia. Only an hour before, his parents had gone in to check on him in his crib and found his body flaccid and his lips blue. They had given CPR and called 911. Little Jake was rushed by ambulance to the emergency room, but he could not be revived. Soon the hospital personnel began to bring in the paperwork, including the consent for an autopsy.

Fran, Jacob's mother, described it this way: "I didn't want to see the fact of his death in writing. They brought me a paper, and it had Jacob's name on it. It took me a moment. I physically winced and shook my head. The lady was very nice. She told me, 'Just take your time.' So I asked her to just point to where I needed to sign because I just couldn't look at the rest of it and see his name there. Because if his name was on an autopsy authorization, that would make it real."

At that early point in the nightmare, Fran's reaction was perfectly normal. Understandably, she was on emotional overload. The horror she was experiencing had a surreal quality. She told me that at the same time she felt unbelievable shock and grief, she also felt somewhat numb. Though she knew her beloved child had died, she just couldn't stand to see it in black and white.

I also observed this form of denial in operation when I made regular visits to my friend Mary, whose thirty-two-year-old son had lost control of his vehicle and hit a tree. He lay in a coma with a blood clot deep in his brain as we sat together in the ICU waiting room. She chatted cheerfully with all the guests that came to offer support. She smiled and even joked. I never saw her cry or even express the depths of her concern for her son. (Of course, that doesn't mean she didn't do it when she was alone.) Yet I knew how very much she loved her son.

Benevolent denial was at work, protecting her so that she could take in the facts little by little and maintain the hopeful and optimistic attitude she needed to go through this grueling phase of her son's recovery. She focused on the positive aspects of the doctors' reports and her own observations of the ways his condition was a little better today than it was yesterday. Though she intellectually acknowledged the seriousness of the injuries and the horrible possible outcomes, she did not dwell on those. You could say that she was in denial of the intensely negative possibilities, but was that a bad thing to do? I think not. When you get down to it, optimism and hope usually require a healthy dose of this type of denial.

I often work with cancer patients. Are their lives really threatened? Could all kinds of devastating things occur, no matter how long they live? Absolutely yes, on both counts. But consider how it would rob them of quality of life if they spent their time obsessing about potential death or pain. In a way, they have to be able to "deny" those things in order to live and make the most of their time. Yes, they must acknowledge their medical needs, take care of themselves, and undergo needed medical treatments. In addition, they gradually have to come to acceptance and peace about the possibility of making a transition out of life on this earth. However, if they don't have the emotional skill of shutting out the disturbing awareness of the worst, they won't be able to create the best today. (In fact, no matter where we are in life, that's an essential skill.)

WHEN DOES DENIAL BECOME DESTRUCTIVE?

Up to this point, we've talked about how denial can be beneficial. So how do you know when denial is becoming harmful?

Let's begin this discussion by looking at an example from the arena of addictions, a therapeutic specialty responsible for educating millions about the self-destructive potential of denial. Maybe the reason you are reading this book relates to addiction in a loved one or yourself. In the unlikely event that you have not been touched by addictions, you'll see from this example the self-sabotage rampant in people who practice pathological denial, either after a tragedy or as a habit in their daily lives. Meet a man I'll call James, who could be the poster boy for unhealthy denial.

Jennifer had sought my assistance to prepare her to conduct an "intervention" with James, her alcoholic husband. As you may know, an intervention is a factual, firm, and loving confrontation by a small group of people who care about an addicted person, with the goal being to persuade the individual to seek treatment. I had coached Jennifer and other family members to prepare a list of James's behaviors that were indicative of an alcohol problem, and we had rehearsed what to say in response to his likely defensive maneuvers.

When the big day came and the intervention was in progress, four nervous but determined family members stayed the course, one by one sharing their observations, their concerns, and their feelings. Predictably, James had an explanation for everything.

Jennifer had just shared the fact that James had been drinking in the mornings. His response: "Well, at least I'm not like those real alcoholics. I always have breakfast before I start drinking."

More often than not, interventions are catalysts for dramatic turnarounds. Unfortunately, in James's case it was not. His denial was so firmly entrenched that, despite the potential (and ultimate) loss of his wife, his job, and his dignity, he was unwilling to face the truth about himself. On the continuum of unhealthy or healthy denial, James was at the far left. That's pretty obvious to us, but it was not so obvious to James.

Because denial is largely subconscious, it's tough to know when you've crossed that point on the continuum when denial has become a problem that is impeding your recovery. Though we all use defenses to protect ourselves from pain when we are troubled, there is a time to dig deeper and face up to the pain so that you can heal.

THREE LEVELS OF DENIAL

Denial may be experienced at three levels. Which of these do you recognize in your current or past reactions?

You Don't Acknowledge the Facts

It's not uncommon to screen out information, pretending to yourself that certain facts don't exist. People may tell you things, you may read about things, or even see them with your own eyes . . . but you convince yourself there's no way that could be true. Later, you look back and ask, "Why didn't I see it?" You did, but at the time, you refused to acknowledge it. Denial is a powerful distorter of perceptions.

I remember a rather extreme example of this. I worked with a client who refused to believe that her son, who had been lost at sea in a storm, was dead. Because she never saw the body, she kept expecting him to come home, though five years had passed. Her denial of the facts lasted unusually long, as most of the time people soon come to terms with what has happened, though they don't want to admit its significance in their own lives.

You Don't Acknowledge the Practical Significance

You may acknowledge a fact, but not admit to yourself how big it is or how much it will affect your life in practical ways. This is what happened to David as he minimized the importance of some of his wife's newly distant behaviors:

"I told myself, 'Everybody goes through a few marital problems.' I didn't want to admit to myself what I later learned: my wife had been having sexual conversations with a guy on the Internet, had met him in a neighboring city on three occasions, and that was only the tip of the iceberg."

You Don't Acknowledge the Emotional Impact the Event Has Caused

I think this one is the most often used form of denial. You know what happened, you know it's significant—but you assure yourself and those around you that you are fine, in control. In other words, you either numb out, deceive yourself into thinking it really doesn't matter that much, or pretend to yourself and others that you are "strong."

Then little by little, as you become ready and able to handle it, the deep emotions often begin to surface, sometimes in a startling way. When this happens, you may think you've had a setback, but actually, you'll be moving forward in your recovery because you've progressed to an emotional readiness to deal with the realities.

It's a little bit like this. My friend's elderly mother has a problem with her stomach that really needs surgery. Yet she is about one hundred pounds overweight. The doctor wants her to lose at least fifty pounds before surgery, as he fears the possible complications from the extra weight. She hasn't been able to do that yet, but let's say that she did. When she has the surgery, she's going to have lots of pain, less energy, and less mobility for a while. Is she worse? Some of her symptoms are. She's in a more medically vulnerable state. But the reality is, she's better. She's on her way to genuine healing of the deeper problems.

That's the way it is when denial starts to break down and the emotions break through. There's pain. You feel worse. You feel vulnerable. But you're getting better. You've taken the next step toward real healing. Otherwise, you don't admit what an emotional wallop the traumatic experience has packed. As a result, the emotions build and begin to exact an even higher toll than is necessary. The inevitable reactions are delayed, and they deepen.

YOU HAVE A CHOICE: DENIAL OR REALITY

As we've already seen, denial can pad the initial blows and give you time to regain your equilibrium before taking the full brunt of the facts. However, its adaptive value is relatively short term.

More often than not, as time passes, denial is a barrier to good problem solving and adjustment. Its antidote is a healthy dose of reality. It's your choice. To help you make the best choice, let's explore the results you can expect from each option.

Denial Ups the Damage

While offering you temporary relief and a false sense of well-being, unhealthy denial exacts a high toll. Dan was among those who found that out the hard way. Dan's beloved wife, the mother of his one-year-old son, was killed in a one-car accident on the way to work. Here's what he told me.

"'I'm fine . . . really.' I must have used that phrase a thousand times. It started when two people from work came to tell me about the accident in which my wife was instantly killed. When they told me about it, I said, 'Okay, thanks for telling me. I've got to go find out about my son.'

"They offered, 'We'll drive you.'

"I said, 'No, really . . . I'm fine.' And I was very irritated that they wouldn't let me drive. My thought was, 'Okay, I've got this. I'll go and take care of things, and it'll be fine, and I'm sorry you had to tell me that, but I've got to go deal with this.' And I was just amazed and angry that they wouldn't allow me to drive myself after just having told me my wife was dead.

"And that was really pretty much the way I pursued the whole recovery process . . . I'm fine, and I can deal with this. Which, of course, I really wasn't."

Dan's reaction was understandable, given the immediate and overwhelming responsibility he felt for taking care of his son. He had to keep life going, no matter what. However, he shared with me later in the interview that swallowing his emotions cost him big-time, as it does so many others. Maybe you will personally recognize some of the following side effects:

1. *Unhealthy denial cuts off information needed for problem solving.* Dan never denied the fact that his wife had died. However, he failed to acknowledge feelings that boiled inside him after he lost the love of his life, his best friend, the mother of his long-awaited child. Without the awareness of how much pain he was really feeling, he could not learn healthy coping skills to deal with the pain. How could he deal with emotions that "didn't exist"? Yet the emotions did exist. The harder he tried to push them beneath the surface, the more they intensified.

Dan didn't feel that he could afford to acknowledge the true emotional impact of his wife's death. Another person, Jackie, experienced a level of denial that had even greater immediate, life-threatening consequences. To make matters worse, her denial was actually encouraged by the professional whose help she sought.

She told me, "I didn't have any of the classic symptoms, and I was very young. I was never sick. I was a single mom with a teenage son, and I was super busy. I had a very high-stress job, and I was a volunteer at the International Ballet. I did everything. One day I went to sign up as a volunteer for the ballet. I realized I felt too bad to do it, and I had to admit I'd been feeling bad for a while. I started to think about the fact that my normal routine had become to go home and take a power nap before I could go on to the next thing on my schedule. I had a small pain on my lower right side so that if I ate very much, it hurt. The logical solution? Just don't eat much. After several weeks, my 'solutions' hadn't changed the problems, so I finally decided to go to the doctor.

"I told the doctor, 'I don't feel well, but it's probably no big deal.'

"He said, 'Let's explore what your life is like. What do you do?'

"I began to tell him about being a single mother, having a teenager, having a stressful job, doing volunteer work. I avoided telling him about the intensity of the pain I was in, and I noticed he really didn't want to go there either. In fact, he stopped me with a reassurance: 'No wonder. Anyone would be tired with all the things you have on your plate. Maybe you need some medicine to help you stay calm.'

"So I took the tranquilizers, and I didn't let any of it slow me down. I kept on pushing. I was at work every day.

"Nevertheless, the pain was insistent. It became more and more difficult to ignore it. I finally decided it might be wise to seek a second opinion. Thank God, the second doctor chose to do a barium enema. We were all shocked when the test showed colon cancer. I had to have surgery immediately."

Jackie's strong will and determination, normally wonderful qualities, endangered her life. Unfortunately, the doctor's good intentions to calm Jackie's anxieties almost killed the patient he was trying to help.

Jackie's physical pain is similar in a way to emotional pain. Her pain was her body's red flag, waving to signal her to pay attention, to investigate the cause of the discomfort. This is instructive for those of us who experience emotional pain, sometimes long after tragedy. Pain that doesn't go away can be ignored for a while. But it's wise to stop, find out what's going on, and deal with it.

It's hard to admit the truth when the truth is painful. But

think about it this way: if something is occurring inside you, it is affecting you whether you acknowledge it or not. If you have pain, don't you want to know its origin so that you can work on it? Why not face the facts so that you have the information you need to begin to address the problem?

Jackie's pain eventually got through. What is your pain telling you? Maybe you are finished with something in your past, but the past isn't finished with you.

Some say the truth hurts. But does it really? We'll talk about that momentarily.

2. *Unhealthy denial makes you more defensive.* If there are facts you are trying not to see or feelings you are trying not to feel, you won't be overjoyed when others point out what you are ignoring. You may change the subject, secretly irritated. Or you may snap back some sarcastic comment. You may be more prickly, your fuse shorter than usual. If you listen carefully, you may hear yourself explaining to yourself or others why the apparent

> *Maybe you are finished with something in your past, but the past isn't finished with you.*

facts are not the real facts. You may even begin to detach yourself from people who keep pointing out what you don't want to hear, or even those who keep quiet about the beliefs you know they have. When you adopt the stance, "Don't tell me anything I don't want to hear," you shut yourself off from information essential to your recovery.

Another example came from a client I worked with recently, a mother who did not want to believe that her child was taking part in the rampant drug abuse she was hearing about among the students at her teenager's school. Despite rumors to the contrary, and in the face of evidence supplied to her by a concerned teacher, she continued to cling to false self-assurance. After all, she had raised him right; he knew better than such behavior. She wouldn't even hear me when I urged her to look at the handwriting on the wall. As a result, I'm convinced her son is still using drugs. And the likelihood is, right now the problem is growing into a monster.

In other words, when you dig your heels in, bristling at any suggestion that you don't know how you feel or what's true in your life, you miss the opportunity to address issues that are crying for your attention. Like the proverbial snowball growing as it rolls down the hill, denied and ignored problems become more pervasive, gradually taking over your life. Unfortunately, the only way out is for the pain to escalate to higher and higher levels until you can ignore it no longer. Trust me, that's not the best way to face the facts.

3. Unhealthy denial makes you susceptible to addictions as a means of escape. People in denial are easy prey for addictions of all kinds. That's because though you don't admit the pain, you still feel it. You feel you have to do something to bring relief.

Temporarily pleasurable substances and activities become seductive. Some sink into such life-engulfing habits as excessive drinking, drug abuse, or inappropriate sexual behavior. Others fall into the more socially acceptable addictions like workaholism or maniacal busyness. All of these can serve as temporary anesthetics, dulling your consciousness of the emotional pain you can't seem to shake. Yet their use is habit-forming. Though they provide temporary relief, it doesn't last. You turn to the substance or activity over and over, finding it less and less capable of giving you what you need. Despite this, denial prevents your admission that your behavior is out of control, handicapping your ability to correct your course. Slowly, you can become entrapped in addiction.

4. Inappropriate denial alienates you from available support.

When you refuse to acknowledge your emotional and practical needs, you cannot connect with resources that could speed your recovery. There are people in your life who want to be there for you, but they can't if you won't let them.

In addition to your family and friends, there are professionals who can facilitate your healing and help you get your life back on track. Books, recordings, and other information can help you know what to expect and how to deal with this crazy time.

With these resources available, why would anyone refuse to take advantage of them? Why would anyone let denial stand in the way of connecting with potentially helpful people or knowledge? One reason is fear, the fear of acknowledging the problem and dealing with the unknown. Another cause is pride, the type of pride that makes you resistant to admitting to being "flawed," or, in your eyes, "weak." It's been said that pride goes before a fall. Don't let yours cause you to trip and sink even deeper in the emotional hole dug by the bombshell that hit your life.

5. *Unhealthy denial keeps you stuck in an unreal world.* The world you may try to create is one in which "nothing bad can really affect me, I am in control, I'm never wrong, and nothing is my fault." This fake world, however, is never safe from the intrusions of reality. Though you may maintain bravado on the outside, a hidden anxiety nudges your insides. You forge ahead, trying to pretend everything is okay, but it's not . . . and you know it. The energy you need to move ahead in your life is being used up, and an emotional time bomb is ticking.

Reality Brings Repair

While denial sabotages your ability to move forward, the courage to face reality has important benefits. Let's look at three of those.

1. *Reality brings long-term relief of pain.* As we've all heard

before, "The truth hurts." Is that statement true or false? In a way, it's both.

It's true, because at first it hurts when you acknowledge the facts and feelings of a painful situation. In fact, when you begin to let yourself feel gut-wrenching emotions, the hurt can be almost unbearable. It's easy to want to run from that and ease the immediate pain by moving back into denial. You may be able to do that for brief intervals without a problem, giving you a breather from the pain. But if you stay there, you'll regress.

Even though the truth sometimes hurts short term, in the long run truth is your only salvation. Though it's initially painful, giving yourself access to the facts and being in touch with your emotional struggle gives you the information you need to do the hard work of healing. A life without truth is a life not worth living. Without truth, you cannot be your true self.

It was Jesus who said, "You will know the truth, and the truth will set you free."[1] But, as we all know, first it can really tick you off!

2. *Reality allows more effective problem solving.* In the scientific method, or any other method of problem solving, the very first step is, "Identify the problem." Before you can even begin to brainstorm ideas and create strategies to make things better, you have to have the facts you need to understand and conceptualize the problem accurately.

Without accurate problem definition, you may have the best of intentions, the strongest of resolves, and the most diligent of improvement efforts. However, you'll have disappointing results if you throw solutions at the wrong issues.

My pastor, Dwayne Higgason, told me about a recent experience that illustrates this point. Dwayne had purchased a carbon monoxide detector for his home. He was awakened in the middle of the night with the "beep, beep, beep" of the alarm. He stumbled out of bed to check to see if there was a problem and to reset the detector to silence the sound. Satisfied that there was no source for carbon monoxide in the house, he went back to bed. Momentarily, he was dismayed to hear the beeping again. He got up again, this time actually removing the battery to be sure that the noise would stop. At last, he would be able to get some much-needed sleep.

No sooner had his head hit the pillow than the alarm sounded yet again. Totally frustrated by now, he stomped into the kitchen, grabbed the detector, and stuffed it into a drawer, covering the noisy offender with towels. He had barely made it to his bedroom before the dreaded beeping sounds wafted throughout the house. This time he would be sure. He yanked the detector out of the drawer and took it out into the garage, where he threw it into his truck and slammed the door. Okay, there was absolutely no way now for this bionic machine to act up . . . no battery and the device was outside closed up in the truck.

Unbelievably, Dwayne had just closed his eyes when the familiar "beep, beep" rang in his ears. He sat up on the bed and reasoned, "This is impossible. Where is the beeping coming from?" All of a sudden, it hit him. It was his turn to be on emergency duty for the church. The beeping was coming from the pager sitting nearby in its cradle!

Dwayne had diligently tried multiple methods for correcting the wrong problem. His remedial corrective strategies were quite logical, *if* his conceptualization of the problem had been accurate. It was not. Realistic information is what you need to accurately define and address your problems.

3. *Reality facilitates your healing.* It takes a lot of psychological energy to dam the emotional flood. Exhaustion is the result of the constant tension created by the inconsistencies in what you are trying to believe or portray versus what you know in

your innermost "knower" to be true. All of that energy could be used instead to take you toward the real work of emotional healing.

Last week I was talking with a woman I'll call Cindy who had been creating big purple knots on her head from banging it against the wall of trying to "be good enough" to get her abusive, woman-izing husband to change. She said a strange thing to me: "I feel much better now that I've given up hope."

At first I internally resisted that statement, because I so believe in the power of hope. Then I realized what she was saying. She had come face to face with the reality that she was working from a false definition of the problem. She saw the futility of her efforts to be a better wife so that he would want to change. His efforts to blame her were misplaced, and his change (if he chose it) was his respon-sibility. Therefore, having faced that reality, she was free to address the real issues within herself—how she could set appropriate boundaries, take care of herself, and get out of the situation if that's what it took.

Like Cindy, when you get honest with yourself about the truth of your circumstances, about what you are feeling, and about what you can control, you've taken a most important step. You can begin to do the things that really matter.

ARE YOU IN DENIAL?

Maybe you've already recognized that you've been living too far from reality, or maybe you're still not sure. Your first action step will be to assess where you are right now by taking the following "Denial Quiz." Then I'll share with you seven more important strategies for courageously facing your truth so that you can move ahead in your quest for recovery from the trauma you have suffered.

Please use this scale to rate yourself on the statements that follow, indicating how true each is for you.

1—Very untrue of me
2—Untrue of me
3—Neutral
4—True of me
5—Very true of me

_____ 1. I believe I'm doing much better emotionally than others seem to think I am.

_____ 2. I've been able to stay strong, never or rarely showing my pain.

_____ 3. I try to stay busy so that I don't have to think about what has happened to me.

_____ 4. I find myself getting emotional at strange times, overreacting or secretly fighting tears about something that doesn't even seem to relate to me.

_____ 5. Comparing myself to others who have been through tragic experiences, I think I'm doing quite well.

_____ 6. I keep doing the same things over and over in an attempt to make my life better. Though I haven't seen the results I want, I believe if I only keep doing them long enough, things will change.

_____ 7. When something upsetting happens to me, I tell myself that it really doesn't matter to me.

_____ 8. I've always prided myself on my ability to keep excellent control of my emotions.

_____ 9. Since experiencing the trauma, I've been much more easily irritated, and I often take it out on people who don't deserve it.

_____10. Others have tried to convince me to get help, but I know I don't need it. I can handle this myself.

_____ Subtotal

_____ Total (Multiply subtotal by 2)

Interpretation: While there are other possible explanations for a high score on a given item, a pattern of "true" or "very true" responses strongly suggests that you may be relying heavily on denial to cope and temporarily alleviate your pain. If you are past two or three months from a life-altering event, there is a strong probability that higher scores indicate an unhealthy use of denial.

Use these general interpretive guidelines to give you an idea about where you are right now:

85–100: This is an "alarming" score. If you continue your course of running from reality, you will be highly likely to compound your problems and make your recovery much more lengthy and complex.

60–84: A score in this range is "high." This suggests that you are definitely in a danger zone; you are probably using denial in a way that could impede your progress.

45–59: If you fall within this range, you are about "average" in your use of denial as a coping mechanism. While there does not appear to be cause for alarm, you may want to implement the denial busters that follow to be doubly sure that your recovery plans are based firmly in reality.

30–44:   A score falling in this "low" range suggests that you are dealing appropriately with the facts of your situation as well as acknowledging your emotional realities.

20–29:   A score in this range could mean you're totally facing reality, or it could mean you're in denial that you're in denial. You might want to have a trusted, close friend or relative respond to the quiz on your behalf and compare your responses.

BEGIN NOW TO CHOOSE *REALITY*

Now that you've begun to acknowledge your use of denial, you can begin to implement seven action steps that enable you to move forward in dealing with your current reality.

Actively Seek Information

Rather than trying hard not to see what's happened (or happening), face the facts. Something terrible has happened to you, and it's devastated you on some level. It's understandable that you might want to curl up in a ball and not go anywhere near it, but if you do that, fear and anger will grow and take over your life.

Courageously and actively, seek out the facts about your situation and the facts about yourself and your reactions. Deliberately put yourself in direct contact with situations in which you are unable to deny the facts. This may run totally contrary to your natural inclinations because it produces high anxiety, but do it anyway.

Earlier in this chapter, you met Fran at the ER, having just lost her seventeen-month-old son Jacob. Even at this very early stage, she and Jake's father grasped the importance of this principle. The way they had to do it was unbelievably tough, but they did it, and they were glad.

She told me, "The thing that we did that helped, though it was really difficult, was, we asked to see the body. The nurse said 'yes' immediately, but another staff person asked, 'Is that something you are sure you want to do?' I told him, 'Yes, I want to see the body.'

"It was a good thing, because then I really knew he wasn't there anymore. She let us both hold him. She let us cut a little lock of his hair. She assured me they would take good care of him. It was very difficult. We wailed and we cried. But it helped us break through the denial. Making ourselves face it brought home the finality of Jacob's death."

Ask Yourself, What Have I Been Trying Not to Notice or Believe?

Getting honest with yourself means asking some tough questions. Put each of these questions at the top of a sheet of paper, and spend some time writing whatever comes to mind. Don't evaluate it or judge it at first; that may inhibit the expression of some truths you need to see. Just write down whatever pops into your head in response to the questions that follow. Write fast, and don't worry if there are duplications.

- What do I find myself trying to ignore?

- What is it that, when someone mentions it, I become defensive?

- What have I noticed, but explained away?

- What am I trying to believe?

- What evidence against that belief am I discounting?

- What am I pretending not to know?

> *What is, is.*

Now, look back over what you've written. What patterns do you see? Why is it so important to you to refuse to acknowledge some of the evidence? Most probably, it's to avoid pain, and that's understandable. However, you can't avoid the realities forever. The facts are the facts. What is, is. Take a deep breath, take in the realities, and begin to consider how you will deal with them.

Acknowledge Your Humanity, Including the Emotions That Come with Stress

It's okay to be human. Really! It's not possible to be superhuman, at least not long term. Really. Feeling is not only Okay, but it's also good, though it feels bad. (Did you get all that? Read it again.)

The sooner you acknowledge to yourself the truth about what you are feeling, the sooner you will regain power over the chaotic emotions that threaten to control you. Denial is not the way to master your emotions; honesty is. More about the "how-tos" of this later.

Understand That Tears Don't Mean You've "Lost It"

Tears are nature's way of healing after loss. Tears are *not* a sign of weakness, evidence that you are out of control, or something that won't stop once they get started.

I know, I know. Especially if you are male, you've probably been taught, "Shake it off. Big boys don't cry." You may have even been rewarded or praised for your lack of tears in your current horrific process, with others praising you for "being strong" (meaning stoic).

Despite all of that, tears are often the river through which healing flows. If you're not comfortable with this important form of expression when you're around others, get behind closed doors or go to a special place in the woods. Crying relieves emotional pressure. That's why people often refer to having a "good cry."

Talk with Caring Relatives and Friends About the Experience and Your Reactions

Scientific research verifies that talking about traumatic events does combat denial, but it also brings other benefits. Sharing your thoughts and feelings verbally can also alleviate distress, improve immune function, and lead to a healthier experience of life.[2]

Why is this true? Major traumatic events exact a heavy psychological toll by challenging your basic beliefs about yourself and your world. To the extent that your basic assumptions about life were shattered by the trauma, you have to somehow integrate the information that is contrary to your preexisting patterns of belief. In other words, you have to make some kind of sense of it.

One of the ways you can do this is to gradually and repeatedly expose yourself to traumatic stimuli, including thoughts, memories, and images related to the trauma. I've already begun to encourage you to do that.

The other process, which is hard at first, is to talk with others about the experience. By talking with supportive and empathetic others, you will learn to think about and tolerate more disturbing trauma-related thoughts than you could on your own. In addition, talking with receptive and helpful others can help you make sense of a traumatic experience, get information about coping strategies, or gain control over your emotions. As you expose yourself to different points of view and as you experience acceptance and understanding, you'll be better able to accept yourself.

Of course, you will want to carefully select the people with whom you choose to share, especially at first when your feelings are so raw. You know the people in your life who are understanding and supportive, so talk with them. Also, it can be very helpful to discuss your experiences with others who have been through similar situations. While every person's experience is different, it's comforting to see the similarities and to know that you're not crazy and you're not alone.

Journal Your Thoughts and Emotional Reactions

Research has also shown that writing about your experiences and feelings is therapeutic, helping you to regain power over them. Further, journaling has been shown to provide the same benefits as talking . . . relieving stress and making you more physically and psychologically healthy.[3]

Journaling is, after all, talking without a listener. It's like conversation, but there's no one on the other end. No one, that is, except you and God. Writing about your feelings allows you to listen to yourself. You become more conscious of what's going on inside. That gives you the information you need to begin to address the problems.

Sometimes your thoughts are all over the place, and you can't get hold of them. When you first begin to journal, your writing may follow this bounce-around pattern. No problem. Don't worry about it making sense. The patterns and insights will begin to emerge after a while.

Many of my clients resist journaling because they think they have to create a publishable masterpiece or that they have to write in their journals every day. In fact, one person said to me, "I'd rather suffer than journal!" No wonder, if you have unrealistic self-expectations about the process. Journaling is not about the art of writing, nor is it about communication. If you were communicating with someone else, you'd have to take into account what the other person needs to learn. No, journaling is about self-expression. You're writing about what you need to say, not what someone else needs to hear.

Further, you don't have to journal every day or on a set schedule. When something triggers feelings, or when you find yourself overreacting to some situation, these are good times to write. Just sit and reflect. Then pretend you pushed a tape recorder in your head and record your thoughts and reactions. You'll be surprised what you learn.

Don't Be Afraid to Get Professional Help

"No way! I'm not crazy!" you may protest at the suggestion to seek professional help. Of course you aren't. You're a normal person who's been through a horrible experience. The coping methods you've used before with life's ordinary challenges may have been dwarfed by the "bomb" that blew up your normal life. Anybody would have been thrown way off by this.

I've been a practicing psychologist for over twenty-five years, and only a tiny portion of the people I've worked with have been "crazy" (and, as you might guess, I don't like that word). Most have been everyday people like you who have hit life's brick walls.

Maybe you're worried about what people will think if you see a "shrink." While admittedly seeing a mental health professional has carried a stigma in the past, I'm thankful that those attitudes are changing. People with a reasonable degree of education and realistic life experience know that when you are experiencing any kind of health problem, it's wise to see a specialist. If you had an accident and crushed a bone, you'd see an orthopedist for the repair work. You wouldn't go to your next-door neighbor or your sister. Why, then, when your psyche has been involved in a serious "accident," would you choose not to consult an expert?

Carefully following the recommendations in this book will move you along. However, there are additional benefits of sitting down face to face with a caring therapist who has training and clinical experience in dealing with trauma. You'll feel comforted by the fact that you'll be heard and understood, but not judged.

While in some cases seeing a therapist is not absolutely essential, almost all people who have been blindsided by trauma could profit from the knowledge, expertise, and coaching of a professional. Don't be embarrassed to take advantage of the opportunity to expedite your progress down this crazy emotional highway. It's unfamiliar territory. An experienced personal guide can be a big help.

Talk with friends, your minister, your family doctor, or another trusted professional to get a recommendation for a mental health professional in your community. Do it sooner rather than later. Don't forget, research shows that early intervention helps to prevent more complicated symptoms from developing.[4] But even if it's later, don't hesitate to make an appointment with a therapist who can help you.

MY COMMITMENT TO *REALITY*

Today I choose reality, courageous emotional honesty with myself and with others I trust. Though denial may give me temporary emotional protection and false comfort, I won't linger there. I won't pretend I don't know, command myself not to feel, or stay so busy I don't have to think. No longer will I live behind the mask of being "in control" while my insides feel anything but.

I realize that I need facts to solve a problem. Therefore, I will actively seek the information I need (though it is sometimes painful), knowing that the knowledge ultimately makes me stronger. I choose to face the facts about my situation and the facts about myself. I accept that I am a fully feeling human being and that experiencing and expressing emotions is not a sign of weakness.

No longer will I lie to myself, for I recognize that real strength comes from integrity, authenticity, and truth. Therefore, though I may feel afraid, I bravely take this step into reality, knowing that bravery is unnecessary when there is no fear. I choose to gain control by giving up control. I reject denial. I choose to be real. This day, I choose reality.

2

"Poor Me"

I had the privilege of working in evacuation shelters with survivors of Hurricane Katrina, which devastated the Gulf Coast and other areas of my home state of Mississippi and our sister state, Louisiana. In the chaotic days following the torrential winds and floods, I was struck by the understandable shock and disbelief of the people I tried to comfort. However, even at this early stage, I could already hear the words that were either seeds of life-debilitating victimhood or life-restoring responsibility.

———

"Everything I have is gone. From the satellite pictures they showed us here at the shelter, I can see it. Water up to the roof of my house. Who knows when we can even get back in there? We made it out with the clothes on our backs. I have no idea whether my sister, brother, and aunt are dead or alive. I can only hope and pray and just try to get through one day after another here."

45

———

"The people working here at this shelter don't care what we're going through. I told them I wore a size 7 shoe, and they brought me a 7½. And we had chicken again today. It's the third time this week. Can you talk to them and see if I can get a better cot? The person next to me has a different kind, and it looks a lot more comfortable."

———

"I'll tell you one thing about this Hurricane Katrina. She made me find out what's really important in life. Material things . . . those can be replaced. It's people and faith and love that are the real things. Times like these show what people are really made of. I'm determined, if I have anything to do with it, that some good is going to come from this. With God's help we will come through this together, and we'll come out better and stronger on the other side."

One week after Hurricane Katrina devastated the worlds of thousands and shook a nation, these individuals were exhibiting the attitudes that would make or break the rest of their lives. Still in shock, some were simply taking one day at a time—a wise thing to do, since letting their imaginations run wild about what might be facing them was simply too much right then.

The victim mentality was evident in the constant complaints of others. Their theme song was "What Have You Done for Me Lately?"

Thankfully, most of the folks I worked with were not in this category. I especially remember one couple who volunteered to clean the bathrooms every hour, a powerful example of doing what you can where you are. I could hear the seeds of true recovery in the words of those who had already begun to use this traumatic event as an inspiration for greater determination, deeper faith, closer relationships, and a more purposeful life.

Even at this early hour in the aftermath of tragedy, everyone had begun to make the choices that would make their recovery possible—or not.

THERE'S NO WAY AROUND IT; I *AM* A VICTIM!

Most of you reading this book have truly been victimized in one way or another. In many of your cases, somebody victimized you—through crime, abuse, abandonment, betrayal, or negligence, or by taking advantage of your goodness. Others of you don't have a person to point to, but you were a victim of circumstances. You were in the right place at the wrong time or the wrong place at the right time. Some of you have lost someone you loved through untimely death. All of these are ways of being *victimized.*

But that doesn't mean you have to assume the posture of a "victim." (From now on, when I put "victim" in quotes, I'm referring to the self-sabotaging attitude I'm about to describe.)

Victimlike thoughts, words, and behaviors, through repetition, become success-stealing habits. Sometimes those thoughts, words, and actions seem quite logical, given what you've been through. But you have to be really careful. No matter what losses you incurred when you were originally victimized, if you become a complaining, finger-pointing, poor-me person, you will ensure that your losses will grow bigger and bigger for the rest of your life.

> *If you become a complaining, finger-pointing, poor-me person, you'll ensure that your losses will grow bigger and bigger for the rest of your life.*

You probably didn't have much of a choice about the first victimization. But if you elect to adopt the whining, what-have-you-done-for-me-lately stance of a chronic "victim," the subsequent losses will be of your own making.

Maybe you're asking yourself, "With all those downsides to becoming a victim, why would anybody go there?" Glad you asked.

THE TEMPTATIONS OF VICTIMHOOD

"Victimhood" can be emotionally tempting, especially after going through a traumatic experience. This is particularly true if even before this personal trial occurred, you already had the tendency to shift blame and responsibility. Consider these three enticements to becoming a "victim."

"Victims" Don't Have to Be Responsible for Their Own Attitudes and Actions

The awareness of your contribution to your own problems can sting at first. It hurts to face the fact that you're not perfect and to realize that you are responsible for the choices you are making in the midst of your heartbreaking circumstances. In addition, personal awareness brings with it the challenge to change. Change is hard, so it's tempting to deny your own responsibility and believe instead that others are the culprits.

Mary spent years with a "victim" mentality. She was a professional dancer getting rave reviews and expert predictions that she had a stellar career in front of her. That was before the serious injury to her ankle that dashed her hopes. Mary would not be able to dance again. She went through years of feeling victimized by life as she struggled within herself to find her way (which she eventually did). Dancing was her life. It was all she had ever wanted to do.

Mary told me, "I was finally able to make a breakthrough after taking responsibility for the choices I had made prior to the injury, like not staying in peak shape by going to dance class every day. Until I had this realization, I felt like a victim. Even though I was the one who injured myself, I was caught up in self-pity because I felt like the world had done this to me. After I accepted the fact that what happened was caused at least in part by the choices I made, I was able to forgive myself and move past it."

Unlike Mary, others can find no legitimate way they contributed to their particular "injury," so they feel justified in continuing to blame the world for their troubles, failing to recognize that they have choices now that determine their destiny.

The "victim" option can be enticing because it seems more comfortable to continue as you are, never having to face up to your own responsibility while expecting others to change. More accurately, you could say that ignoring the need for personal change seems more convenient, but ultimately it's not more comfortable. Choose the "victim" way of thinking, and your discomfort will only increase as your life grows more miserable.

"Victims" Get Others' Sympathy and Support . . . for a While

Another temporary reward of being a "victim" is that when you're feeling really upset and depressed, others tend to offer you more sympathy and help. In other words, you are rewarded for being down-and-out. While support from others can be healthy, it's also possible that sympathy can reinforce unhealthy complaining. A basic psychological principle is, behavior that gets rewarded gets repeated. So in order to get more nurturing and sympathy, you may get into the habit of talking about how bad things are for you and how the world has treated you unfairly. However, that practice will backfire after a while.

Consider, for example, the experience of Denise and John. Their daughter, Donna, was a twenty-two-year-old mother who had been through sexual abuse from a neighbor early in her life. Despite all their efforts to give their daughter professional help as well as their love and support, in her teen years Donna chose to abuse drugs. Her lifestyle became that of a full-blown addict. Denise and John gained custody of Donna's precious three-year-old, but they were unable to convince their daughter to seek help.

Denise and John explained, "She was on Welfare and Medicaid, but she wouldn't even go down there and get the money. Someone almost choked her to death in the bad neighborhood where she hung out, and she lost all of her insurance cards, the baby's Medicaid card and Social Security card, everything.

"She'd call her brother and play on his sympathy. She'd say, 'I've got this problem. Mama and Daddy just don't understand. Will you help me?' Then he'd call us and say, 'She says she's going to do better.'

"We'd tell him, 'We know, son. We've heard it. We've heard it all. She's made promise after promise. But it's always the same. She blames everybody, then she turns around and refuses to take advantage of any opportunities that she has. We'd do anything in the world to help her get back on her feet and get going again in her career. But all she does is complain and blame. We just can't support her in this negative, destructive lifestyle.'"

I'm not saying that you shouldn't talk about what's bothering you, to share your pain and receive caring from others. However, that's not the same as being a chronic complainer. Chronic complainers don't just share their thoughts and feelings with others; they expect them or the universe to fix it! They assume no responsibility for action themselves.

After a while, if you're on the slippery slope toward the "victim" mind-set, you need friends who gently encourage you to action and responsibility with words like:

- What do you think you could do right now in this situation?"

- I realize it's difficult. Let's go for a walk to get some fresh air and a fresh perspective."

- Maybe you don't realize it, but you talk most about things you have no control of, such as . . . Let's make a pact to begin to focus on small things we can do to make your days a little better."

If you're wise, you'll respond to those nudges, and you'll listen to the Lord's whisper in your heart that says, *It's Okay. You can do it. I am with you.*

If you are not so wise, and if you persist in victim-like behaviors, you're going to wear out your support people. They will eventually either leave physically or emotionally, some sooner than others. In some cases they'll still be there, but their growing irritation with and resentment of you will begin to erect emotional walls. Don't be shortsighted and think that the attention you get from excessive complaining is worth it. The positive attention won't last, nor will the satisfaction you get from it.

"Victims" Feel Self-Righteous and Justified

Annette, a young woman who was diagnosed with crippling multiple sclerosis, described how she played the victim to feel self-righteous and justified in her behavior.

"It's hard not to sink into a victim mentality. My version of it was to be a militant disabled person. I learned the disability laws and demanded that everyone conform. If they didn't, I was on the attack. If adults stared at me in the wheelchair, I'd stare back. When a newly diagnosed person would say to me, 'We're not all strong like you,' I'd shoot back that they had better toughen up. I had plenty of self-righteous indignation. I had unhealthy pride in my knowledge and my toughness. Over time, I learned that I had to lighten up. I saw that it was not true strength to put everyone else down. If I was going to lift myself up, I had to be attuned to lifting others up as well."

The feeling of self-righteousness can be very tempting following a major disappointment or setback. Annette tried to make herself feel better by comparing herself to others, and she "won." She felt a false sense of pride and power. If she could successfully deflect any responsibility from herself, she could sanctimoniously assure herself that she was not like "those people."

Why does the experience of trauma make you more vulnerable to the quest to come out on top in comparisons with others? When you've been through a life event that sent you reeling, the hunger to regain some kind of power can be ravenous. Making yourself feel good by putting someone else down is one way to do that, albeit a destructive way.

That momentary rush of pleasure from feeling superior to someone else ultimately robs you of the ability to develop true strength. When you are in denial about things you need to work on, about ways you need to mature and grow, and about your own opportunities to learn from adversity—you miss it. You're busy looking at the speck of sawdust in someone else's eye while ignoring the plank in your own. You blindly keep repeating the same mistakes while being quick to point out the errors of others.

It reminds me of the story about a woman who went to her doctor complaining of pain. He asked her, "Where are you hurting?"

She answered, "I'm hurting all over." When the doctor asked her to be more specific, the lady touched her right knee with her index finger and yelled, "Ouch! That hurts!" Then she touched her nose and winced, saying, "Yeow! That hurts too!" Then she touched her left shoulder. "Even that hurts!" she informed the doc.

The doctor carefully checked her over, then told her, "I have determined your diagnosis. You have a broken finger."

You know, if the world and everyone in it seem to have a problem, maybe, just maybe, it's your feeler that's broken!

QUIZ: ARE YOU A "VICTIM"?

It's important to take an honest look in the mirror. Is it possible that you've unwittingly slipped into the "victim" mentality? If you suspect that you may have become a "victim," it's critical to become aware of it and to know what kinds of attitudes and habits may be holding you back.

Take the following short quiz to see if any of these behaviors or habits are sabotaging your recovery and harming your relationships. Put a checkmark beside any items that describe you.

_____ 1. After all I've been through, I've learned you just can't trust people.

_____ 2. I admit I have a tendency to blame others when things go wrong in my life.

_____ 3. I often have pity parties.

_____ 4. People have told me that I complain too much.

_____ 5. I feel angry when people try to get me to make personal changes and begin to move on. They just don't understand.

I suggest that after you've made your responses, you also ask someone close to you to respond honestly to the quiz with their observations of you. Listen openly to any feedback you receive from this informant.

Now let's talk about each of the five items in the "Victim Quiz."

1. *After all I've been through, I've learned you just can't trust people.* If you've been disappointed, betrayed, or otherwise harmed by some individual, at first it may be difficult or impossible to trust that person or even people whom you perceive to be in any way similar to him or her. However, to turn that bad experience into a distrust of everyone is an overgeneralization that breeds relationship-destroying paranoia. "Victims" assume the worst, leading them to jump to negative conclusions about others' motives and behaviors. Though you've been hurt, there are still so many good, safe, and nurturing people in the world. Don't forget that.

2. *I admit I have a tendency to blame others when things go wrong in my life.* Certainly, it's important not to blame yourself when others are responsible. In the chapter on guilt, we'll identify the reasons that's destructive. Other people who've deliberately contributed to the trauma in your life are accountable for their own actions.

However, you can go to the other extreme. You can become bitter and angry at the world. Thus, when anything goes wrong, you are all too ready to assign the blame to anyone but yourself. In other words, it's never your fault. That's what "victims" do.

A healthier perspective, one that keeps you from being stuck where you are, is an approach that makes you neither overresponsible nor underresponsible. You realize what you can control and what you can't. You do not hesitate to work on changing what you can—the personal attitudes or actions that are within your power. That's "responsibility."

3. *I often have pity parties.* It's one thing to grieve about the sad and horrific experiences you've been through. You feel sorrow about your losses, and that's both normal and healthy. It's erroneous to think you can or should just stuff all feelings, suck it up, and be totally tough. Sometimes, as a part of the normal grieving process, you will feel some self-pity.

However, it's quite another thing to wallow in pity and to embrace that "poor me" mentality, especially over time. You may secretly believe that God owes you a pain-free life. You tell yourself things like, "Nobody cares what I'm going through," or, "My situation is worse than anyone else's."

Betty adopted a "poor me" mentality after a fall down the stairs that broke her hip. She later told me, "I learned to stop the pity parties the hard way. Right after the accident, everybody came around trying to cheer me up. Then I started to notice I was alone more and more. At first, I just felt sorrier for myself because others didn't understand, and they had abandoned me. I was convinced that this was one more piece of evidence that the world was against me. Oh, sure, I was going to rehab for my physical injuries, but I was really mad about the whole thing.

"One day a friend who I knew really cared about me had the courage to say, 'Betty, I want to help, but you're making it very difficult. No matter how I try to encourage you, you have a 'but' for it. I know you've been through a hard time, and I want to be there for you. But your constant complaining and your refusal to do anything but the minimum to make your own life better is getting very frustrating. We've been friends a long time, but I'm not sure how much longer I can take it.'

"At first I was irritated and defensive, but then I began to think about it and realized she was right. Slowly, I started to work on my attitude. I tried to figure out what I could do to get better on the inside."

Like Betty, "victims" are hosts of perpetual pity parties. The problem is, one by one the guests become exhausted and leave. In fact, the host may also tire of the festivities, but may not know how to get out. Don't let that happen to you.

4. *People have told me that I complain too much.* "Victims" do complain a lot, expecting someone else to fix it. This tendency to externalize, to look to other people for the solutions, is a hallmark of the victim mentality. Then when the situation is not fixed to their satisfaction, they complain some more. Thus they become chronically negative, habitually noticing and zeroing in on what's wrong. Complain more than you act? Take responsibility for doing what *you* can do.

5. *I feel angry when people try to get me to make personal changes and begin to move on. They just don't understand.* It's true: no one knows exactly how you feel and how you're struggling. And it would be natural to feel irritated with people who judge your actions without having a clue about how difficult things are for you after the trauma you've experienced.

However, the key is to look at how long your struggle has lasted and how frequently you complain instead of doing something. If, over time, those who know and love you best continue to encourage you to take small steps to get back up, and you continue to resist vehemently—you could be in danger of becoming a chronic "victim."

YOU HAVE A CHOICE: VICTIMHOOD OR RESPONSIBILITY

I want you to fully understand the choices you have. That way, whichever way you elect to go, it will be with informed consent. You'll know the consequences of each course of action so that you can weigh costs and benefits and choose accordingly.

Victimhood Is a Losing Game

In describing the characteristics of "victims," I've let you in on some of the consequences of choosing the course of chronic victimhood. In case you aren't yet convinced, allow me to share with you four more reasons that it's in your best interest to give up the blame game.

1. *You create personal misery by interpreting your life events negatively.* The quality of your everyday experience is not determined solely by what happens or what others do or say to you. No, the "world you live in" is created by what you focus on and the way you interpret the everyday events in your life; that's your private experiential world. If you have a habit of seeing the world through a negative lens, always perceiving and believing that you are misunderstood and mistreated, you'll reside in the negative, miserable world that you have created.

2. *You become increasingly angry and frustrated because of your lack of power.* One of the major problems with the "victim" mentality is that it complicates your already intense reactions to the lack of power and control. Here's how. If someone else needs to change for your life to improve (a feat you cannot accomplish), you live in perpetual powerlessness. In other words, you are powerless because you've defined the problem in a way that takes you out of the equation. You've convinced yourself that there must be a solution out there, if only someone else would do what he or she is supposed to do—find it and fix it!

If you frequently put yourself into an out-of-control position by blaming others and by failing to assume responsibility and take action, you doom yourself to a life of frustration and inaction. You hate that feeling of powerlessness, but you keep making yourself powerless by putting the responsibility for change into someone else's hands. You can't make them do it, so you are perpetually out of control. Why would any person want to do that to oneself? That's no way to live.

3. *You may strike out at the "offender," but it's never enough.* As the "victim's" resentment grows, there is a temptation to try to make others pay. The rationale is, "You made me hurt, so it's only fair that you hurt."

There are two big problems with this, however. One is, revenge does not satisfy. Yes, you may feel pleasure temporarily, but that doesn't last. When you get caught up in it, revenge is never enough because it doesn't relieve the pain. True pain relief comes from spiritual and emotional healing, not from human efforts to even the score. The second problem is that your desire to strike out tends to spread and generalize. Soon you're not just railing against the offenders, but you develop a vengeful, hateful attitude that affects all those around you. Your loved ones suffer because they "can't do anything right." Your work life can also suffer, as your bosses and team members grow more impatient with your attitude. All of that leads us to the next problem with the blame game.

4. *You develop "perpetrator paranoia."* Every "victim" needs a "perpetrator." Yet sometimes the real perpetrator is elusive. The person(s) you believe caused your trauma may not be anywhere around or may even be dead. Or, you may have experienced a significant loss, but it seems there's no one to blame but the universe.

When this happens, people who have bought into the "victim" mentality can find themselves on an unwitting quest to hunt down and put down serial people they mentally label as some kind of "perpetrator." If you succumb to that temptation in order to justify your thinking, you may vilify certain bosses, coworkers, acquaintances, tech support people, doctors, or anyone else who you tell yourself has malicious motives. Even family relationships can become battlefields.

For example, Ann's husband was demoted from his job as a

manager in a grocery store. They said it was because of his attitude, but he said he "knew" that wasn't the real reason. He left and went to another grocery chain, but unfortunately, he took his "victim" attitude with him.

Ann described it this way: "Charlie became so difficult to be around. He'd come home from work with the latest tale of how his coworkers were deliberately trying to make him look bad, and how his boss really wanted him gone. I'd listen to the stories, and for the life of me, I couldn't reach the same conclusions about their motives as he did. And from his descriptions of his hostile responses, I could see how he wasn't chalking up any stars for his personnel record. If I gently suggested another way to look at it, he turned on me. He yelled that I was always putting him down. He screams at the kids too. I really don't know what to do next."

When you have perpetrator paranoia, you magnify the faults of others while denying your own. You see an evil motive behind even positive behaviors, frequently telling yourself what "they" are trying to do. In other words, when people either are trying to be helpful or are just going about their day in a normal way, you imagine that they are up to no good. You are convinced that if you let your guard down for a moment, "it" (whatever "it" is) will happen all over again.

5. *You become a very unpleasant person, damaging your work and personal relationships.* Matthew, an airline pilot who lost his job after 9/11, described it this way: "I fell into a self-pity pool big-time. Everywhere I went, I felt compelled to explain to people what had happened, how unfairly I had been treated, and how badly the airline had screwed me. I'm sure it got very old to listen to."

> *Self-pity has no resurrection, a sinkhole from which no rescuing hand can drag you because you have chosen to sink.*[1]
> —ELISABETH ELLIOT

Have you ever been around someone who constantly talked about how others and the world in general have failed to meet their needs? A person who couldn't be pleased? One who had a short fuse, and you never knew if you were next? What was your response to that person? Most of us would want to spend as little time with that person as possible. If it was a person you had to be around, you'd put up internal walls to protect yourself emotionally from the unpleasantness or downright harm.

Responsibility, the Choice That Produces Personal Power

I hope that by now you're realizing that becoming a victim is no way to go. That price tag is much too high! The alternative to that is responsibility.

Responsibility means that you look at your situation and your life honestly and accurately—acknowledging what you've lost and clearly seeing and embracing what you still have. It's choosing every day to do all you can with what you have. It's looking for and practicing gratitude for small and large blessings. You don't wait for someone else to change, apologize, or act on your behalf. You muster all the energy you have and some you think you don't have, and you determine to learn and grow and move, millimeter by millimeter.

> *Things turn out best for people who make the best of the way things turn out.*
>
> —AUTHOR UNKNOWN

When you make that decision, you'll be amazed at what begins to happen. Resources you never imagined will come into your life. People whose encouragement you need at that moment will cross your path. You'll stumble across a book or a television program that speaks to your exact situation, right then, right there. When you are committed to healthy, responsible living, God will send you just what you require to continue your healing. That, my friend, is a spiritual principle that works.

Another reason that responsibility increases your power is that you focus on the "haves" rather than the "have nots." A basic psychological principle is, you see what you look for; what you look for, you'll find. Focus on what's wrong, and you'll find that. Search for what's right, and that's what you'll see.

As Janet told me, "Now I am very aware if I get into the victim or blame mode. I force my mind to focus on my list of 'gratitudes' instead. When I first started the list, though, I couldn't think of one thing. I had to put down, 'still breathing.' Eventually I added to the list. As soon as my mind started going down the negative thinking road, I would read my gratitude list over and over. It helped tremendously. You can't firmly hold a positive and a negative thought in your brain at the same time. I learned to focus on the positive."

Taking responsibility requires some good, honest work—but it is so worth it. The benefits to this mind-set are far-reaching. Let's talk about four more of them.

1. *No one else has to change for your life to improve.* Have you been down the dead-end street of trying to persuade, cajole, threaten, or force someone to change? I have. Several times, unfortunately.

I know what it's like to be in a relationship with an alcoholic, trying to love enough, convince enough, control enough, and, yes, rescue enough to get him to change. I believed that my happiness depended on his putting down the bottle. Getting him sober was certainly a worthy goal and one that would have improved the quality of life for all of us, that's true. But my focus was in the wrong place. I needed to spend my energy on educating myself about my own behavior and creating the best life

> *Though life may have rerouted you or erected some barriers in the street, you can keep moving—when you choose responsibility.*

possible despite less-than-ideal circumstances. My own development would have progressed further had I spent more time praying rather than in obsessing about how to get him to change. When you change in a positive direction, others are invited to come along, but they don't have to in order for your life to improve.

2. *You are not stuck trying to get someone else to change.* You know the feeling when you're supposed to be somewhere important and you get stuck in a traffic jam? It's no fun to be immobile, especially when you need to be about some important business.

That feeling of immobility is similar to the frustration you feel when you're stuck trying to get someone else to change. You can get yourself out of the emotional traffic jam you're in.

A first step is to assume responsibility for whatever actions are possible for you, where you are today. The choices of others don't have to hold you back from exploring alternate routes for your journey. Though life may have rerouted you or erected some barriers in the street, you can keep moving—when you choose responsibility.

Not long ago, I interviewed Michelle Nichols, professional speaker and columnist for *BusinessWeek*. Michelle lost her eight-year-old son Mark due to brain cancer. Michelle's attitude personifies the benefits of the action-oriented approach.[2] She told me, "Someday I'm going to meet Mark in heaven and he's going to say, 'I had to go so soon. What did you do with your time left on earth?' If all I can say is, 'I watched every episode of some sitcom or soap opera,' what the heck do I have to report? I want to do something with that time. When you die, you have no more chances to do cool things on earth. It is over. There are no do-overs.

"God has put in me the spirit of optimism and the will to continually go forward. Really, who benefits if you just stay in the chair and never rise again? It's not going to bring your child back. If God had wanted to take us both, he'd have done so. But he didn't, so I know I have to get going and keep going!"

3. *Action relieves anxiety.* When you're anxious, something deep inside cries out, "Do something!" (This may be covered up by the fear that screams, "Hide!") The truth is, we are biologically wired for "fight or flight" when we feel threatened.

When you take action—that is, you do something, even if it's a little thing—you feel relief. You are actually cooperating with your body's arousal system that gets you prepared for action in the presence of perceived threats. You can use that energy to problem solve and to inch your way toward solutions.

> *All appears to change when we change.*
> —HENRI-FRÉDÉRIC AMIEL

4. *People respond more positively to you when you are behaving responsibly, so you receive more healthy support.* When you are taking responsible action, you're much more pleasant to be around. Even if that action is internal—that is, working on an attitude, a reaction, or a thought habit—the encouraging people in your life will celebrate because they want you to succeed. If they're smart, they know they can't do it for you. So when they see you nudging yourself out of inertia, they want to support you in that effort. As you begin to take responsible "baby steps," you receive the emotional applause of your friends and loved ones. Thus, you gain the courage to go a step farther, and farther, and farther.

BEGIN NOW TO CHOOSE RESPONSIBILITY

Rejecting the role of "victim" and embracing responsibility involves changing how you think and what you do. The "how you think" part involves digging pretty deeply because in a way, we'll be talking about the basic way you see the world and yourself in it. This choice involves changing your expectations and how you approach problems in your life. So don't think you're going to zip through the upcoming sections without some soul-searching and some initially uncomfortable work on habit change. Let's start with the mental habit that is foundational to the "victim" perspective.

Reject "Externalization" (lie)

Externalization is the erroneous belief that your happiness (or lack thereof) depends on people and circumstances outside yourself. It's not difficult to buy into this faulty assumption when you live in the American culture. All you have to do is turn on the television for fifteen minutes to have four commercial announcers teach you about all the things you just must have to make you happy and without which your life will be totally incomplete. As I've been on speaking tours abroad, I've learned my country is not alone in spreading the gospel of externally-produced happiness. Who among us is totally immune to the seduction of advertising?

The assumption of responsibility for your own happiness and your own life involves a switch to an internal focus. The relief of your pain, the resolution of your confusion, the reestablishment of some kind of routine, a positive change in your habits, the rebuilding of a meaningful life—where do these all happen? They happen inside. God provides the inner strength, wisdom, and resources; you provide the choices and the practical actions.

Listen to yourself! Tune in to how often you attribute your discomfort or your problems to external sources. Externalization is easy to do, since you've been through some very abnormal external circumstances that caused you pain. However, what has happened is not going to change. It's already happened. What's done is done. The only thing that can change now is *you*.

You can become more attuned to your tendency to externalize by writing down your thoughts when you're feeling upset. Once again, push that "Record" button in your brain and transcribe the recording, writing only on the left side of your page. What are you talking to yourself about? Are you talking more about your circumstances and what someone else should do, or are you zeroing in on how you can respond to those circumstances?

Then use the right side of the page to challenge yourself and to move yourself into a way of thinking that restores power to you. Next to those external kinds of thoughts, write about what *you* can do differently within those circumstances, or how you can think differently so that you focus on things over which you have more control. Resist those beliefs that your pain will be fixed by something that happens "out there" rather than "in here."

Know the Difference between a Problem and a Condition

A problem is something you can do something about! A condition is something you can't. It's critical to know the difference.

Too often, when describing what we think are our problems, we're talking about conditions.

- "My problem is, my husband is running around on me." (If that's a fact, then that's a condition. Your problem is, how are you going to respond to his behavior?)

- "My problem is, my wife was killed in a hit-and-run accident." (Using our definition, that's a condition. Your problem involves all the ways you will react, adjust, and restructure your life.)

- "I've definitely got a problem. My house was washed away by the storm surge of Hurricane Katrina. The insurance company won't pay. They say it's flood damage, not wind damage. I'm left with a slab and a mortgage." (As painful as that situation is, that's not a problem; it's a condition. The steps you will take now to reestablish your life—that's the problem.)

Don't spend the majority of your time bemoaning conditions. Define and get to work on the problems.

Accurately Answer the Question, Who's Responsible for What?

Your challenge is to sort out the answer to the important question, who's responsible for what?

I still remember a lesson I learned as a six-year-old. I was in the room the day a fellow pastor paid a visit to my dad.

"Arnold, I need your help," he said. "In my sermon last Sunday, I quoted a scripture off the top of my head. My people have challenged me on it, and I can't seem to find it in the Bible. I need your help locating it."

"What scripture did you quote?" my dad asked.

"Every tub's gotta sit on its own bottom," the minister replied.

Too compassionate to the man's plight to giggle (as I did in the corner of the room), my father patiently pointed out biblical passages that stated the principles of personal accountability, though the bottom of the tub was not to be found among them!

> *A problem is something you can do something about! A condition is something you can't.*

After the man left, Daddy turned to me and said, "My friend made a mistake in his quote, but never forget the real message. Wherever you find yourself in life, Bev, and no matter what other people do, you can always choose what you are going to do. God's not going to be asking you what others did. He'll be talking with you about what you did."

That's the principle I most want to communicate to you in this chapter. You are responsible for your own attitudes and behaviors. No matter what others choose to do, your task is to manage yourself and your own reactions.

If others expect you to do for them what they need to do for themselves, you'll be doing them a disservice to take responsibility for them over and over. When you see that you've been into unhealthy rescuing, set limits on how you're contributing to others' irresponsibility. Here's a warning: the recipients may

> *Though others may do things to us, we are responsible for what happens in us.*

not be pleased with that. But stick to your guns. Do what is healthy for all concerned, even if it's temporarily unpleasant.

If you choose to remain a "victim," you'll fail to seize the power to change yourself. You will only get better as you begin to do things differently.

Someone once said, "If you could kick the person responsible for most of your troubles, you wouldn't be able to sit down for months!" That may not be accurate in some cases. However, it is true that though others may do things *to* us, we are responsible for what happens *in* us.

Relinquish the Temporary Pleasure of Blame Shifting

I know, there's a little adrenaline rush when you talk to yourself about how someone else is to blame and how that person needs to pay. But as we've seen, it's a false feeling of power because it doesn't undo what's done or redirect your life in a positive way.

Lasting pleasure comes from developing positive relationships with others, from meaningful and purposeful living, and from spiritual renewal. These have none of the negative side effects of a blaming, hostile approach to life.

As George Herbert wisely said, "Living well is the best revenge." Give up the habit of blame. It's poison to your spiritual and emotional health.

Give Yourself Compassion, but Not Excuses

Giving yourself compassion, but not excuses, can be a tricky balance. The side of the scales you have trouble with depends on your emotional habits before your life was turned upside down.

If you've always expected yourself to be in control and prided yourself on being a pick-yourself-up-by-your-bootstraps, push-past-any-limits kind of person, you may find it difficult to give yourself the grace to be human and struggle. In the same way you would express compassion for someone else in trouble, give yourself a break. You've been through an extraordinarily difficult experience, and these reactions are anything but normal for you. Extending compassion to yourself is not necessarily a way of shirking responsibility. Honestly recognize that during a healing period, you just can't do things the way you've always done.

> He that is good at making excuses is seldom good at anything else.
>
> —BENJAMIN FRANKLIN

At the same time, don't take the "victim" stance of using your tragedy as an excuse to remain inert. After some of the initial shock and deepest of grief pass, gently nudge yourself to begin the healing process. Identify parts of your regular routine that you can reclaim. Recognize your realistic limits, while doing some things you really don't feel like doing.

Shift Your Focus to What You Can Do Differently

A classic symptom of "victimhood" is the focus on what someone else should do to make your situation better, the expectation that someone else should change. As we've already seen, this puts you *more* out of control in an already out-of-control situation.

Instead, practice focusing on your "response-ability." Just like it sounds, *response-ability* is the ability to respond differently. No matter what has happened, no matter what others have done, you always have the power to choose how you are going to respond.

This doesn't mean that others are not legitimately accountable for their actions that caused pain. However, if you obsessively focus on those people, you'll miss opportunities to do what you can do to restore sanity, order, and purpose to your own life. You will have unintentionally given the perpetrator(s) ongoing power over your life.

Take back control of your life by working on yourself. Examine and challenge the negative thinking that almost always invades your life after an emotional catastrophe, and implement action on the ten positive choices. Begin to rediscover a purpose and find ways to rebuild a meaningful life. These are all "inside jobs." Take response-ability now.

Learn the Skills You Need

When the rules of the world have changed, when your familiar resources are gone, when your life has morphed into some unrecognizable form—your old ways of doing things just may not fit.

Consider Martha's challenges. She told me, "Jack handled all of our business stuff. He was so good at that, and numbers just scramble my brain. Who could have known that he would die of a heart attack at fifty-one? I have no idea what we have or even where to start. It's hard enough just losing him. Now I have to be responsible for this, too? It's just too much."

Sometimes when life blindsides you and you're reeling emotionally, you also have to develop new skills to survive in the overwhelming world that's just been created for you. It seems like it's the worst possible time to have to learn something new; it's all you can do to hold it together and get through the day. Yet learn you must because you don't have the luxury of not learning. Don't be afraid to ask for help. Find an expert in what you need to know, someone who has the heart of a teacher. That might be a therapist, a financial consultant, a career coach, or a disability specialist. Whatever the skill you need to develop, there are professionals who specialize in showing you the best and simplest ways to get there.

Take an Honest Inventory

To do the personal work to move yourself out of the "victim" way of thinking, spend time thinking about, praying about, and writing the answers to these questions:

- What do I have to work with currently (not what I don't have)?

- How have I been sabotaging my own progress?

- What is within my power to control?

- What small, positive action steps are possible now?

Make a Reasonable, Stepwise Plan and Act on It

Based on what you've learned about yourself in your personal inventory, make a plan. Not a grand plan—you're probably not ready for that. Just a plan for little things you can do this hour, this day that will get you moving slowly in a positive direction. Mind you, this will not be totally comfortable.

Everyone must row with the oars they have.
—ENGLISH PROVERB

If you've been too long in a passive mode, managing to avoid anxiety through unhealthy denial, you may have to stretch a little. However, your plan should break tasks down into manageable parts—not overwhelming, but in your "stretch reach." As you implement your plan, celebrate the tiniest movement. You'll be encouraging yourself to do more!

Your general plan is to take charge of your insidiously negative thoughts. When confronted with any of the ten choices, take the high road. Every time you do that, you will be implementing one of the most influential of the choices: the choice for responsibility.

MY COMMITMENT TO *RESPONSIBILITY*

I choose responsibility. Though I may have been victimized, I refuse to become a victim, wallowing in self-pity. Though I had no control over what happened to me, I choose to exercise control over my own thoughts and actions. I do the hard work of changing the habits of negativity, strife, and blame.

I realize that I cannot change someone else, nor does my recovery depend on someone else changing. Therefore, I focus on the resources I have and the actions I can take. I identify small steps that move me ever so slowly along the pathway that leads to the rebuilding of a meaningful life. I search for the blessings among the struggles and determine to be thankful for them. Today, I choose responsibility.

3

"I Have a Thousand Questions"

CHOICE #3: WHY OR HOW

When the nightmare occurred, Jenny Kerry had already been fighting exhaustion, both emotionally and physically. Her husband, Frank, had become more and more debilitated with the progressive neurological disease that was stealing his ability to speak clearly, care for himself, and move independently. At this point, he moved around only with the assistance of a walker. Jenny was juggling to maintain financial stability by working as a nurse at the local hospital.

One fateful day Frank unsteadily made his customary daily trip across the yard. Entering their barn, he encountered an unbelievably horrible sight. His mother-in-law was hanging from a rafter in their barn, murdered. He used his cell phone to call 911, and then his wife.

The next morning as Jenny and Frank were in the midst of gut-wrenching grief, there came a knock at the door. As he attached the handcuffs to their wrists, the gruff police officer announced, "Jenny and Frank Kerry, you are under arrest for the murder of Mattie Jenkins. You have the right to remain silent . . ."

Of course, the local television media covered the saga in vivid detail. The news was the talk of the small town.

Before being cleared of all charges, Jenny and Frank spent two terrifying weeks in the local jail—incarcerated while they were still reeling from the shock and grief of having a beloved family member murdered. Separated from each other, they received anything but sympathy from the officers who were mistakenly convinced of the couple's guilt.

When Jenny and Frank finally walked free, they were anything but. Members of the media cruised their street and swarmed their property. Going to the grocery store entailed dealing with whispers and suspicious stares. They received accusing phone calls and letters. Jenny suspected that some of the harassment came from her own sisters and other family members.

Within three weeks of their release from jail, Jenny and Frank were awakened in the middle of the night by the stifling smell of smoke. Jenny was barely able to get her handicapped husband and herself out alive from the burning house. The fire department later determined the fire was arson. Neither the murder nor the arson case has ever been solved.

Jenny told me, "I asked the 'whys' over and over again. Why did all of this happen to me? Why did I have to go through one thing after another, any one of which would have been almost too much to handle? Why did they think I did it? I've never done anything to hurt anybody. I've spent my life as a nurse, trying to help people. Why would someone kill my mother, who was such a sweet and loving person? Why on earth did all of this happen?"

Maybe you can relate to Jenny's experience in some way. Life came after her over and over, having no mercy when she was going down for the count. She didn't have time to recover from one thing before she was blindsided with another and another and another.

After you go through the unexpected unthinkable, it's natural to want some answers. Questions, all of which contain "why" as the underlying issue, cry out for answers.

- Why did this have to happen?

- Why did it happen to me?

- Why did this happen to me now?

- Why did he/she do this?

- Why didn't I see it coming?

- What did I do to deserve this?

- Why didn't God stop it? (More about this question in chapter 4.)

- Why didn't I do something differently, something that would have changed the outcome?

WHY: THE ENDLESS QUESTION

Why do we instinctively want to ask why? Are there underlying assumptions that give rise to the questions? And what are we unconsciously trying to achieve by searching for elusive answers?

Hidden beneath the queries are three shaky assumptions: (1) there are practical or cosmic reasons for everything, (2) you should be able to discover these reasons if you try hard enough, and (3) when you know these reasons, everything will make sense.

There has been considerable debate about whether "everything happens for a reason." Some search for the immediate cause or divine purpose of tragedy, believing the reasons are there if they could just be skillful enough to discover them. Others believe that we are only specks in the universe, randomly subject to its whims. They would claim that we should simply accept whatever happens and deal with it without expecting a Supreme Being to justify Himself.

My personal belief contains elements of both. Sometimes there are direct causes and things we need to change to prevent future similar events from occurring. In those cases, we must take a fearless look at what we can do differently in the future. In other cases, we are randomly included in a tragic event. No one gets a free pass, and being a good person doesn't exempt you.

Whether or not there are actually tangible, identifiable reasons for what happened to you, you will probably never be able to find all the answers you seek (in this life, anyway). Even when you find an answer, it doesn't fully satisfy you. It always seems like more information would help you feel settled about the matter. You ask the same questions over and over again—to yourself, to God, to friends, to the coffee table, to whomever will listen. The problem is, rather than relieving your anxieties, you only increase them when you feverishly dig for details, tidbits, and hidden causes surrounding your traumatic experience. For one thing, it causes you to focus obsessively on the past, which cannot be changed, and to ignore the present.

WHY DO WE ASK WHY?

So why do we continue to question along the same venue when the results aren't satisfying? I think that there are six primary reasons.

You Believe the Answers Will Help You Regain Control

When adversity strikes, it sends you reeling. After all, this wasn't supposed to happen to you.

While it can be argued that we never (or rarely) have real

control in life, we all like to think that we do. Whenever you go through unexpected trauma, you are reminded of your powerlessness, for often there was absolutely nothing you could have done to prevent it. It just happened. You don't like being powerless, so you fight it. One of the ways you do that is by the search for information.

You've probably heard the saying "Information is power." Up to a point, there's truth in that. For instance, people in the workplace who are in the communication loop are more likely to wield power; accurate and complete information empowers them to do their jobs well. In a relationship, people who take the time to seek information about the other person's thoughts, feelings, and needs are more adept in developing connections. Additionally, actively seeking rather than denying the facts lays the foundation for effective problem solving. However, you will be disappointed if you believe that you actually can find *all* the answers and that if you could, it would totally relieve your sense of powerlessness. Answers help, but they're not a cure.

People who are caught up in these beliefs end up trapped in an obsessive search cycle. Because the information they uncover provides only temporary relief, they tell themselves that the next answer will surely settle their anxiety and quiet their mind once and for all. And so it goes. The tidbits they uncover are reassuring—for a while. Ultimately, though, they are disappointing because the new information cannot convince them that they are really in control. (Reality always upsets that applecart.)

More often than not, we are actually seeking deeper answers that are elusive and unattainable. If we are unable to accept the inevitable truth that answers are not absolute, our quest will continue and we will become addicted to the search. The bottom line is, rather than giving you control, incessant questions really cause you to feel more and more out of control.

Searching for Answers Gives You Something to Do

When you realize there's nothing you can do now to change what happened in the past, you feel powerless in another way. To combat that feeling, you have the urge to do *something*, even if it's the wrong thing.

In addition to the psychological urge to do something, there is also a physical basis for that urge, as we discussed previously. When you are feeling threatened, your body responds with physiological activation that urges you to take some kind of action, whether it's the right action or not. Searching for answers is seductive in that it's something to do when you can't figure out anything else. Unfortunately, this is emotionally exhausting because what you are doing is not really helping. The actions you are taking are not going to regain your lost power.

You Believe You Will Get "Closure" If You Ask Enough Questions

"Closure" is a popular concept in our culture. You hear it all the time when journalists interview people who are struggling to overcome various catastrophes. They talk about some moment in the future when they'll find the answers they're struggling for or when life will be worth living again. "We just want closure," they say.

In my many years of clinical practice, I've interviewed hundreds of people who thought the same thing. They had hung their hopes on some piece of information or event (though usually it was impossible to articulate exactly what this would look like) they believed would lift their confusion and relieve their angst. Yet almost invariably, when I asked them later, "Did you really achieve closure when such-and-such happened?" they said no. The anticipated experience didn't close the wound; it just deepened it. Knowing more only presented them with additional painful facts to process and deal with emotionally. Or the new knowledge raised more questions than it answered.

You Want to Relieve Guilt

Another reason you continue to ask why is that even when logic says you could not have changed what happened, or when others reassure you that you weren't at fault, you are not entirely convinced. You might not be able to point directly to what you could have done differently, yet you're positive that you're just not seeing what you did wrong. You search for errors of commission or omission, examining yourself for secret sins or past mistakes that may have somehow brought on this misfortune.

The problem with this approach is that if you look for it, you *will* find evidence to support your own theory that what happened was your fault. After all, who can't find something we've done wrong, either just prior to the event or in the more distant past? Nobody's perfect. However, these mistakes may have nothing to do with what went wrong. Sure, if you can see that something in your behavior contributed to what happened, you need to correct it. Anything you can do to keep disaster from striking again is worth your attention. However, don't obsess about real or imagined wrongs, and don't waste time or energy punishing yourself for them. You have enough problems to deal with right now without heaping unnecessary ones onto the pile.

Once I was working with a six-year-old boy whose parents had just announced they were getting a divorce. His childish response exemplifies what I've heard from many an adult.

"My parents are getting a divorce because of me," Galen said.

"Oh, really?" I responded. "What makes you think it's because of you?"

"I just know it is. I took my shovel and dug up a bunch of holes in the backyard. I think that's why they're mad at each other."

Of course, there was absolutely no connection between this child's misdeeds and his parents' divorce. Yet this explanation, though painful to him, was appealing in a way. If he was the one who had caused the breakup, that meant there was nothing wrong with his parents, on whom he depended for security. That made his world safer. Often children feel less helpless if they take responsibility. If they're the ones who caused the problem, then just by being "good" again, they think they can fix the problem. Like Galen, if you define the problem as something within your power to cause, you can regain a sense of power by telling yourself you won't do that again, and then everything will be all right in the future.

Another purpose of searching for guilt is that there's always the chance you'll "prove" yourself innocent. Secretly, you hope to relieve the burden of guilt. In other words, if you find you were not at fault, at least you can be absolved, and that will be one hurt you won't have to feel any longer.

You Think If You Just Keep Digging, You Can Rewrite the Ending

The logical mind knows that nothing will change the past, but sometimes false hope springs eternal. You begin to think, "Maybe if I do this . . . then . . ."

I interviewed Shari some eight months after the fatal morning that redefined her world. A professional woman with a sharp mind, Shari found that her usual rational skills were suddenly seduced by the wishful thinking that underlies "What if?"

It had been a perfect, clear morning for their daily 6:00 a.m. walk. As usual, Shari and her walking partner of six years donned reflective safety gear. Chatting and laughing, they turned onto their street, with Shari on the inside and her friend closest to the road. Without warning, she heard a sickening screech and in an instant her friend was thrown into the air and on top of the car that had careened around the corner. Shaking off a moment of paralysis, she ran to where he lay and attempted CPR. He didn't move. He died almost instantly.

After the accident, Shari wrestled with questions:

- Why didn't the driver see them? Was she on a cell phone or putting on makeup? If only she had been paying attention.

- What if she hadn't gone back in the house to get her reflective gear before she left? Could that three minutes have made the difference between life and death? If they had not been in that exact spot at that time, maybe her friend would still be alive.

- She really hadn't felt well that morning. What if she had chosen to stay home? Would he have gone on? Would he have been in that exact spot or closer to the side of the road? What difference would that have made?

- Why didn't they hear the car coming? Maybe they could have jumped out of the way.

Can you see what Shari is searching for in her questions? Embedded in her queries is the attempt to magically turn back the clock and make the situation turn out differently. But what happened, happened. No amount of imaginary revision of the scene will change it.

You Want to Protect Yourself and Others in the Future

The desire to protect yourself and others in the future is actually a good reason to search for answers, provided you keep your responses level-headed. Of course, you want to make the world safer for yourself and those you love. But how do you know if the desire for safety has become obsessive, either diminishing the effectiveness of your precautionary measures or becoming downright harmful? Consider the aftermath of the tragic death of infant Damien.

When six-week-old Damien's vomiting wouldn't stop, his parents took him to the emergency room. After the doctor examined the baby, she gave him meds to stop the throwing up and then reassured them, "It's probably just a stomach virus. Give him plenty of liquids, and he'll probably be fine in a few hours." He was not. The autopsy revealed meningitis.

How could this have happened? Carolyn, Damien's mom, read everything she could get her hands on about meningitis. In fact, she bought volumes on every possible childhood illness and practically memorized them. At any sign of tummy upset, crankiness, the smallest sniffle, or dozens of other symptoms she had read about, she rushed her four-year-old daughter Emily to the pediatrician. The "mild diagnosis" the doctor provided gave no comfort to Carolyn. She was sure that there was something the physician was missing and worried about it incessantly. Carolyn also kept Emily away from other children, fearful that she would pick up germs. No birthday parties, no Sunday school, no playing with kids in the neighborhood.

Carolyn was determined to prevent the painful loss of another child. However, her understandable concern turned into an obsession that robbed Emily of the opportunity for a well-rounded, healthy life.

Consider these two key issues. First, is your search for protective strategies yielding new and practical information you can actually use? Or are you asking the same questions over and over without being able to define specific, legitimate steps that will prevent related harm in the future? If you aren't sure, you may be getting stuck. Second, what specific wise actions can you take to provide greater security for yourself and your loved ones in the future without becoming so overprotective that you severely limit your life? Yes, of course, take responsible action when there are obvious ways to change bad habits or make your life more secure. But be cautious about taking this too far. Your attempts to build a wall around you and your family that will keep out all possible harm may actually be doing more harm than good. A free life always holds some risk, and to feel your aliveness, you must learn to tolerate risk. Don't isolate yourself from new people or opportunities for growth in a misguided, frenetic attempt to guarantee safety.

YOU HAVE A CHOICE: WHY OR HOW

Maybe you're saying to yourself, "Once I find my answers, I'll be able to move on." Maybe so, maybe not. You might end up getting stuck in the quest to discover all the whys and wherefores. Let's consider a few results of this choice.

Endless Whys Aren't Wise

A friend of mine, Captain Dave Carey, is a motivational speaker and author who often shares his experiences as a POW during the Vietnam era.[1] He also encountered a more recent life challenge when his wife, Karen, underwent an unsuccessful, grueling battle with breast cancer.

Dave described the months of questioning why Karen's breast cancer had recurred several times and why it spread. Then he said, "Throughout Karen's long battle, we talked a lot and wrestled with so many questions. I can remember it as though it were yesterday. We were sitting at the table and crying and talking once again about our confusion. Why was this happening to us? Then, it finally dawned on us. 'Why?' was not a good question. First of all, no matter what the answer to that question was, we weren't going to like it. And second, whatever it was, the outcome and the reasons for that outcome were not in our hands, but in God's hands.

"The Bible says that we are the clay, and cannot the potter do what he wishes with the clay? I had read all that stuff before and intellectually agreed. But I tell you what, when you have to experience it, it's hard. It's hard to realize that God is working a plan here, and that's okay.

"But suddenly the truth dawned on us, and we quit asking why. As a matter of fact, we quit so much wrestling with this whole thing. We began to focus on what we had to do that day."

Dave and Karen continued to do everything within their power to restore Karen's health, but they stopped asking questions to which they would probably never receive satisfying answers. They came to a point where they realized that they were wasting their emotional, mental, and spiritual energy on questions, rather than on enjoying the time they had left together.

Still not convinced? Still hanging onto the belief that if only you could find the answers, then everything will be okay? Let's dig a little deeper and examine three consequences of holding on to obsessive questioning.

1. *You fall prey to "analysis paralysis."* After a traumatic occurrence, many people respond with an insatiable search for the perfect answer. This can lead to being stuck in an endless quest for more information that will help them analyze the event and, hypothetically, come to understand it. Some people naturally tend toward perfectionism, details, and control, and these people are even more vulnerable to analysis paralysis. Each new bit of information, far from satisfying their curiosity, only convinces them that there is so much more to discover. So the search continues.

Yes, it helps when you have a level of understanding, but that is not always possible. The problem is that while you're searching and scraping for the next answer—believing that this one will be the key—you're sitting still. You fear that if you leave some stone unturned, you might miss an important piece of information you need to map out the solution. You're constantly "getting ready to get ready."

2. *Relationships deteriorate when you incessantly question people.* I've seen this one played out hundreds of times with clients who are struggling to recover from a betrayal perpetrated by someone they trusted. Discovered affairs, for instance, are prime emotional territory for the broken-record approach to asking questions:

- "How could you do this to me?"

- "Why did you do it?"

- "Will you do it again?"

- "How can I ever trust you?"

- "Who are you, anyway? I thought I knew you."

Even if the other person is repentant and really wants to make things right, that individual usually doesn't have very good answers to these questions—not the first time the question is asked, much less the seventy-third time. Yet the questioner is certain the offender is withholding critical information, and the accuser wants to be absolutely sure the other person is being held accountable.

Let me say before I go farther that it's reasonable to want to know why something happened so that preventative actions can be taken. So when does questioning become problematic, heaping unnecessary and additional injury onto a relationship you are trying to salvage?

- When you've asked the same question over and over, and you're not getting any new or helpful information.

- When the question–answer process is making both of you more frustrated and angry.

- When you become aware that the motive behind your repetitive questioning is more to punish than to save the relationship.

If your ultimate goal is to have a healthy relationship and, in particular, to restore one that has been damaged, maybe it's time to stop picking the scab off the wound (pardon the graphic image). Instead of constantly asking what happened, it may be time to begin to create a positive vision of what can happen now. Spend some time talking with your loved one about how he or she would define a quality relationship and how you two can work toward those things you collectively or individually value. For instance, what kinds of things can you do to enjoy each other's company again? Are there activities you used to like doing together that you've gradually dropped? When you were dating, what kinds of loving acts showed the other person that you cared? Can you begin to do things like a "thinking about you" phone call in the middle of the day, planning a special date, or leaving a loving note for the other to find? Perhaps you could block out some time—even fifteen minutes a day—to just sit together over a cup of coffee and talk about not only the events of the day, but how you reacted to them.

3. *You grow more frustrated as you continue to search for answers that you're never going to get.* "But I should be able to find

that out," you may be saying to yourself. I can see how it feels that way, but it just may not be possible. I remember talking with Ben about his experience.

Ben's wife of twenty-three years, Mona, packed up and left while he was away at work. She left a note with no explanation; she just said she'd had it. She wouldn't return his calls to her cell phone. Ben then went to Mona's new apartment, which he had managed to locate, but she wouldn't come to the door.

> *If you look backward too much, you'll soon be headed that way!*

He kept riding by there, hoping to see some clue that would help him understand and come to terms with her leaving. On one other occasion a few days later, he again went up and knocked on her door. No one answered, though her car was in the parking lot. The following afternoon Ben had a call from the sheriff's department, informing him that he was now under a restraining order; he was not to go within five hundred feet of her apartment.

Ben thought he simply couldn't go on unless he figured out what caused Mona to leave. He called her mother, her sister, and her friends, trying desperately to learn why Mona had abandoned him—to no avail. He mentally replayed hundreds of scenes from what he believed was a solid marriage, making himself miserable by second-guessing his every action.

Mona's attorney relayed her desire for an "irreconcilable differences" divorce. Ben finally signed the divorce papers, but well over a year later, he was still emotionally stuck. He could not free himself to pursue another relationship, afraid that he would repeat the phantom mistakes he believed he must have made in the past.

If your search, like Ben's, is wasting valuable recovery time because it's making you more frustrated, it's not worth it.

Frustration easily turns into anger, and anger easily hardens into bitterness. Does this sound like it's heading in a good direction? If you look backward too much, you'll soon be headed that way!

Is your questioning making you feel better or worse? Are you feeling more control or less as the answers are not forthcoming? If your plan isn't working, maybe you should consider abandoning it.

DON'T LET THE WRONG QUESTIONS
TAKE YOU CAPTIVE

Another possibility to consider is, maybe you've been asking the wrong questions. That's one of the things Captain Dave Carey, whom you met earlier in this chapter, learned during his lengthy tenure as a prisoner of war in the "Hanoi Hilton." Dave and his fellow prisoners learned, as you can, that some questions are more helpful than others.

> *To dry one's eyes and laugh at a fall, and baffled, get up and begin again.*
> —ROBERT BROWNING

Captain Carey, then a twenty-five-year-old naval aviator, was shot down from the skies of North Vietnam on August 31, 1967. He spent the next five and a half years as a prisoner of war, enduring beatings, torture, and humiliation. He made it clear in my interview with him and in his book, *The Ways We Choose*, that he did not allow himself the luxury of "Why me?" questions for very long. Instead, his priority was how to survive, mentally and physically. He admitted, however, that it was hard at first to adjust to the idea that he was not invincible as he had believed.

"Scott Peck wrote in the first line of *The Road Less Traveled,* 'Life is difficult.'[2] I quickly learned how true that was. There will be joy and sorrow, happy times and sad times. But many of us believe, 'No, life and work are supposed to be easy.' When things go badly, we say, 'Why me? Why is this happening to me?' When things are going well, however, you don't hear anybody saying, 'Why me? Why is this happening to me?' If I have the mind-set that bad things shouldn't happen to me, work and life are going to be very frustrating because life is not perfect."[3]

Rather than becoming mired in the "whys," Dave said he and his fellow POWs quickly had to figure out the "hows":

- *How can we stay in touch and avoid deadly isolation?* So they invented creative ways to communicate with prisoners in other cells. Dave and his cellmates had thick calluses on their knuckles from rapping patterns on the walls.

- *How can we keep our minds active so we keep from going crazy?* So they instituted "entertainment night," when cellmates put on performances and recitations for each other.

- *How can we keep ourselves off the guards' radar screen to avoid interrogations and beatings?* So team members rotated the responsibility of lying on the filthy floor during communications, their eyes straining to see any approaching guards under the cracks beneath the door.

The "how" mind-set helped Dave and his fellow POWs to survive, physically and mentally. And so it is with you. You, too, have the task of using all the resources you have to turn your own times of "psychological incarceration" into learning experiences. Like

Dave and his fellow prisoners, we can learn to create our own freedom, wherever we are.

Turn Your Attention to "How"

As you await release from your own personal prison, do what Dave and his fellow POWs did. Rather than getting stuck on "why," turn your attention to "how" by asking questions like these:

- How can I deal effectively with the adversity I am facing instead of drowning in it?

- How can I learn what I need to learn so that I can get through this and become stronger on the other side?

- What can I learn beyond the crisis that I can use for the rest of my life?

- How am I going to make the right adjustments to adapt to the realities of my life now that it's changed?

- How will I take what I have left and make the best future I can?

- What choices can I make so I can spend the rest of my time on earth living up to my potential as a human being? How will I use my innate gifts?

Can you see how these are better questions than "Why me?" or even "Why?" "How?" is a process-oriented question that inspires you to seek a path of action that may or may not work on the first try. The beauty of it is, if your choice doesn't work, you can tell right away; the results are verifiable. I might tell you to work out on a treadmill to burn off excess energy, but if you try it for a week and it doesn't work, you can say to yourself, "Well, that was fun, but it didn't do the trick because I couldn't turn off my thoughts.

Maybe I need to do something more creative. I'm going to try expressive painting instead, see if I can get my emotions on the page through images. I think I need to understand myself better, and I can't do it through words."

When you ask "why," on the other hand, it invites an abstract answer, and usually the response is not verifiable. "Why did this happen to me? Because I dropped the ball. Because I should have been more alert; I should have been stronger/wiser/better/smarter," and so on. How do you know what you should have been? How do you know for sure if it would have made any difference? Maybe you were just in the right place at the wrong time.

When you are in the midst of deep and enduring suffering, your whole being wants relief. You want to move on and breathe freely again. This is the life force at work, pushing you toward survival. You honor God and the life energy He gave you by using your intelligence to make choices that head you in the right direction. Asking why doesn't necessarily head you in any direction; it often keeps you stuck in a quagmire because you cannot attain a satisfactory answer and because so many "why" questions have blame as an underlying agenda. Asking why is often just another way of asking, "Whose fault is this?"

If you think of yourself as a "prisoner of war" doing battle to save your own life (you are, in fact, trying to save your future), you will want to ask questions that provide answers you can actually use. Let's explore some of the reasons that "how" questions help you significantly more than those repetitive "whys."

HOW "HOW" HELPS

Once you begin to focus on discovering what to do and how to do it, you're well on your way to getting unstuck and moving ahead. Let's think together about how (and why!) this is true.

91

"How" Is an Easier Question to Answer

Go with me into the bedroom of Madge and Bill, where she's asking him the broken-record question for the umpteenth time: "Why did you gamble away your paycheck? Why? You've got to tell me."

Bill's frustrated answer is an honest one: "I don't know why. It just happened."

As you have probably experienced, it's difficult to answer when someone demands to know why you did something. You may have a reaction to the word *why* that dates back to childhood days when your mother caught you with your hand in the cookie jar. Remember? When she asked, "Why did you do that?" in *that voice*, you shrugged your shoulders and mumbled, "I don't know." There's something about that word that just shuts down your brain.

What if Madge were to ask her husband questions like these:

- "Billy, how did this happen?"

- "When you began to think about going to the casino, how did it progress?"

- "What kinds of things can we do to prevent this from happening?"

- "How will you respond differently if you find yourself in a similar circumstance again?"

- "How can we seek help for this out-of-control behavior? I'll be glad to participate and do my part."

Billy might still find this conversation a difficult one emotionally, but he'll at least be more likely to have access to the information he needs to talk about the situation with his wife.

"How" helps you focus on behaviors and conscious thought patterns that are much easier to identify and discuss.

Asking how lets you trace the traumatic event, step by step, using the information available. Through simple research, you can often find out what happened, filling in your own knowledge or memory gaps. You can also go back and examine the context in which it occurred, in some cases learning how the problem started in the first place. Most importantly, you can use the resources available to you to learn how others have dealt with similar situations and how professional caregivers advise you to work through the process.

This information won't necessarily resolve your big problems, and nothing will undo what's already been done, despite any wishful thinking. However, it will move you ever so slightly in the direction of reclaiming your life because you will learn more about what led up to the tragedy and identify any parts of it that you might be able to change in the future.

"How" Gets You Unstuck and Moves You into Action

"How" implies action. You don't have to know the big plan when you ask the question. You don't have to look for answers that will last the rest of your life. All you have to do (which can be a tall order when you're overwhelmed) is to look right in front of you and find out what you can do this hour, this day. Change out of your pajamas and get dressed. Write one thank-you note. Pick up the phone and dial the number of that person who said, "I'm here if you need me." Put on your hiking shoes and take a ten-minute walk around the block.

"How can I get over this?" is too big a question. "How can I do this one thing this morning?" is better because you can manage to find an answer, and you can act on it.

Don't know how to do it, or how to get started? Seek help from a professional coach, psychologist, counselor, social worker, or clergy. Or enlist the help of a buddy.

People want to help, but they usually don't know what to do. You might have a friend who would love to be there while you take those baby steps, but he or she doesn't know what you need right now. Don't just say, "Save me!" Think about it and ask for something specific: "I need to get out of the house, but it just seems so hard right now. Would you be willing to come over and take a fifteen-minute walk with me in my neighborhood?"

Perhaps you don't even feel like getting started. I've been there, and I know what it feels like to have your energy totally depleted. But here's the secret: you have to actually do it *before* you feel like doing it. As you get going, you'll gain momentum and fresh insight, and that will raise your energy level for the next task.

Because "How" Is Practical and Action-Oriented, It Reduces Your Anxiety

When a horrific situation leaves you shaken to the core, even modifying your view of the world, you're in a scary place. All your familiar landmarks have shifted. The ways you coped with little mishaps in the past are not up to the gargantuan tasks you face now. Mixed in with the shock, anger, grief, and other emotions is anxiety—a terrible, churning anxiety. The world is no longer a safe place.

Earlier in this chapter, we talked about the body's response to threat, which is to gear up for "fight or flight." Your nervous system is aroused, preparing itself to confront the threat. Sometimes the potential foe is vague, "out there," and nebulous, yet the sense of dread is very real. If you stay in that state long enough, you become emotionally and physically exhausted.

When you take constructive action, you are giving the body what it is wired and poised for. It wants to move, to rise up against the threat. This fills your need so much better than obsessively searching for elusive information. You're still acting on an internal push to "doing something," but when you ask how instead of why, you have a better chance of doing the right thing.

> *When one door of happiness closes, another opens; but often we look so long at the closed door that we do not see the one which has opened for us.*
>
> —HELEN KELLER

Choosing to take small actions makes you mentally, physically, and spiritually healthy because you are heading in the right direction. Even mental action that involves searching for a new perspective, planning for the future, or rehearsing constructive steps in your imagination begins to relieve anxiety and nudges you forward.

Carolyn, whose son was murdered, described how small actions helped her cope. "Have you ever seen a windshield shattered by a rock? That's what I felt like. My face, my whole body. I was shattered. The pieces were everywhere. I tried to work, but I felt like I was having a nervous breakdown.

"After I built my strength a little, I started using my lunch hour to work out at the nearby gym, usually walking on the treadmill. I couldn't lift weights yet like I used to do, but I would walk on that treadmill. And I would just walk and walk and walk for forty-five minutes. I'm not kidding you, when I'd get back to work, a lot of the tension was gone. Just getting some of that nervous energy out was a release."

When your action level goes up, your anxiety level goes down. (Caution: be sure that the action you take is constructive. Destructive actions like hitting a wall, yelling at someone, or getting drunk may momentarily relieve anxiety, but these actions have negative side effects.)

BEGIN NOW TO CHOOSE "HOW"

Ready to get out of the frustration of "why?" and into the more productive mind-set of "how?" Then go to work on these action-oriented tasks.

1. *List the "whys" you've been stuck on, and write what you've hoped to gain by your continued pursuit of those answers.* Why are you still asking why? Consider these possible motivations: Is it control? The relief of guilt? The rewriting of the ending? Protection for your future? Consider why you are on a continued search for these answers. Then ask yourself this important question—is it working?

> *Change "what if" to "what is."*

2. *Write out the following statement: "I cannot rewrite the ending of things past. What's done is done."* Now say these sentences aloud several times. That, my friend, is the sad truth. What has happened to you is not going to change. I know it's hard, but isn't it time to acknowledge that, both in your head and in your heart, instead of pursuing an illusion?

3. *Change "what if" to "what is."* This is a cousin to number two. Don't spend any more of your time detailing all the possibilities that never materialized. Instead, look at the facts. Assess your current reality as it is, not as you wish it were.

Here's a very important part of this exercise. Begin to write about what you have left, the positive side of your "what is." Focus especially on those people, opportunities, and things for which you are thankful. These are the resources you can use to rebuild your life.

4. *Begin to ask and write about the "how" questions.* Here are a few sample "how" questions you can begin to ask yourself.

- How did it happen, step by step?

- How can I identify the resources I have and focus on those?

- Though I haven't been through anything this big before, how can I call on the methods and strengths I've developed in past crises to help me now?

- How can I build the skills I need to function in this strange world in which I now live?

- How can I structure my life to be safer?

- How can I build a more secure routine without limiting my life by a concrete wall of paranoia and distrust?

- How can I take what I'm learning to strengthen myself and to help others?

God provides thread for the work begun.
— JAMES HOWELL

5. *Think action!* Action doesn't have to be an impressive leap; it can be a tiny creep. The important thing is that it be movement, inch by inch. What little thing can you do today that you didn't or couldn't do yesterday? If what you thought of still seems impossible, can you identify a smaller starting point, one you really can manage? (Hold it! Don't discount that action as insignificant just because you scaled it down. You are where you are. No judgments.)

If you're having trouble with getting yourself in the action mode, call on an encouraging buddy or a professional to help you. Asking for help is action too!

Nothing is too difficult. You only need to know how.
— YIDDISH PROVERB

6. *Think future.* When you're in the throes of grief, it's hard to think about the future. But imagine it this way: "If I were to have a future (though it may seem unlikely right now), what would I want it to look like? If I were to have relationships, what kind would I want? How would I want to see myself?"

Now here's the kicker: "How would I prepare myself for such a future? What do I need to work on within myself to free me for a better life, should that become possible? How might I go about improving myself in these areas? What small behaviors could I adopt today that could possibly bring about an improvement that I could continue to build on?"

The best question, my friend, is "How?"

MY COMMITMENT TO *HOW*

I choose to move into action by asking, "How?" No longer will I be paralyzed by the search for the unanswerable. No longer will I frustrate myself by asking, "Why?" and "What if?" and "Why me?" over and over again, only to be met with deafening silence or answers that torture me.

I recognize that I cannot rewrite history; I can only change my actions and attitudes today. I cannot always comprehend what others do or why they do it. Their minds are not open to me. I can only try to understand my own motives and continue with my own growth. As long as I reside in this human body, I may never understand some of the things that happened to me, but that will not stop me from believing by faith that something good is in store for me in the future.

I relinquish my obsessive quest for "why," and I commit to focus on "how." I zero in on how I can fill this twenty-four-hour day with activities that inch me along in my journey of recovery. I search for ways to learn to live through circumstances that I never chose. In so doing, I will teach myself to deal with this pain and move through it.

With God's help, I will put the pieces of my life back together, perhaps in a different way, but it will work. And through courage and action, I will learn how to live again. Today, I choose how.

4

"How Could God Let This Happen?"

Six years ago, Amanda's twenty-two-year-old daughter, Krista, became romantically involved with a drug dealer. She became pregnant and married him. Since that time, Krista's been hooked on cocaine, shot over a drug deal, kidnapped, and beaten in the head with a gun. She has sometimes prostituted herself for drugs. She leaves home for weeks at a time. Her parents and her child have no idea where she is, but they imagine the worst. Their fears are close to reality. Despite numerous attempts to get Krista into drug rehab, she either refuses or walks away soon after admission.

Amanda said, "At first, we really struggled with God about this. I cried out to him, asking him, 'Why did you do this to us? We've served you. We raised her right.' We never had much financially, but we had our morals. We see people do bad things all the time, yet none of this has happened to them. So we wondered, how could God let this happen to us?"

Earlier I shared with you that I lost my father, a dedicated minister, to cancer when he was thirty-eight and I was nine. It made no sense to me then, and I have to say it makes no sense to me today.

My logical mind thinks, he was serving God, doing so much good for others. I needed him. Why would God take him?

Some forty years later, my mother was diagnosed with Alzheimer's disease. She, too, was a wonderful person who spent her career teaching children and her life in serving others. As I watched that disease ravage her mind and steal her memories before her death, I couldn't help asking God the same questions. "Why would you let this happen to her? It just doesn't seem fair."

Have you been there? I have, on many more than these two occasions. I'm reminded of an incident that involved my oldest grandson, Joseph, when he was about six.

My daughter Amy had all three boys gathered in her arms as they sat outside watching Steven, their dad, trying singlehandedly to build a roof on the storage building. The helper who had committed to be there had not shown up. Steven wrestled with the lumber in the hot sun. Amy kept praying softly, "Lord, please send someone by here who can help him."

After a while when no one had come, Joseph announced, "Mama, I think Jesus is asleep!"

Sometimes it feels that way, doesn't it? I wish I could tell you that I have the magic-bullet answers: do this, do that, and you'll have this all figured out. I wish it were so.

I still don't understand. But I have come to acceptance. My questions no longer keep me from a close relationship with God. I have faith, I believe, I trust God. I have found in the myriad crises in my life that He is faithful, always providing love and strength as I've worked my way through my doubts and questions. I've never lost my basic faith in Him, though I admit I've been mad at Him a few times.

Whether you come from a Christian perspective as I do, or whether you approach these challenges from another spiritual vantage point, there's no way around it. "How could God let this happen?" is a deeply spiritual issue, and this chapter deals frankly with it. I enter into this difficult discussion with you as a fellow struggler, not as an expert with all the answers.

LIFE CHALLENGES YOUR FAITH

Tragedy has a way of testing your faith. After you've come through the darkest days of this emotional winter, your faith will be altered. No question about that. You will be either stronger or weaker spiritually.

I pray that you will be among those who are able to come to terms with the soul-shaking questions about God's role in this horrible mess. If you can do that, your faith will grow. You will come out of this a more resilient and peaceful person. But that is often a grueling process, one in which you may experience confusion, disillusionment, anger, or doubt. And lots of questions, such as:

- Did God cause this?

- If God is all-powerful, why didn't He stop it?

- I was taught that God would watch over me and protect me. What happened?

- I prayed and believed, but it didn't work. Why not?

- How can I trust God after this?

- I'm really angry with God. Is He angry with me?

Is it okay to ask these questions? Yes, that's part of the recovery process. And God is not upset with you for asking them.

Think about it this way. Think about a relationship you have with someone you really care about, such as your spouse, child, or close friend. Now imagine that something happened that caused your loved one to question your motives or to believe that you had chosen to do something hurtful. Would you want that individual to stay away from you and refuse to talk about his or her concerns, holding them in and carrying them for years? Or would you want the opportunity to discuss it and to be around the person to reassure him or her of your love and commitment? I don't know about you, but I'd definitely want my loved one to talk with me about his or her perceptions, questions, and struggles.

God is like that. He wants to communicate, even when the communication is not all positive and polite. He's big enough to handle your questions. He's not going to desert you or zap you because you feel anger toward Him. He's patient enough to guide you through a slow, painful process. He's faithful, even more than committed earthly parents who love their children through the worst of circumstances. He's there for you, even when you feel like pushing Him away.

Mary, a missionary in Guatemala, learned through a difficult experience that God is big enough to handle all our questions—even our not-so-nice ones. She was house-sitting for a missionary couple who were away on a trip when robbers broke into the house. Mary went through a four-hour ordeal in which she was tortured and sexually assaulted. She survived it, but her pain was quadrupled in the aftermath by behavior less violent but perhaps even more hurtful.

After the robbery and assault, Mary returned to the U.S. Soon afterward, she received a letter from the missionaries, demanding that she pay them for the items that were taken in the robbery! They made no mention of what she went through, just bluntly demanded the payment. She was crushed even more deeply when she received a letter from the mission director, in effect her boss and spiritual leader, supporting their demand. Never did she receive a call from anyone to inquire how she was doing.

Doubts are the ants in the pants that keep faith moving.
—FREDERICK BUECHNER

Mary questioned God, and she was disillusioned about people she had viewed as God's representatives. She described it this way: "I went through a stage where I would just try to get alone and talk with God. There were many times when I shook my fists at God and said, 'I don't understand this emptiness, and I don't understand why I'm standing here before you and before people . . . emotionally naked . . . ripped apart. All this darkness is here, and I don't understand that. We used to have good times walking together. You used me to help others. Why am I going through all of this now?'

"A minister told me, 'Mary, God's big enough for you to get mad at, and it won't bother Him. I've known people to shake their fists at God. He's big enough for that too. So you need to talk to Him and tell Him how you feel. Tell Him what you're thinking. Just get it out. You can communicate.'

"It's taken a long time to get past the distrust of God and people and to feel a little bit more normal. But God never abandoned me, no matter what so-called religious people did."

As Mary's experience demonstrates, it's just fine to question God. God doesn't topple off His throne in shock when you are honest with Him about your doubts and your anger. You may not get specific answers to all your questions . . . maybe not even most of them. But as you work to achieve acceptance, you'll find more peace. Sometimes it takes some time—and a lot of soul-searching.

THIS WORK BRINGS OWNERSHIP OF YOUR BELIEFS

Remember when you were a child and your parents laid down rules, rules, and more rules? Those were their rules, and you had to follow them. Your parents may have tried to explain their reasons to you from time to time, letting you know why it was best for you to do what they required. But for the most part, they probably just expected you to trust that they knew best and to do what they said. At least mine did.

As you grew older, you carried some of those rules in your head. Some you continued to try to obey, some not. Then came more life experience, and you began to see firsthand what your mom meant, why your dad always required that. In other words, you tested those rules for yourself. In the crucible of your own life laboratory, some of the rules became encoded as values. Values—deeply held personal beliefs and principles—come only after real challenges and personal encounters with God that teach you the truth at a heart level.

The spiritual work you do after tragedy has the power to do just that: to create firm beliefs rooted in spiritual wisdom, to implant values in the place of lightly examined rules. If you make wise choices, then renewed, stronger, deeper faith can emerge from the ashes.

WHAT DO YOU BELIEVE?

We've already seen that traumatic events can challenge your spiritual beliefs and assumptions. Let's look at some of the beliefs that can cause confusion during adversity. I'll share a few thoughts with you about each of them, rooted in a combination of biblical teaching and other ancient wisdom, personal experience, and insights gleaned from others who have successfully dealt with hardships.

Belief #1: If You're Good, God Won't Let Bad Things Happen

Marty could hardly believe his ears! He had devoted the past twenty-three years to the company. He'd uprooted his family seven times, willing to go where he was needed most. His performance reviews had been good, and he'd been promoted up the ladder. Retirement was only six years away.

He'd had to work many extra-long hours since they announced the merger, getting things in order for the planning meetings they'd have with their new colleagues. When the VP of Operations called him in, he expected an "Attaboy!" for his hard work and an update on their next steps.

Instead he heard, "Marty, I'm sorry, but your position is being eliminated. You know how it is with these reorganizations."

Rabbi Harold S. Kushner's book *When Bad Things Happen to Good People* has been a bestseller for years, and for good reason.[1] As the title describes, it addresses one of life's greatest enigmas.

We know intellectually and logically that good people do go through bad circumstances. But when it happens to us, our true beliefs are uncovered. We assume that if we're "good," we deserve good results. Think about your typical response when adversity strikes: "What did I do to deserve this?" Prompting this question is a deeper belief: "If something bad happened, I must have been bad, because bad things don't happen to good people."

You see, we've helped ourselves feel more secure in the world by telling ourselves, "If I just live right and treat others as I would want to be treated, everything will be Okay." Not necessarily. True enough, by "living right," so to speak, you clearly stack the deck in your favor. You increase the probability that you will experience a positive life. It's more likely that you'll get back what you put out. But, unfortunately, they don't sell an insurance policy that protects you from hardship and catastrophe.

No matter how faith-filled, how honest, how kind, or how saintly you are, you will have trials and tribulations in this life. But don't get down and out about it. Keep the faith, and you will eventually overcome.

Once a seminar participant told me, "The only fair in life is a carnival." Sometimes I think that may be true. You will delay your healing indefinitely if you get stuck in the unrealistic fantasy that life should be fair. Repetitive thoughts about fairness reignite anger, revenge fantasies, and destructive behavior.

Misunderstandings and unrealistic expectations about how life works make you especially vulnerable to becoming caught in the fairness trap. Don't think you fall into this category? Take this quick, two-question quiz to find out.

1. *True or false? Treat others the way you want them to treat you, and they will.*

   False. The Golden Rule is not a rule. Of course, when you treat others with respect and kindness, this significantly increases the probability that you will be treated the same way in return. But your actions fall far short of guaranteeing reciprocity.

   All people have choices. Some people lack strength of character. Other people respond negatively when they find themselves in a difficult situation. Whatever the circumstances, it is foolhardy to expect that you'll be liked, respected, and treated fairly by everyone you encounter, or even by all those you've been kind to in the past.

2. *True or false? When you invest, you can expect a return.*

   Often false. No one invests hoping to lose. However, there are no guarantees.

   I've seen hundreds of people stay in horrible personal situations because they've been there so long, invested so much. They hope against hope that one day, things will turn around. It's a gamble with odds akin to those enjoyed by the addicted gambler who feeds the slot machine over and over, believing that this time the payoff will come.

When a personal or financial investment fails to pay the expected dividends, it's easy to get stuck in the anger of, "It's just not fair." True, it's not fair. But if it's where you find yourself, you must come to terms with the harsh realities and get moving. Gather the resources you have left and begin to rebuild.

The bottom line? *Get real.* We live in a world that very often is not fair—not by our definitions, anyway. An unrealistic expectation that fairness in this life is one of your "inalienable rights" will only bring you a string of disappointments.

Do what's within your power to be fair to the people in your life, remembering all the while that treating others well and doing good in the world does not assure that you'll always receive good in return. It definitely increases the probability, but it doesn't guarantee it!

The rain falls on both the good and the not-so-good folks; it doesn't discriminate. In this world, we all will have troubles. But be encouraged! When you hold on to your faith in God (and more importantly, He holds onto you!), those trials won't take you under. The fires you're walking through won't burn you up.

Do bad things happen to good people? Absolutely yes. Not one of us is exempt from those tests. Now let's look at a second tricky concept that often causes us to stumble spiritually.

Belief #2: God Can Do Anything He Wants To

God can do anything, because He's God. (And I'm not. That's a hard lesson!) However, though God could do whatever He wanted, He has chosen to limit Himself in this phase of the earth's history. Let's consider three key factors in this: our freedom of choice, divinely ordained natural laws, and God's divine timetable.

1. *Our freedom of choice.* God gave each human being what theologians call a "free will," the ability to choose attitudes, actions, and lifestyle. And because other people have been allowed free will, they often make negative choices that affect us.

Listen to the way Jeff described it: "My twenty-four-year-old son had absolutely nothing to do with the fact that he was robbed and beaten by a home invader. He was there minding his business; but that man chose to break the law and assault my son."

Was this crime God's will? No, it was the will of the person who chose to perpetrate it. God knew it, though, and He allowed it because He put into place a system in which people can exercise their own wills.

2. *Natural laws.* God has spun into motion natural laws and earthly processes that affect us all. Consider weather disasters, for instance. Sure, you hear stories about a tornado skipping over one house and hitting another. Is there a divine design to that? Most of the time, probably not. Sometimes moral people get hit, and scoundrels are spared.

Or think about this. If an airplane, for whatever reason, becomes unable to fly, it's coming down . . . no matter how many good people are on it. The cause? Gravity, one of the earth's natural laws.

3. *God's divine timetable.* I've studied this one through Scripture, prayer and communion with God, and consultation from trusted spiritual leaders. You may not totally agree, but I hope you will reflect with me on the intriguing concept that God's permission of suffering is actually an act of love.

I believe that the time will come when God sets it all straight. Evil will forever be put in its rightful place. The evil spiritual forces will meet judgment and lose their power to seduce and torment others. All those who have elected to follow evil will also be called to account. There will then be peace in heaven and on earth because evil will have been removed.

At that point, however, the days of opportunity to commit to God's pathway of love and goodness will be over. Every human will have made his or her eternal choice because the clock will have stopped on the time of loving, merciful invitation to choose God's plan.

I believe that one of the big reasons God continues to allow evil in the world is to extend the time of opportunity for the members of the human race to choose divine love and mercy. Unfortunately, as long as evil is permitted to remain in the world, suffering will be here too. In a paradoxical way, then, God's permission of suffering is a demonstration of His love.

"But," you may argue, "some of the things that happen don't involve human error or even evil. They just happen." I agree with you. There are freak accidents and other horrific events that just happen. God could stop them, but He sometimes doesn't. We don't understand why. We may never understand why.

I recently interviewed Rosemarie Rossetti, Ph.D., author and speaker, one of my colleagues in the National Speakers Association.[2] Her life changed in an instant because of an accident that resulted in a paralyzing spinal cord injury. Her story is representative of the millions each year who suddenly experience a life-altering tragedy without any human error involved. It just happened. In a later chapter, you'll hear more from Rosemarie on what she learned during her courageous and lengthy rehabilitation. But for right now, I just invite you to listen as she shares what happened.

"The story begins on June 13, 1998, our third wedding anniversary. It was Saturday afternoon—a Caribbean blue sky, no wind, no rain, not a cloud around. My husband, Mark, and I loaded the bikes onto the back of our car and drove from Columbus to Granville, a small town about forty-five minutes east of Columbus. We parked the car downtown, and I got out of the passenger seat. I had no way of knowing it, but that moment was when I took my last step.

"I got on the bike and started riding the trail, laughing and talking and having a wonderful time, when all of a sudden Mark heard what he thought was a gunshot. He slowed down, looking to the right. That's when he saw it. He yelled to me, 'Look over there. Something's falling.' And I remember looking to my right and seeing a few leaves falling to the ground. Instinct told me to speed up. He shouted, 'Stop!' What he had seen was a tree that was halfway on its way to the ground. And within an instant I was crushed by a three-and-a-half-ton tree that was followed by a live power line. I was pinned, crushed, and knocked unconscious on my bike underneath an eighty-foot-tall tree. I had two broken vertebrae in my neck and five crushed vertebrae in my back. I didn't have any head injuries; the helmet protected my head.

"I woke up, and there was Mark and the other two cyclists who happened to be on the trail. Mark was screaming. The three of them leveraged themselves and got me out and laid me on the bike trail. And I just lay there looking up at my husband.

"I asked, 'What happened?' He told me a tree fell, and all I could say was 'Why, why?' I'm lying there in excruciating pain. He had no answer, of course. 'It just fell. It just fell.' And I was just crying. I couldn't move below my waist, so I knew it was very serious."

As time went on, Rosemarie searched for answers about why the tree fell. She was told by experts, "It could have been a bumble-bee that landed on it, or a bird, or a leaf expanding, or a little extra dew on the tree, or a little wisp of wind. It didn't take much. The tree was rotten." And why at that second? "We can't know why. It just happened. It could have been the proverbial straw that broke the camel's back."

Rosemarie says that she questioned nature, but she did not have an issue with why God let it happen. Not so for so many others.

Here's another belief that deserves some challenging thought.

Belief #3: Prayer Always Works

Does prayer always work? That depends on your definition of *work*. If you mean that prayer always results in a positive response to your request, you must not have had much experience with prayer.

I believe that God hears and answers all prayers. I personally experienced miraculous healing from systemic lupus almost thirty years ago, and I've had many other wonderfully positive answers to prayer. However, there have also been times when I prayed just as earnestly and believed just as strongly . . . but I didn't get what I was asking for. Often what I was asking for wasn't some selfish material wish. It was something really good, something that seemed in line with God's principles, something I thought would help someone else or me in all the right ways. I was experiencing the other side of answered prayer—God's answer was "no" or "wait."

What I also found is, prayer works to change *me*. It may not change my situation, but when I truly communicate with God, over time, my thoughts and attitudes are rearranged. I benefit because my connection with God produces hope and positive action. The chorus of testimonies about this phenomenon is made up of millions of people across the centuries.

Scientific evidence also backs up the healing effects of prayer. True, certain scientists may describe what happens as the placebo effect or the power of expectations and belief. Call it what you will—studies show that prayer, meditation, and faith change not only your spiritual and psychological health, they impact your physical health as well. Prayer helps to remove stress, reversing the burst of hormones that can suppress immunity. When the believer "steps into the familiar space" of prayer, the threatening environment fades into the background, again reducing stress and bolstering the body's natural defense systems.[3]

Belief #4: When You Have Faith, You Can Visualize It, Act on It, and It Will Come to Pass

In religious faith, as in pop psychology, there is much talk about visualization. It's true, one aspect of faith involves seeing something positive before it happens, believing that it exists prior to actually seeing it demonstrated, and acting in ways that support its coming to pass.

Is visualization a magic way for your faith to get you what you think you should have? If you say the right words and give commands to the universe, do you automatically attract the fulfillment of your wishes? Nope. In fact, one of the hurdles you have to cross after life-changing trauma is accepting the losses of so many things you visualized. They were good things, you hoped for them, you legitimately expected them . . . but they will never be as you imagined. Not after the unexpected unthinkable occurred.

> *The universe is not your genie!*

Contrary to the "secret" espoused to eager readers, the universe is not your genie! Things don't always happen as you hope, imagine, and send forth. The real secret, however, is that God sustains and energizes you, no matter what!

Here's an interesting thought to ponder. Rather than having faith in God, some people have faith in "faith." Do you have a neat faith formula that is always supposed to work—in other words, faith in your faith? Or is your faith in the sovereign God? The answer to that question makes a big difference. Faith in God means hanging tough, even when things don't work out the way you wanted. It means holding onto God's hand, even when you don't have the tools to decipher His overall plan.

Belief #5: When You Have Spiritual Faith, Life Will Make Sense

Genuine faith in God gives life a sense of meaning. However, that doesn't mean that life will always make sense! Far from it. It's a pipe dream that all the puzzle pieces will fit nicely and that nothing but obvious blessings will pour on you constantly.

God does not always choose to explain the tragedies and hardships that come into our lives. He doesn't require our signature of approval. We must never forget that He is God. Our trust in Him must not be contingent on our comprehension and understanding of all the struggles that come into our lives.

From where we sit, life just may not make sense. However, for so many reasons, trust in a loving, all-knowing, sovereign God does.

YOU HAVE A CHOICE: DOUBT OR FAITH

While you may have many spiritual questions, you do have choices. You can choose *doubt,* reasoning that a loving God could not, would not have allowed this to happen to you. In the perspective of doubt, God cannot be relied upon and trusted. Better watch your back and just take care of yourself.

Alternatively, you can hold on to *faith,* trusting in God's loving character even when the evidence you see is confusing, determining to act on beliefs consistent with hope and love, taking comfort in God's promises to see you through whatever happens to you.

Let's look at a few of the costs and benefits of these two choices.

Distrust and Doubt Wear You Out

Maybe you think it would be easier to just stay where you are . . . questioning, eternally questioning. Stay away from a God you don't understand. But there is a big price tag to that. Let's look at a few of the consequences of distrust.

1. *At a time when you need it most, you have nothing solid to hold on to.* When everything is dimly lit, shifting, and uncertain, the last thing you need is to feel disconnected from God and other sources of your spiritual strength. The relationship with an unchanging, ever-present God can be the anchor that prevents your shipwreck when you are going through the raging storms of life.

2. *You feel a need to depend totally on yourself at a time when you are not yourself.* When you don't trust God, and you don't feel that others understand, you have no one left to depend on but yourself.

Listen in on my conversation with Gregory, a promising young businessman who had to file bankruptcy because of an unforeseen market change. He said, "I look in the mirror, and I wonder if I even know myself anymore. To make matters worse, I thought I had it all under control, and look what happened. When I started the business, I prayed about it. I thought I was doing the right thing. It's hard to pray now. But I don't trust myself either."

Gregory found himself in a position of total reliance on a person in whom he'd lost confidence—himself. I would argue that the arrogance of self-reliance is never a good idea, but it's certainly a scary thing when your world's been upended.

3. *The distrust can grow into hardened cynicism.* It's a short trip between spiritual distrust and a cynical, what's-the-use-anyway attitude. *The Merriam-Webster Online Dictionary* defines *cynical* as "contemptuously distrustful of human nature or motives."[4] When your legitimate questions begin to morph into a belief that God is up there just waiting to squash you if you make a wrong move or

for no reason at all, that erroneous belief can pour concrete into your soul.

Consider how Sandi responded to a devastating material loss. She was so proud of her new dream home. She and her husband, John, had scraped and saved for five years for the down payment and even some new furniture. When the home had finally been completed three months ago, she'd carefully displayed the treasures that had been handed down from her mother, who had inherited them from her grandmother.

Sandi looked back with pride on her home as she, John, and their two children pulled out of the driveway and headed to Chuck E. Cheese. Who on earth could have guessed that this would be the last time she would see her beautiful home intact?

She couldn't believe her eyes when they rounded the corner two hours later. The back half of their house was already engulfed in flames. Frantically, she dialed 911 on her cell phone. The fire truck sped to the scene, but the destruction of their beautiful home was unstoppable. Nothing could be saved. They lost it all.

Afterward Sandi struggled with her view of God. How could He let this happen to them? They'd worked so hard. Just when it seemed things were leveling out, that their dreams had come true—poof! Literally, everything went up in smoke. It made sense to her that God had been just a little perturbed that they were so happy and had slapped them down a notch or two. This fit with the cynical view her father had always had, and now it appeared that he had been right all along.

She said, "Trust a God like that? No, thank you. All this stuff about 'God is love.' Where was He when those new electrical outlets sparked and caught my drapes on fire? Where was His love when my family heirlooms went up in smoke? When our family pictures and the memories they represented were incinerated? What kind of God would allow that kind of loss? I don't care to hang out with anyone who is that cruel. I think I'll just keep my distance from now on."

The problem is, the longer Sandi stays away from God, the more convinced she may become of His untrustworthiness. As in human relationships, trust in God is not reestablished in a vacuum. Why? Because there's no opportunity to test your negative expectations, so you continue to believe that your worst fears are true. As risky as it feels, the rebuilding of trust only comes through contact. If Sandi chooses to cut herself off from God's support and sustaining power as she's going through this loss, she'll miss the chance to experience His loving nature.

> *Faith keeps you right side up, even when your world turns upside down.*

Faith Yields Health and Wholeness

Faith, on the other hand, brings a sense of security and comfort, even (especially) when the circumstances around you are chaotic and incomprehensible. This isn't just a "religious" concept either. Growing scientific evidence reveals the positive impact of faith on your health. Let's explore three of the major benefits of faith.

1. *You have personal stability in an unstable world.* This world can't be trusted to deliver your dreams intact. You can be blindsided by events that wreck your well-laid plans and your concepts about how things should and will be.

Faith keeps you right side up, even when your world turns upside down. No matter what your circumstance, your internal world is not so easily shaken when you firmly believe that God is constant; He never changes; He loves you with a quality and depth of love you could never comprehend; and if you open yourself to Him, He will empower you, giving you strength and practical help.

2. Research shows the practice of faith makes your mind and body healthier. The empirical evidence for the positive impact of faith is overwhelming and exciting. When I came through graduate school (more than a couple of years ago!), we were subjected to the un-informed opinions of people like Sigmund Freud that religion exerted a negative and neurotic influence on mental health. Many of us knew differently from our own experience, but back then, matters of faith were looked upon with skepticism or downright disdain by much of the scientific community. Of course, we all know that it's possible for religion to be practiced pathologically, such as when people use it to rationalize hatred, prejudice, aggression, and judgment of others.[5]

Many studies now document the powerful connection between faith and both mental and emotional health. Harold Koenig, M.D., associate professor at Duke University Medical Center, provided an excellent systematic review of research on this topic in his book *Is Religion Good for Your Health? The Effects of Religion on Physical and Mental Health.*[6]

Dr. Koenig drew confident conclusions from his review of hundreds of studies about the relationship between religion and health. He demonstrated that the practices of church attendance, prayer, Scripture reading, and devout religious commitment, particularly within the context of an established Judeo-Christian community (excluding cults like those involved at Jonestown and Waco) are associated with better mental and physical health. Check out a sample of the results Dr. Koenig cited for the health implications of the active practice of faith.

Mental Health

- The use of faith for coping is statistically related to higher self-esteem.[7]

- Devout religious commitment is associated with lower rates of depression and quicker recovery from it,[8] higher morale and well-being,[9] and marital satisfaction.[10]

- Frequent church or synagogue attendance is correlated with lower suicide rates,[11] lower rates of anxiety disorders,[12] lower rates of alcohol and drug use,[13] more social support,[14] and higher life satisfaction.[15]

- Private religious activities like prayer and Scripture reading are associated with greater well-being and life satisfaction,[16] less death anxiety,[17] and lower rates of chemical dependency.[18]

- Interventions for depression and anxiety that incorporate religious concepts with secular approaches bring about faster recovery than secular approaches alone.[19]

Physical Health
- Frequent church attendance predicts lower levels of physical disability in older adults, including faster recovery from hip fractures.[20, 21]

- Intensity of religious commitment and frequency of church attendance are associated with lower perceived pain levels in end-stage cancer patients.[22]

- Frequent church attendance and religious commitment are correlated with lower blood pressure and lower risk of stroke and heart attack.[23] In fact, the risk of heart attack for nonreligious men is four to seven times higher than that of religious men.[24]

- Religious commitment and frequent attendance at church/synagogue are associated with lower mortality in general, a finding so robust it was found in 80 percent of the studies that examined this association.[25]

Whew! If that doesn't convince you, nothing will! Science documents what millions of people could tell you—a strong faith in God delivers great value!

3. *You experience hope, which promotes persistence and fights depression and discouragement.* Hope and optimism are often central features in religious belief and practice. Hope is generated when you believe that there is a divine Someone who is able to bring you through the worst of times and who gives you creative ideas and abilities to do day-to-day, minute-to-minute problem solving.

Hope is a central element in all recovery. When you have hope, you are willing to stay positive, to keep trying, to believe that you will survive, and to determine that somehow good will come from your suffering. Faith in a loving God is a wellspring of hope.

BEGIN NOW TO CHOOSE *FAITH*

With the authority of scientific research, along with years of experience with the psychological and spiritual realities in my own life and countless others', I encourage you to choose faith as a resource to sustain and move you on your journey after personal crisis. Below are six key ways to do so.

Know the Truth: Big Struggles Are a Fact of Life for Everyone

Sooner or later, every person will encounter disappointments, heartaches, and tragedies. No one is excluded from that group, no matter how well we try to live nor how lovingly we treat others.

Don't be surprised or shocked by trials. Expect them, and refuse to sink into cynicism when (not if) they happen.

> *Constant sunshine is not the projected weather forecast.*

Now I'm not suggesting you become a pessimist, not enjoying today because you're always waiting for disaster to strike. I'm talking about realistic optimism—living today to the fullest and having hope for tomorrow while understanding that constant sunshine is not the projected weather forecast. It's all about knowing that no matter what comes your way, God will provide the resources to get through it. It's recognizing that in the worst of circumstances, He will reach toward us with love and hold us in His strong, gentle arms. And it's being aware that without a doubt, you'll have the opportunity to test that. That's realistic optimism.

Acknowledge That There Is a Divine Plan You Cannot See

As humans, we are bound by time, space, and knowledge constraints. Our experience is limited to the physical, mental, and spiritual planes in which we live.

If you believe in an all-knowing, ever-present, personal, and loving God (and I do), you can find comfort in the belief that He is not limited as we are. We get a snapshot; He has the panoramic view of eternity. He knows how He plans to help us continue to grow and mature.

Hanging over my fireplace, I have a beautiful hand-woven tapestry I purchased on an African speaking tour. The colors are magnificent, and I'm amazed at the intricacy of detail. Yet, when I turn this work of art over, the pattern on the front is indistinguishable. I see gnarled, ugly knots scattered across the weave. Our lives are like that. Miraculously, all of our gnarled, ugly experiences are woven into a pattern that, under the skillful hand of the Master Weaver, becomes a beautiful life.

Trust that despite your pain, everything you are going through will be used for good if you allow it. From this vantage point, it may look very ugly. But what is meant for harm can be turned on its evil head and be employed for a positive purpose. If you love God and are committed to His purposes, He will see to it that happens.

The prophet Jeremiah wrote: "'For I know the plans I have for you,' declares the LORD. 'Plans to prosper you and not to harm you. Plans to give you hope and a future'" (Jeremiah 29:11). I've had so many experiences in which I felt harmed, but in hindsight, I can see that I didn't have the capacity to grasp it at all. It wasn't over, not by a long shot. I was like a toddler trying to learn quantum physics.

God's plan is much bigger than we are. Though we may hurt now, we can find security in the fact that we have a Father who gets it, who understands it all, and who cares for us more than we could ever imagine.

Learn the Difference between Faith and Trust

The choice I'm encouraging you to make in this time of trouble is *faith*. Right now, though, I want to take you to an even deeper challenge, moving your heart to embrace a very difficult component of faith—trust.

Faith by its traditional definition is easier, if you ask me. You "see" it before it happens, relying on a principle you believe to be true. Then you act on what you believe, which helps to move you along the road to that positive destination. You believe that you comprehend a plan and a system, and you do all you can to align your actions with how things work. As a result of faith, determination, and hard work, you finally achieve the outcome. Allow me to share a personal experience with this process.

Some thirty years ago, I was diagnosed with systemic lupus, which I had apparently had for about twelve years at that time. The arthritic-type symptoms had become debilitating, and my eyes had

123

developed serious complications. I saw the best doctors and took the medicines they prescribed, but I also could read. The medical books said there was no known cure for this chronic and potentially fatal disease. I knew that if I were to be healthy again, there would have to be divine intervention.

I searched the Bible for answers. I discovered that a significant part of Christ's ministry was healing, and I came to believe that He had not changed. I talked with others who had experienced miraculous restorations of health. Space does not allow me to go into all the details of the months of learning. I deepened my faith. I told others what I knew was happening (despite their knowing, pitying looks): that God was healing me. I took care of my body in practical ways. The bottom line is, when I was finally retested, all my diagnostic markers were normal. I remain healthy three decades later.

But it doesn't always work that way, and I don't know why. I don't believe that my faith was superior to that of someone who didn't get healed. I don't understand why sometimes circumstances don't change, despite prayers and positive actions.

That's where trust comes in. As I told you, trust is harder but absolutely essential if you are to weather the chaos of life without losing hope. When things don't make sense, when you've been exercising faith until your faith muscles are sore, and when you still are staring your unflinching negative situation in the face—that's when you trust. You don't trust in a system, and you don't trust in your ability to "work a system." You trust God.

You know how it is when you deeply trust someone in your life? Someone could report to you that he or she saw this individual doing something, implying that he was up to no good. Your reaction would be something like, "Well, I'm not sure what he was doing, but I know him. I know his character; I know his heart. So I'm sure there must be some other explanation." You don't really have an explanation for what was reported to you, but you know there must be a good one.

When you have a relationship with our living, loving Lord, you know His nature. Even when you are puzzled by what He seems to have allowed, you trust.

Realize That Sometimes God Delivers You *from* Trouble, but Sometimes He Delivers You *in* It

I live in Hattiesburg, Mississippi, about one hour north of the Gulf of Mexico. For two hours (which seemed more like two decades), I rode out 120 mph winds during Hurricane Katrina. My experience was miniscule compared to so many others who experienced total devastation from even stronger winds and floods.

During this harrowing experience, I asked God to teach me something about weathering all of life's "hurricanes," and I believe He did. Among other things, I learned that after you've done all you can to prepare, your task is simply to trust that God is with you in it and He will see you through it. Here's an excerpt from an article I wrote for my e-newsletter, *The Magnetizer,* the morning after the storm.

> The storm is raging. No more boarding up windows or shopping for storm supplies. The furious winds are howling. Loud "cracks" probably signal the snapping like toothpicks of the tall pines that surround our house. Wham! An unknown missile slams into the boarded glass windows. Thank God they're boarded! What can I do? Absolutely nothing.
>
> The only thing I can do now is to be quiet, listen to the wind, and breathe. It's time to be still, listen, breathe deeply—and to know that He is God. I've been praying—but now it's simply time to rest, fully conscious of the One

who is neither surprised nor frightened by the storm. Be still, listen, breathe . . . be still, listen, breathe . . .

This place in the arms of God is like the eye of the storm, strangely calm while surrounded by miles of hurricane-force winds and swirling debris. Literally, peace in the midst of the storm.

That's what trust is all about—realizing that God's love reaches into the scariest places, where we can be still and know that He is God. Since that time, I've spoken with many who sustained unbelievable damage to their property during that storm. Almost to a person, the resounding testimony is this: if it weren't for God and for the thousands of volunteers devoting themselves to helping others, we simply would not have made it through.

God didn't deliver all of us from that storm, but He surely has taught us about His nature and His sustaining power in it.

Ask for Wisdom and Strength for Today

The twelve-step support group folks have it right when they focus on "one day at a time." Really, sometimes you do well if you can make it through this hour or this five minutes. If you look too far ahead, you'll get overwhelmed and shut down. If you spend too much time looking backward, trying without success to change history by wishing it away, that preoccupation will rob you of today.

Today is what you have. There's quite enough to deal with today.

You will be given what you need when you need it. The time when you need wisdom is right now. You need to know how to take the knowledge you have and apply it in the tiny aspect of your overall situation you're facing at this moment. God has promised that if you ask for wisdom, He'll give you a generous portion.

Strength? He has that for you too. When you're exhausted and feel that every bit of your own strength has been squeezed out of you, have faith that your resources are a long way from depleted. The divine supply is ready to flow into you when you ask. You may not be "jumping stumps," as we say here in the South. But you will have the strength you need for what you have to do right now. After all, that's all you really need.

Act Like a Kid Again

Sometimes we try to complicate faith. You'll see writers advance formulas that look like they might have been stolen from NASA. Yet faith is really simple. It's based on relationship with and trust of a loving God.

One day when my grandson Ethan was two years old, his older brother Joseph was sick in bed with a virus and a high fever. Their mother, Amy, was taking care of Joseph and, knowing her, she was praying all the while. Ethan came into the room, toddled over to his brother's bed, closed his eyes tight, and put his little hand on his brother's hot forehead. He prayed simply, "Lord, touch him." Interestingly enough, Joseph's fever broke almost immediately.

Those whose faith serves them best in times of trouble (and at all times) are those who simply come as a little child, trusting that our loving heavenly Father is always there to listen, to offer practical help, and to provide heavenly hugs.

Surround Yourself with Emotionally Healthy, Encouraging People of Faith

Faith is contagious. You are likely to become more and more like the people with whom you surround yourself.

Choose to place yourself in the company of optimistic, faith-filled people. These are not "Pollyanna" people who just think you ought to perk up and forget it. They are folks with some experience with the realities of life but who have chosen to grow, learn, and make the best of life's sometimes harsh realities. Having "been there," they are living testaments to the fact that, with God's help, you can make it.

MY COMMITMENT TO *FAITH*

I choose faith. Though I do not always understand God's ways, I do trust His heart. His nature is love, and I know that He will lovingly carry me through this. He never promised me a trouble-free life; quite the contrary. But He did promise me that He would never leave me nor forsake me, that He would always be with me to comfort me, encourage me, and pick me up when I fall. He invited me to rest in Him and to draw on His peace when the storms come. My heart says "Yes!" to that invitation.

Though I have faith and act in faith, I don't rely on my faith. I rely on the God I trust, the one in whom I place my faith. I know that there is absolutely nothing that I've been through, no emotion I've felt, that the Lord doesn't understand because He's "been there."

Trusting in His love, I have peace in the middle of my storm. I have hope when my circumstances look hopeless. In fact, I have everything I need. Today, I choose faith.

5

"Of Course I'm Angry!"

CHOICE #5: BITTERNESS OR FORGIVENESS

I noticed the scowl on the face of Tai, a Vietnamese engineer, as I taught the management team about the business and personal impact of hardened anger and of the power of forgiveness. I was sure he wasn't the only one in this room who felt the emotions his face seemed to reflect. After all, the company was about to downsize, and many were unhappy with the edicts that had been handed down from corporate.

Tai never spoke up in the group that day, though others were quite verbal. It wasn't until we sat together on the long ride back from the remote retreat location that I learned what he had been thinking.

"I heard what you said today about how grudges make you sick in your heart and body. But I can never forgive the Communists. They don't deserve to be forgiven."

"Tell me more about it," I invited as I grabbed my notepad to capture his story.

"I had dreams for my life," he said. "I left Vietnam in 1982 in a thirty-foot fishing boat with sixty people on board. We landed on

Malaysian soil after four scary days and nights at sea. One year later, I considered myself and my family very lucky to have been admitted to the U.S. under political asylum status. But I'm getting ahead of myself. You see, the horrible images of the eight years before keep coming back to me. The Communists invaded my country and destroyed my dreams.

"What kind of crime did I commit anyway? Was it a crime to be born in a religious family? Was it a crime to attend an American college? Was it a crime to work for a living? Unfortunately, it was, from the Communist perspective. Religion was considered a tranquilizer to the People's Movement. Being educated in an American school was enough to qualify me as a traitor to the 'people.' Working with government-owned Air Vietnam meant collaborating with the enemy. So I was put into the 'reeducation camp' [prison].

"Four years in reeducation camp seemed decades. Day after day, I built the hatred in myself because the Communists came and took away our country's prosperity and our hope. The guards acted like monsters . . . abusing people, treating people like animals, laughing at people's suffering. They tried to weaken our bodies by hard labor and undernourishment in order to control our minds. Out of twelve hundred prisoners in the camp, four hundred died in one year.

"After fifteen years, the hatred is still boiling inside me as much as it was when I was in the camp. In all the years living in the U.S., I've never touched a book on Communism. I refuse to watch any movie about Vietnam. When I talk to someone who says one word that seems like favoring Communism, I walk away. My wife has begged me to go with her to visit family back in Vietnam, but I cannot set foot there because of what happened."

A PRISON OF YOUR OWN

This man's experiences are very different from yours . . . or are they? Yes, you're in a different time and place, but I'll bet you've had similar emotional elements. Every one of them can fuel anger and, if you let them, beget bitterness.

Loss of Power and Control

This man was literally in a prison, and you're probably not. However, when life hands you painful experiences against your will, that loss of control can make you feel trapped. You can experience "imprisonment" in an emotional world you never imagined. Bitterness can make the bars in your cell so thick and strong that there's virtually no chance of escape.

Undeserved Punishment

This Vietnamese man did not commit a crime, yet he received four years of cruel punishment. Some of the most difficult offenses to forgive are those you perceive as totally undeserved. Oh, sure, you may question, "What did I do to deserve this?" And you may berate yourself for not being able to foresee the future and protect yourself. But deep down, you know that this injury was an undeserved violation of your rights, of your person, of something or someone you love and value.

Loss of Things Valued

The psychological losses were the ones that fueled this man's anger the most—the loss of freedom, the stealing of dreams, the horror of witnessing harm to others. It's usually not the tangible, material losses that fuel anger most. It's the intangibles—those deeper ones that invade your core values, your past pains, your expectations of fairness, and your beliefs about what's right. It's those psychological losses that convince you that your life has been unfairly snatched from you and that someone needs to pay for that.

Difficulty Letting Go

My new friend was still living in the prison from which he had been physically released years before. He was unable to release himself from the emotional prison that continued to keep him from walking free and rejoining life. He had not even been able to go back and spend time with beloved family because of the hatred he associated with that whole country. Until we spoke that day, he never realized the similarity between his own hate and the behaviors of the cruel Communist guards he despised. Those men had kept him locked up. Tai was choosing to let bitterness consume him, and therefore his ongoing psychological incarceration was assured.

Have you found it difficult to forgive someone you believe contributed to your pain? You will never be free as long as you hold on to the bitterness and hatred that poison your spirit and take away your joy. The heavy steel doors and barred windows of your emotional prison can be opened by the keys you hold in your hands. In this chapter, I'm going to show you how to choose to place those keys in the lock, turn the latch, open those big doors, and release yourself into a world of positive possibilities.

By the way, I was delighted to receive a letter from Tai about a year later and to learn that he had chosen to enjoy the freedom of forgiveness. He wrote, "I still hate Communism, but I have forgiven the Communists. It's unbelievable the difference it's made in my life. In fact, I'm excited about planning my first trip with my wife back to Vietnam this summer. I can't wait to see my family again!"

ANGER AFTER TRAUMA IS NORMAL

Let me tell you before we take this any farther that it's perfectly normal to feel angry when you go through tragic experiences. You've hit a brick wall. What's happened doesn't seem right or fair. Your rights have been violated and your hopes dashed. Everything in you rises up and screams, "No! This shouldn't be!"

You may be especially prone to anger if what happened to you occurred because of carelessness, negligence, or outright malicious action. Even when your loss came about because of a natural disaster or a freak occurrence, you can project intense hostility toward individuals you perceive to have had responsibility either before or after the fact (such as insurance companies refusing to pay after a natural disaster).

> *It is easier to forgive an enemy than it is a friend.*
> —MADAME DOROTHEE DELUZY

In fact, your susceptibility to deep hurt and intense anger can be predicted in part by two factors: the level of human involvement in your trauma and the depth of the relationship you had with whomever you believe contributed. The closer and more trusting the relationship with the person who harmed you, the higher your expectations and thus the deeper the pain and anger. If someone you trusted to take care of you, to honor commitments, or to behave in love toward you does the opposite, that's much tougher to swallow.

ANGER IS NORMAL, BUT IS IT HARMFUL?

No and yes. In fact, there are times when the anger can actually be downright helpful. However, in other ways, stored anger can destroy your spiritual, physical, and emotional health. It's important to recognize when you've crossed the line and are unintentionally destroying yourself. Let's figure that one out together.

You may have been taught that a "nice person" or a "good Christian" shouldn't get angry. Wanting to "be nice," you stuff the inevitable resentments that crop up in your routine, everyday life. You smile and pretend all is well when it isn't. If you add to that the natural anger when life drops a bombshell, the anger can't stay hidden forever. Growing anger finally expresses itself in an explosion, in withdrawal from a relationship, or in some physical ailment.

The truth is, no matter how much faith you have or how kind a person you want to be, the experience of anger is a fact of life. That's neither abnormal or sinful. In his letter to the Ephesians, Paul wrote, "Be angry and sin not."[1] Those two instructions appear in the same sentence; they are not mutually exclusive. Anger is not necessarily harmful.

In fact, there are times when short-term anger is both justified and necessary to move you in directions you need to go. For instance, if you're really depressed and lethargic, a good dose of anger can give you the indignation and energy you need to get up and get moving. The energy of anger overrides the weight of despair and avoidance and propels you to "do something." Sometimes anger is the impetus for setting boundaries with people who shouldn't be allowed to continue to hurt you or others. Many an individual has been saved by finally reaching the conclusion, "Enough is enough!"

SO HOW DO I KNOW WHEN ANGER BECOMES DESTRUCTIVE?

There is a point, however, when anger becomes destructive. You need to know if and when your anger has crossed the line, when your heart is in danger of being filled with seething or explosive rage.

CONSTRUCTIVE ANGER	DESTRUCTIVE BITTERNESS/RAGE
✓ Attacks the problem, not the person	✓ Attacks the person, not the problem
✓ Utilizes win-win strategies, believing that both you and the other person have ideas and feelings that deserve to be understood	✓ Attempts to win by causing someone else to lose, "knowing" that the other person is entirely wrong and deserves to be put down
✓ Uses direct, assertive, honest, and respectful discussion	✓ Uses domination, intimidation, or manipulation
✓ Brings issues to the surface so they can be resolved and collaboration can occur	✓ Creates undercurrents that block collaborative problem solving
✓ Is relatively short term	✓ Hardens in the soul and lasts; becomes an attitude through which you view the world

To sum up, the harmful side of anger takes over when you take your anger out maliciously on others, you turn it onto yourself, you allow thoughts of revenge to become obsessive and habitual, and you choose to hang on to the anger.

Rebecca shared with me the understandable anger she felt after being deceived by her husband. As you read her story, you can see elements of both healthy anger and destructive bitterness.

"You're darn right I was angry, and who wouldn't be?" she told me. "When we were dating, he was so thoughtful. He made me think he was totally in love with me. When he proposed, I was so happy. We had a gorgeous wedding. In fact, my parents spent fifty thousand dollars on it. Seven weeks later, we had a new resident in our home. It was the best man in our wedding, who turned out to be his gay lover.

"I was hurt, confused, furious at him for deceiving me, hating myself for not seeing it . . . you name it, I felt it. At first, I honestly felt like killing him, but he wasn't worth going to jail for. Then I felt like doing a civil suit for money, not just a divorce, and I would have if I could have found a way to do it. I'd hear the stories from people who somehow thought it was their duty to share all the juicy details of his life. I'm afraid I wasn't very nice. I told off more than one person, demanding to know where the heck they were before the wedding!

"I wanted to punish him, to hurt him for hurting me. I'd fantasize about surgically removing parts of his anatomy. Why would he take me through this? He knew he was gay before he said 'I do.' This misery went on for months, until one day I realized that he had gone on his merry way, while I was sitting at home full of rage. I had allowed my life to come to a halt, and it wasn't affecting him in the least."

Rebecca was right. The bitterness was only harming her. That is a key insight I want you to get from this chapter.

WARNING: BITTERNESS CAN BE HARMFUL TO YOUR HEALTH!

Several years ago, I shared an office building with a group of surgeons. One day, one of the physicians allowed me to go into the operating room and watch him perform surgery. I knew it would be interesting, but I had no idea God would teach me a very graphic life lesson that day.

I watched as the surgeon used the razor-sharp knife to perform the delicate, life-saving task of repairing an aneurysm in the elderly man's stomach. I had a close-up view from a stool beside the operating table.

I'll spare you most of the gory details, but the task was to cut out the aneurysm and replace it with a synthetic graft. The doctor had opened the man's stomach (at which point I almost fainted), had located the aneurysm, had clamped off the arteries, and had begun to remove the "junk" from the affected section of artery. I was amazed at the amount he piled into the container. This had to be life threatening, I thought. All of this foreign material was blocking the flow of blood. Without the blood supply, the person cannot live.

At that moment, dressed in my surgery garb and totally grossed out, a powerful insight flashed into my spirit. I saw that the artery blockage was a living metaphor for bitterness. Like the plaque that choked out the blood flow, long-term anger also blocks the flow of life energy. Eventually, health deteriorates. You suffer mentally, emotionally, spiritually, and physically.

This man's choices over time to smoke and eat unhealthy foods were at the root of his problems. Like the man on the operating table, the bitter person chooses to hold on to malice, mentally dwell on the offense, and anticipate the satisfaction of revenge. In both cases, the problem grows and its impact spreads.

Imagine for a moment that you released a drop of red food coloring into a beaker of water. At first, you'd see a red dot. Soon you'd see pink water. Like the drop of food coloring, anger that is nurtured spreads, and it soon begins to affect every "system"— your communication with God, your relationships with others, your performance and productivity at work, and your peace with yourself.

Dramatic intervention was essential to save this man's life. Thankfully, under the care of this experienced surgeon, the patient would probably live twenty years longer, freed to do the things he enjoyed. Similarly, the dramatic intervention of forgiveness for a deep hurt is essential if your life is to be restored. Choose not to deal with the bitterness, and your injury eventually could be fatal.

YOU HAVE A CHOICE: BITTERNESS OR FORGIVENESS

I repeat the resounding theme of this book: *choice, choice, choice*! Though your anger may be justified, and though what happened to you may have been just plain wrong, you don't have to let that anger control your life. Your mind has better things to do than to use up valuable space and energy fantasizing about revenge.

> *By putting his hand around my neck, he slowly strangled himself.*
>
> —MINAKO OHBA

Consequences of Bitterness

If you elect to harbor bitterness, nurturing your anger so that it becomes a part of you, you're also choosing some very unwelcome consequences.

1. You can't have emotional peace. Strife and the emotional turmoil that accompanies it are the enemies of personal peace. Bitterness and peace cannot coexist.

2. Bitterness harms your physical health. An abundance of medical research documents the impact of anger on your health in general, but particularly on your heart, which needs to keep on ticking if you're to live.[2]

3. *Your mental sharpness is diminished.* When you give place to the obsessive thoughts that accompany bitterness, or when your rage distorts your perception of the facts in your everyday world, you don't think as clearly or accurately. Your thoughts become distorted by the fact that you can't help seeing and hearing reminders of your hot issues in all the events around

> *Bitterness is a self-inflicted disease of the spirit.*

you. Your emotional radar is turned up to the max to help you detect potential threats. Habitual angry thoughts affect your concentration, and your ability to solve problems is handicapped.

4. *Your career success is limited.* Bitterness about one situation can create a bad attitude that intrudes on your performance in the workplace. Have you ever worked with or around a person who is hostile, distrustful, defensive, and easily set off? How well does such a person function as a team member or as a manager? A hostile approach places a ceiling on your professional advancement.

5. *All your relationships suffer.* Stored anger bleeds into every one of your relationships. You don't mean for it to, but you just can't help it. Before you know it, your bitterness will show up in a short fuse, a critical spirit, and the gradual erosion of relationship quality.

6. *You feel spiritually disconnected.* Bitterness is a self-inflicted disease of the spirit. Out of your spirit come worship, communication with God, and your inspiration for purposeful living. Ever feel that your prayers aren't getting beyond the ceiling? Bitterness in your heart could be the root cause of your inability to perceive God's love and presence in your life.

Anger is like burning your house down to get rid of rats.
—HARRY EMERSON FOSDICK

Despite these consequences, however, many people hang on to unhealthy rage (which can be either silent or vocal) because they don't want the perpetrator to go free and not have to pay for what he or she did. Wait a minute! Think about the harmful outcomes we've just discussed. Who would actually be released if you forgive? Not the offender. That individual is still accountable to God and to the natural consequences of hurting others.

The Freedom of Forgiveness

The idea that you are punishing perpetrators with your thoughts is ludicrous. In all probability, they are out there living life as usual. The fact that you are tied up in bitter feelings is not affecting them at all. It's you who needs release! That's what forgiveness does for you.[3]

1. *Forgiveness unties you from the individuals who have wronged you.* Carrying a grudge is a backbreaking and spirit-rending task that leaves you perpetually connected to the person with whom you are angry. When you forgive, you set yourself free from that individual and release the energy you must have if you are to move on in your life.

2. *Forgiveness allows you to think more accurately and resolve problems more effectively.* When you forgive and heal, those reminders lose the power to set you off emotionally. Your mind becomes better able to focus on the big picture rather than automatically zooming in on all the negative details. Hey, my friend, would you agree that you have plenty of problems to solve and that you need a mind that is free to work on them?

3. *God rushes to help you when you forgive.* No matter what happens, no matter how horrific or undeserved it is, we've been given the spiritual assignment of forgiveness. Jesus modeled that vividly on the cross, after He had been betrayed, unjustly convicted, brutally beaten, humiliated, and nailed on the cross to be

executed. From the depths of His pain as He was dying, He prayed for the forgiveness of those who were mercilessly abusing Him.

Whether or not you are particularly religious, there's no denying the fact that replacing bitterness with forgiveness infuses your life with positive energy and a greater capacity to experience joy.

God wants you whole! When you choose to follow His lead and forgive, He runs toward you with open arms, eager to extend grace to you, restore your peace, and give you all you need to implement your decision. Forgiveness repositions you for amazing healing. God is definitely excited about forgiveness. He gives us the opportunity to become a channel for giving to others the forgiveness He freely gives us.

Dr. Martin Luther King Jr. warned that hate begets hate and wars produce more wars. He said, "Love is the only force capable of transforming an enemy into a friend. By its very nature, hate destroys and tears down; by its very nature, love creates and builds up."[4]

BUST THE FIVE FORGIVENESS MYTHS

I hear you saying, "All right, I can see that there are some problems with hanging on to hostility. But I just can't let it go yet. It wouldn't be right." Your resistance to releasing your anger may be due in part to a belief in one of five myths, any one of which can paralyze you, embitter you, and keep you from moving forward in your life. As you search your soul, do you find yourself endorsing any one of these erroneous ideas?

Myth #1: If I Forgive, I'll Be Letting the Person Get Off Scot-Free

I can't count high enough to number the people in my clinical office and in my seminars whose arguments have gone something like, "He/she doesn't deserve to be forgiven after what happened. I just can't let him/her get away with it."

But wait! Let's think about this for a minute. In fact, I'd like you to go with me into a seminar I was conducting recently for a hospital management team.

There had been some lively (translated: argumentative) discussion about how one should deal with it when a person deliberately or negligently inflicts harm. I decided to have a little good-natured fun with a man who had been particularly vocal, making comments like, "Revenge is sweet, very sweet." I asked him if he'd be willing to help me demonstrate a point, and he agreed.

When he joined me at the front of the room, I asked the rest of the group to picture themselves in my body, standing where I was standing. Next, I requested that they visualize the individual that wronged them, the one they had the most trouble forgiving, and to "place" him or her where their fellow participant was standing beside me.

Can you do that right now, too, in your mind's eye?

I then pulled out a long rope. As the snickers and giggles went through the audience, I slowly and methodically wrapped the rope around his neck, and then mine, around his underarms, then mine, around his waist, then mine.

I'll ask you now what I asked them. How would you like to carry around with you twenty-four hours a day the man or woman with whom you are most angry? Of all people, no! Yet, psychologically, that's what you do when you refuse to forgive; you tie yourself to that individual.

To drive the point home with this management team, I then tried to walk forward. Of course, my "companion" and I stumbled all over each other. He was dead weight when I tried to move ahead.

They got the picture. When you're holding a grudge and you're emotionally tied up, it's hard for you to make progress yourself. The weight of that emotional load holds you back.

How about you? Do you get it? Can you see yourself in that scenario? A woman on the front row of another program got it, too, after I had just conducted the rope demo with a fellow participant.

The lady on the front row exclaimed loudly enough for all three hundred participants to hear: "Oh, my heavens! I just realized something!"

"What?" I asked her.

"I just realized that I've been sleeping with my ex-husband for the past ten years!"

Sensing I had an example before the group they would not soon forget, I stepped toward her with the microphone. I invited, "Will you share with the others what you mean?"

"I can't stand him," she began. "You would not believe all the things he did to me when we were married. Now he's quit paying child support. The kids can't depend on him to do what he says. When I lie down on my pillow at night, my mind wanders to the latest example of his irresponsibility, which leads me to all the other times. What I've just seen here is that I'm still letting him in my bed. I divorced him ten years ago . . . but I didn't let him go."

Bitterness is like acid. It eats the container that holds it.
—AUTHOR UNKNOWN

This woman was learning the secret: it is the person who chooses to hold the bitterness who pays the price. The habit of hostility casts a shadow over your entire life, creating a never-ending nightmare.

Myth #2: If I Forgive, I'll Be Saying That What Happened Doesn't Really Matter

Of course what happened to you does matter. In most cases, what happened was very wrong. You are not sweeping it under the rug, excusing it away, or diminishing its importance by choosing to forgive. As a matter of fact, the enormity of its impact is proven by the sheer amount of faith and courage you have to exercise in order to forgive.

Lydia, whose daughter was shot to death by her fiancé, said it this way: "The trial was surreal. Our family on one side of the courtroom, his family on the other. I had the strange thought, 'This is the seating arrangement for a wedding, not a murder trial.' Then I saw him, and I wanted to kill him. After all this time, there he stood. He was walking and breathing, and my daughter was dead. My fury boiled inside me.

"But I talked with his family members, and I realized that they had lost a son too. I knew that I could not forgive him without divine strength. I asked for God's help, and I got it. On the way home, I told my husband, 'I am choosing to forgive him.'

"Now I would never want him out of jail, mind you, because I wouldn't want anyone else to get hurt. He's a dangerous man. But I no longer give him power over me."

Myth #3: If I Forgive, He/She Will Have Won

We've already begun to see how you are always the real loser when you allow an unforgiving spirit to control you. Your collateral losses continue as the bitterness causes you to become a less effective worker, spouse or partner, parent, and/or friend. Julie found this out the hard way.

Right after Julie learned that her husband, Benny, had been cheating on her with his coworker Ann, she went nearly emotionally berserk. She kept her husband up until all hours with incessant questions, put-downs, name-calling, and more questions. She stormed over to Ann's house and, in front of Ann's husband, dared the woman to talk to Benny again or contact him outside of work in any way.

Bitterness, or resentment, is like drinking poison and expecting your enemy to die.

—Hubert Humphrey

Intense anger after this kind of betrayal is understandable, but it didn't stop there. Even after Benny and Julie had seen a counselor to try to salvage the marriage, and even after the prognosis for their relationship was beginning to improve, Julie was still tortured. Ann's picture had been in the local newspaper with a story about a sales award she had received. This only increased Julie's agony. Ann seemed to be doing just fine, while she and her husband were going through turmoil trying to repair the damage to their marriage. It just wasn't fair.

Julie made an appointment to see her lawyer. Not to file for a divorce, but to file an alienation of affection suit against Ann. Julie just couldn't let her come out on top.

The suit dragged on for over two years. Julie relived the anguish over and over, each time she met with her lawyer, read a new interrogatory, or attended a deposition. Each new legal incident caused a setback in her relationship with Benny.

Julie wanted to win. She did win the suit, but she told me later that it didn't bring satisfaction. In fact, her relationship with Benny is still very tenuous. Julie "won," but with a very expensive price tag. She won, but she lost. If you pursue a vendetta, inevitably you lose. You hurt yourself.

Myth #4: If I Forgive, I'll Be More Vulnerable to Harm in the Future

Forgiveness will not stand in the way of healthy caution in your future. After all, you're not closing your eyes to the realities. You've had the tough, vivid realization that this world may not be as safe as you had previously assumed. Though you've experienced a loss of innocence, you can gain the more mature understanding of how to deal with a measure of danger in life by making safer choices—without becoming paranoid.

Forgiveness does not mean that you keep yourself in a dangerous or destructive situation. In fact, with clearer vision and perceptions undistorted by seething anger, you'll be better able to think and to plan how to prevent harm and to protect yourself.

Myth #5: I'll Feel a Lot Better If I Can Get Some Revenge to Even the Score

I watched a television documentary in which the father of a victim witnessed the execution by lethal injection of his son's murderer. The local television reporter interviewed the father afterward.

"What was it like for you? Did it feel like justice was finally done?" the reporter asked.

The visible hate exaggerated the lines and narrowed the eyes on the tortured father's face as he spoke. "Justice? Justice? That was way too easy. His death was over quickly. My son suffered. Is that what you call justice?"

After eighteen years of waiting for the execution of revenge, it still wasn't enough for this bereaved father. Even the perpetrator's death wasn't enough. In fact, when it comes to revenge, rarely is "it" enough. After it's over, you feel like planning phase 2 of the revenge project! Or some feel guilty about what they've just done. Either way, you can't get no satisfaction. (Apologies to Mick Jagger.)

Oh, yes. One last concept before we leave this topic.

Maybe you are like many who reassure themselves that what they are doing is not harmful. Does this sound familiar? "I think about revenge, but I would never act it out. I'm much smarter and nicer than that. But just you wait. I'll see the day when he gets his, and I'll be happy when I see it happen. After all, what goes around, comes around."

Listen to yourself. You said, "I'll be happy when I see him get what's coming to him." If you flip that over, what you really said was, "I won't be happy until . . ." You just tied your happiness to something that may or may not ever happen, and if it does, you may not be around to see it! Is this smart?

Get out of the revenge business. Fast.

PREPARE TO FORGIVE, MENTALLY AND SPIRITUALLY

If you're ready to embark on the exciting journey of forgiveness, we'll begin by preparing our minds and hearts. Then we'll make the choice to forgive, after which we will continue to affirm that decision during the ongoing process of emotional healing. In just a moment, I'm going to lead you through a series of steps to prepare your mind and heart for the important work of releasing yourself from bitterness.

However, some of you may be thinking about checking out about now because you don't believe you have a need for such strategies. You aren't aware of any feelings of bitterness. Before we discuss the other steps of preparation, I invite you first to dig a little deeper to identify any pockets of unforgiveness in your soul.

Conduct a Personal Life Scan to Identify Anyone You Need to Forgive

Before you conclude that you're home free on the choice of this chapter, I invite you to close your eyes and take a mental trip back through your life. Ask God to bring to your mind any person living or deceased with whom you have unfinished business. Is there a grudge that's slipped beneath the surface of your psyche? Don't limit your personal freedom by failing to deal with those too.

Understand What Forgiveness Is and What It's Not

It's understandable that some people resist forgiving those who have hurt them. They have a mistaken idea of what forgiveness actually is and what it is not.

Forgiveness is not sweeping the situation under the rug, excusing the behavior away. Neither does forgiveness mean that you lie down like a doormat for people to clean their feet on. Additionally, forgiveness is not necessarily a feeling; you may not immediately feel loving toward the person, even after you've truly forgiven. Forgiveness may not even mean that you can reconcile and "embrace" the offending individual at a personal level.

What is forgiveness then?

The simplest and most accurate definition of *forgiveness* I've found comes from pastor and author Dr. Charles Stanley: forgiveness is giving up my right to hurt you for hurting me.[5]

Forgiveness is a decision, a choice. It's a deeply personal and spiritual transaction in which you choose to let go of plans or fantasies of revenge and to release yourself from the burden of psychologically or physically evening the score. If you're always trying to get even, you'll never get ahead!

When you forgive, sometimes it's possible to reconcile with the person. If the other person is willing, you may be able to discuss what happened and make mutual plans for a better relationship in the future. (Caution: Avoid the holier-than-thou approach in such a discussion, saying in effect,

> *If you're always trying to get even, you'll never get ahead.*

"Being perfect myself, I forgive you, you horrible person, for the things you did to hurt me!" Be sure you're willing to take responsibility for the part you played in the problem.)

In other situations, reconciliation of the relationship is not possible. Maybe the other person refuses to change, and if you totally let down your guard, the same thing will happen all over again.

It may be that the person you need to forgive is not even alive. Sometimes you simply have to do business deep inside your heart, a commitment that creates a healing contract between you and God.

Finally, forgiveness is not a magic trick that causes all negative feelings to suddenly disappear. Some people do feel better right away, and it's wonderful when that happens. However, more often loving feelings don't immediately spring forth. The healing of feelings after the decision to forgive is usually a process.

So even after you implement the steps to forgiveness I describe in this chapter, don't expect unrealistically that you're going to feel warm and friendly all over. In fact, the next time you see that individual, you may find yourself in a battle with negative emotions that cause you to question whether you really have forgiven. This self-doubt can lead you right into a thought frenzy about all of the person's misdeeds and can suck you into a mental rehash of the offenses that only makes you angry again.

So prepare yourself not to fall back into that mental turmoil. When you feel those old bitter feelings, immediately focus on the fact that you made a positive choice to forgive. Remind yourself that after the decision comes the process of emotional healing. (Asking for divine help right about now certainly won't hurt!)

Know the Answer to This Question: If You Forgive, Will You Forget?

What about forgetting? If you don't forget, have you really forgiven?

I disagree with many people on this. I believe that as a human with a super-recorder brain, you will have a physical memory of the events, even after you've truly forgiven. So don't tell yourself that if you still remember what happened, you must not have forgiven the person. As time goes on and your recovery from the emotional damage becomes more complete, you'll be able to think about that memory without much emotion. That's the goal, not physical forgetting.

The crux of the forgetting matter is this: are you choosing to remember, to internally rehearse the situation, and to watch and wait for the person to experience payback? If so, go on back to your "forgiveness closet," so to speak, because you have some more work to do.

Take Responsibility for Your Bitterness

In chapter 2, we discussed at length the benefits of choosing responsibility. Remember that responsibility is not the same thing as blame.

In choosing to forgive, you're not reassigning blame. You are simply taking responsibility for your own attitudes, for the condition of your own heart. That's always a divine assignment. It's a spiritual principle that does not change just because someone else behaved badly.

> *He that cannot forgive breaks the bridge over which he must pass himself, for every man has a need to be forgiven.*
> —THOMAS FULLER

What if the other person has not apologized? I'll certainly agree that it makes it easier when the person acknowledges he was wrong and genuinely asks for your forgiveness. In those cases, it's more likely that a relationship can be restored.

However, the fact that a person is either unaware or unrepentant does not relieve you of the responsibility to deal with your own bitterness. Remember, forgiveness does not always mean reconciliation and complete trust. But it does always mean that you release the care of the person and the situation to God, thereby restoring peace and healing to your spirit.

Remember Your Own Need for Mercy

This is a big one for me. I know beyond any doubt I am constantly in need of mercy and forgiveness from God and from others. As I look back on my life, I'm so grateful for God's kindness and grace. Even when I've repeated the same errors, God has not rejected me but has loved me, forgiven me, and restored me. His grace truly is amazing.

I've also made many decisions that hurt others—errors in judgment, careless words or actions, or even hardheaded, willful choices to do just what I wanted to do. Turns out these are not just my business; I've hurt people I cared about and loved. I haven't meant to, but it's happened nonetheless.

I've had my share of troubles in relationships. I could offer plenty of justification, telling you all about what I went through. But the fact is, I contributed too. I could tell you how losing my daddy at an early age probably made an impact on my choices in relationships with men. But the bottom line is, I've experienced more than one marital failure. (That wasn't supposed to happen to *me!*) Many judge that harshly, and it's been difficult not to do so myself. Welcome to the human race, Bev. It's just proof of a principle: we all need forgiveness and grace.

Jesus said, "Blessed are the merciful, for they shall obtain mercy."[6] Unless you believe you're not going to need any, thank you very much, it would be good to "put some mercy in the bank" for use when you need to draw on it yourself. Knowing myself, I try to make as many deposits as possible into that account!

Another spiritual principle in operation here is that you tend to get back what you put out. In other words, when others are in trouble, your attitudes toward them set the stage for how harshly you'll be judged when you make a mistake. Other people will use the very same measuring stick you've been using to judge them. That's a sobering thought.

You're doing yourself a big favor when you develop the habit of mercy. Forgive others so that you will be forgiven. Show compassion and grace to others because you just never know when you'll need to have some coming your way.

Try to Understand the Other Person's Perspective

Before you begin the most intensive phase of forgiving, I want you to try to see the world as the offender may have been seeing it at the time. I know, you may not feel like doing this, and sometimes it's not even possible. Some cases are so extreme that you just have to skip this step. But give it a shot. If you can muster any empathy at all, this step can help to soften your spirit and make the task of forgiveness a little easier.

Reflect for a moment on the people against whom you hold grudges. What do you know about them? Is there anything in their backgrounds that may have limited their abilities to make wise choices? At the time they contributed to your pain, what was going on in their lives? Addiction? Struggles? What kind of role models did they have? How well were they equipped for life? Is it possible that what happened was not intentional? Did it happen because of a careless moment? We all have some of those. If they ended up in a destructive pattern leading to a tragic place, remember how they got there—one step at a time. That's the way we all get into messes and into the habits we have trouble breaking.

Before you protest too much, let me tell you that the goal of this step is not to excuse away cruel, malicious, evil behavior. It's simply an attempt to help you comprehend. Even though you reject the person's behavior, you may be able to understand more about how he or she made the mistake that led to your heartache. Sometimes this helps to plow the soil of your heart so that the seeds of forgiveness can take root.

Ask for Help

Ask God for wisdom and empowerment to carry out this important spiritual and emotional transaction. You're sure to get it, because you're choosing to implement a healing process that He initiated and strongly endorses.

Now spend a few moments praying for the person who harmed you. As you genuinely pray for those who mistreat you, something beautiful begins to happen in your own heart. Tenderness begins to replace toughness. Next, request for yourself courage, strength, and grace. After all, you are about to embark on one of the most important journeys you'll ever take—the journey to forgiveness.

Choose Now to *Forgive*

You've prepared your mind and your heart. Now let's get down to the meat of forgiveness. If you will, you're going to forgive step by step and memory by memory.

"OK, I'll do it," you say. "But how?" I'm glad you asked. We're ready to talk about the nuts and bolts, the how-tos of forgiveness. It won't be easy, but it will surely be worth the effort.

Take these steps one by one. Don't rush. This is life-changing work.

1. *Set aside some quiet time to begin the work.* Pick a time when you are mentally and emotionally fresh and when you're least likely to be interrupted. Do whatever it takes to ensure a peaceful environment, such as getting a babysitter or turning off the ringers on your phones.

2. *Clear your mind.* Get rid of outside clutter by spending a few moments breathing slowly and deeply. Visualize God's hands

outstretched to you, offering to help you in this deeply personal and meaningful process. Think about the positive outcomes you'll experience from this transaction—increased peace, clearer thinking, improved relationships.

3. *Identify the hurts.* Get out a pen and notepad. Write at the top of the paper, "Things (Name of Person) Has Done That Hurt and Angered Me." This person can be living or deceased. Don't hurry through this part. Even if the events that come to mind feel silly, write them down. If things have risen to the top of your mind, they must have bothered you. After the items have stopped flowing freely, stay quiet a bit longer and listen, adding anything else that you think of. When you're identifying the hurts, it's like popping popcorn. The thoughts come fast at first, then there are a few stragglers "popping up."

4. *"Tell" the person what hurt.* Arrange two chairs facing each other. Sit in one of them. In your imagination, place the offending person in the other one. (Note: It's usually not wise to forgive "in person." You can come off sounding self-righteous, saying in essence, "I forgive you. Aren't you fortunate that I'm big enough to do this after what you did, you dirty dog?") But I digress. Back to the chairs.

Look through your mind's eye at the person you have placed in the chair. Tell the (imagined) person with all the emotion you feel exactly what he or she did and how it harmed you. Say it out loud. Talk about each item on the list you have created. Don't leave anything out.

5. *Choose to forgive.* Choose—make a conscious and determined decision—to forgive each offense, one by one, so that you are a candidate for having your own wounds healed. Even if you don't feel warm and fuzzy feelings, by a conscious act of your will make this spiritual transaction. This act is the key to unlocking the chains that have kept you bound.

There is no revenge so complete as forgiveness.
—JOSH BILLINGS

Tell the imagined person in the chair, "I forgive you. I no longer hold you in debt to me for what happened. You are free. And so am I!" Saying this out loud so that your physical ears can hear it helps to implant the decision firmly in your mind and heart.

6. *Affirm your decision.* Make it official. Write your decision to forgive in a place to which you can readily refer, like a notebook, your Bible, or a journal. Date it. Sign it.

If you start to waver and question whether you "really" did it, you can refer back to the commitment you made on this date. It's done.

7. *Act on your choice to forgive.* Whenever and however feasible, demonstrate your commitment to the high road you've taken by doing something kind for the person you have forgiven. Can you make some gesture of good will? It doesn't have to be a big deal (though even a small deal may feel like a big deal.) For instance, if your paths cross, can you look at the person, smile, and say hello? Can you make a habit of praying for this individual? Can you openly or secretly do something nice for the person?

In some cases, you may be able to explore reconciliation. If the other person is open to that and willing to meet you partway, you may be able to sit down together and try to understand each other and reach a workable compromise. I know, sometimes that's not possible. The other person is unwilling to change, and though you've forgiven, you have to protect yourself and those you love. However, the biblical principle is, as much as is possible, be at peace with everyone.[7] Be sure that you are not the one putting up roadblocks to a constructive discussion that could help to resolve differences. You may even want to ask the offending person's forgiveness for your own attitude of hostility. (I know that's a tall order, but that kind of stretch has brought relief to many who were bound with bitterness.)

All of these actions solidify and affirm your decision to forgive. They jump-start your own emotional and spiritual healing.

8. *Deal with the inevitable setbacks.* I can see you wincing as you ask, "You mean there's more?" Don't get discouraged. If you've done the forgiveness work I've described to this point, you will have made enormous steps toward becoming whole again.

However, it would not be fair if I did not let you know that it is possible to have emotional setbacks, even after you've genuinely forgiven. You may be confronted with a situation that reminds you of what happened, and those old angry feelings can resurface. That is the time to remind yourself that you have forgiven. Look back at your written documentation if you

> *Forgiveness is a decision; healing from the emotional injury is a process.*

need to. Reaffirm your decision and behave in the most respectful and loving way that the situation allows.

What if the event that triggered your "relapse" was another offense? In other words, what if the person has not changed, and he or she persists in the hurtful behavior? You may have to forgive and forgive again. You can't afford to have your soul recontaminated by bitterness.

That does not mean that you fail to set limits. Your task will be to continue to forgive in your heart while behaving wisely in your relationship with any untrustworthy person. When possible, give the person respectful feedback, requesting change. If he or she still continues to act in harmful ways, it makes good sense to keep protecting yourself by setting boundaries.

Yes, even when you've genuinely forgiven, your emotional healing may not come instantaneously. You'll know it's in progress, however, when you find yourself thinking about what happened less frequently and feeling its effects less intensely. Forgiveness is a decision; healing from the emotional injury is a process.

Patrick Henry famously said, "Give me liberty or give me death." Come to think of it, that choice summarizes the choice I've placed before you—the freedom of forgiveness or the living death of bitterness.

MY COMMITMENT TO *FORGIVENESS*

This day, I choose to forgive, freeing myself from the emotional poison of bitterness. No longer will I allow hostilities and resentments to contaminate my body, my thoughts, my attitudes, and my relationships. I refuse to have my energy depleted and my talents wasted because of growing, chronic anger. I care too much about myself and those I love to live that way.

Beginning today, I will not allow myself the seductive, destructive luxuries of dwelling on the offenses, fantasizing or implementing revenge, or in any way making myself personally responsible for justice. I won't allow new memories that surface to cause me to embrace again the hardened anger. Neither will I give the offender power to control my emotions again, even if there is a new offense. No, I am choosing to forgive, and I will continue to affirm that choice.

I will maintain my newfound freedom by aligning my thoughts and actions with spiritual and emotional peace. While I will protect myself from lingering, genuine threats by setting boundaries, I will be diligent in showing courteous and kind actions. With God's help, I will be healed as I choose to walk this path of love, step by difficult step. I reclaim my loving nature. I choose forgiveness.

6

"I Can't Forgive Myself"

On August 20, 1995, the unthinkable happened to Abby Shields.

"I woke up that morning, there was no slip under the door that warned me this would be the last day my foster daughter, Beverly, would live. At 1:10 in the afternoon, she fell into the pool in our backyard and drowned.

"I blamed myself. On the way to the hospital in the ambulance, I was so afraid they were going to take my natural children. Bev was my foster daughter, so that made the guilt even more intense because I had been entrusted with the responsibility of taking care of her. I felt like a horrible mother.

"I felt that I must have disappointed God somehow, and this was punishment. I was so angry at myself. I felt defective.

"Because of that guilt, I began to abuse myself. I questioned my worthiness and my abilities, not just as a mother, but as a woman. After all, a woman is supposed to protect her children. I began to withdraw from my husband intimately. The house started falling apart. It was like, why bother? I gained and gained weight. Food was what I used to try to kill myself, a form of mental suicide."[1]

AM I TO BLAME?

It's tough to know what to do when you believe the culprit is you. In the story above, even though Abby was an extremely conscientious person, this tragic accident happened when her back was turned for only a moment. She was convinced that she had been charged, tried, and found guilty, very guilty.

Like many of us, Abby began to punish herself. The more her behavior deteriorated, the more convinced she was that she was worthless. She was caught in a self-perpetuating downward spiral. Have you been there?

The good news is, Abby found her way back through spiritual faith. She has learned how much God loves her, is there for her, and does not condemn her. She's learning not to condemn herself.

As I've talked with people around the world about their own tragic situations, I've had so many say to me, "I believe God has forgiven me, but I can't forgive myself." It is my hope that as you read, reread, and reflect on this chapter, you'll be able to take the important step of self-forgiveness that is so essential for your restoration.

WHAT ARE YOU TELLING YOURSELF?

Like most emotions, the feeling of guilt is based on your thoughts—that is, what you are telling yourself about your situation. Guilt implies that you "committed a crime," not doing something you were supposed to do or doing something you were not supposed to do. The "evidence" you give yourself may be real, imagined, or exaggerated.

You may say, "No, it's others who lay a guilt trip on me. That's why I feel guilty." Sorry to disagree, but the principle still holds. They can say things to you that are intended to produce guilt, but unless you buy into it, the guilt feelings won't find a home. Those invitations to guilt always come with an RSVP. You have the ability to examine what you are saying mentally and to determine if

> *Invitations to guilt always come with an RSVP.*

what you are telling yourself is legitimate, true, fair, and balanced. Let's look at some of the things you are likely to say to yourself when you're in a mode of self-blame.

"I Should Have Known Better"

Let's acknowledge something and get it out of the way. We all know better than we do! There is a sense in which there is almost always some truth in the statement, "I should have known better." We're honest-to-goodness human beings. We often don't think clearly at the right time, especially when emotions are clouding the picture. That's not meant to be an excuse; it's just a fact.

In the cool light of day, we can look back and say, "I should have done this," or "Why didn't I see that?" or "I knew better. Why didn't I do better?" Consider, for example, the experience of one young lady who "should have known better."

Katie met and fell in love with a man she met at church. In her words, he was "handsome, caring, spiritual, attentive, and sophisticated." She married him five months later. Too late, she learned that her husband was a con man. He cleaned her out financially and devastated her emotionally.

She said, "I knew better than to marry anybody in five months. I'd been in an eighteen-year marriage that was horrible. I thought in eighteen years that my ex, Lanny, had done everything possible to tear me down. But this guy, in three years . . . it was unbelievable.

"I think about how stupid I was. I knew better than to get married that quickly. But he did and said all the right things, and

I wanted to believe I'd finally found happiness. Instead, what I got was a nightmare. To think about what I put my daughters through!"

Katie made the decision to marry this smooth-talking deceiver when she was emotionally vulnerable from the hurtful experiences of her first marriage. She saw in this man what she desperately wanted to see.

There are times when you know plenty in hindsight, but you had no way of seeing what was to come at the time you were making your choices. What seems so clear now may have been hidden or obscure when you went through the situation.

If the choices you made were really a violation of principles you knew to be moral and right, learn from your mistakes. Commit to making better choices in the future. True repentance means that you turn around and *move* in the opposite direction. It doesn't mean that you stay stuck where you are, bemoaning the past choices you made and condemning yourself unmercifully.

If you are being unreasonably self-judgmental about any of your decisions, you need to give yourself a break. You made the decisions that seemed right to you at the time, based on the information you had then. Don't apply the standard of all the knowledge that has now come to light. Of course, hindsight always has better vision.

"I Should Have Seen It Coming"

Sometimes, looking back, you can see that there were some warning signs. However, at the time, you may have "not seen" (correctly interpreted) them. In other situations, there just may not have been any apparent indicators that your trouble was coming. Let's look at both of those situations.

A few months after her husband's suicide, Bethany told me, "Why didn't I see it? I knew he'd had some depression, but I never imagined he would actually shoot himself. He just went into the bathroom at work and did it. He kissed me that morning as he walked out the door, told me he loved me. I should have recognized that he was really telling me good-bye. He bought a new gun awhile back. He has lots of guns, though. He'd been quieter than usual, but I just wrote it off to all the stress at work. But I'm his wife. I should have seen it coming. If I had known he was planning to kill himself, I could have stopped it!"

Bethany struggled with many difficult emotions in the wake of her husband's suicide. She was judging herself, believing that she should have been a mind reader and assigning to herself the power of overriding another person's will.

Sometimes a tragic situation appears out of the blue—wham! There was no way to anticipate it, no way to prepare for it, no way to prevent it. It's hard to accept that we are not invincible. We may fantasize that somehow we should have seen it coming, restoring our feeling of power and control. However, this is unrealistic. We are not clairvoyant. The self-criticism that comes from this way of thinking is undeserved and destructive.

"But," you may protest, "I should have picked up on the signs that were there. Why didn't I?"

A principle of human perception sheds some light on this subject. We have a tendency to ignore or misinterpret information that does not support what we currently believe. That's not necessarily pathological; it just is.

Now follow me. If you are an optimistic person (which is healthy!), you're likely to give a positive spin to the events in your life. You're less likely to obsess over or even pay attention to negatives on the horizon. Thus, the tendency to major on the positives, a good quality, may have contributed to your "not seeing it coming."

Another principle of perception: You tend to read others' behaviors from your own frame of reference. Here's an example.

Ellie overheard her husband in a compromising phone call with another woman. When Ellie confronted her husband about it, he apologized and said it would never happen again. She believed him.

She said, "He said he was so sorry, and he cried. So I thought, 'OK, that's the end of that.' I wanted to believe the best. I cared about my marriage. And I wanted to move on. But I should have had more sense. The two years that followed were some of the most confusing and hurtful times in our marriage. I didn't know what was going on, but I knew things weren't right. I kept feeling like I was doing something wrong because I've always been able to make things Okay. Then I found out that the affair had been going on the whole time. I shouldn't have been so trusting. I've forgiven myself now, though. I feel like I did the best I could with where I was and what I knew at the time."

Ellie was a trustworthy person, making her more likely to be a trusting person. In other words, she assumed that her husband (a minister, by the way) was a person of his word.

(If you are a person who has been unfaithful, do not take this to mean that an episode of untrustworthiness dooms you to a lifetime of it. It's possible to learn from this heartache and change your course. Ellie and her husband are doing very well three years after this chapter in their lives.)

But back to my previous point: don't give yourself a hard time if you were too trusting. Dependable people tend not to be paranoid about others (unless they have had the experience of being betrayed and thereby become more suspicious). You may not have seen it coming because you just don't think that way. You don't go around looking behind every bush for evil motives. You're not expecting and searching for the worst because you try to focus on the best.

"I Am Terrible, Worthless, a Failure"

A third mental guilt trap is to go beyond judging a behavior to judging yourself, placing a general and negative label on yourself based on real or imagined misdeeds. The problem is, the more general your negative self-talk, the greater its destructive impact on your life.

Abby, the person you met at the beginning of this chapter, did just that. She judged herself unmercifully as a worthless woman and a bad mother. That type of negative labeling snaps shut the trap in which unhealthy guilt places you. After all, if you "are" that way, how can you change? What motivation can you stir up to change and grow if you're just a "hopeless case"?

TODAY'S GUILT OR YESTERDAY'S WOUNDS?

If you had a guilt habit prior to the more recent crisis you experienced, you will be more vulnerable to getting stuck in it now. Do any of these statements describe you?

- One or both of your parents used shame to try to manage your behavior.

- You grew up in an atmosphere of criticism, perhaps even being told about your worthlessness on a regular basis.

- You've carried guilt about something you did in the past, having been unable to forgive yourself for it.

If any of these are true, the hill to your self-forgiveness may be a little steeper—but not impossible to climb. You'll need to identify those old voices, talk back to them, and extend to yourself the grace you did not receive earlier in your life. This will help you prepare for the work of forgiving yourself for your perceived failures in this difficult phase of your life.

SHOULD YOU FEEL GUILTY FOR SURVIVING?

Some people emerge from trauma, especially trauma involving bodily harm or threats to life, with a kind of guilt called "survivor guilt." Usually, survivor guilt comes from a comparison between your positive fate and the injury experienced by those around you. You may secretly believe that it would have been better if you had been the one to be hurt or even killed.

I spoke at length with a veteran of World War II, a hero who participated in the deadly first wave at Normandy. More than sixty years later, he shared with me his terrifying experiences.

"After our boat was hit, we had to swim and then wade ashore, keeping our guns out of the water if we'd been lucky enough to locate them. The bodies of our buddies were floating all around us. Once I got ashore, I was separated from my troop, what was left of it, for hours and hours. I stepped over more bodies as I walked around in a daze."

This man spent three grueling years on the front lines, surviving against all odds. This charming gentleman with dancing eyes, a ready smile, and quick wit secretly suffered nightmares, flashbacks, and other typical symptoms of Post-Traumatic Stress Disorder over the course of his lifetime, but he had never filed for any kind of VA pension.

"I couldn't do that," he explained. "I came home alive. So many others came home in a box or came home without legs and arms. I made it though without any significant physical harm. What right would I have to collect a pension?"

We finally convinced him that the "internal injuries" he had sustained during his brave service were deserving of recognition just as certainly as those who were awarded the Purple Heart for the physical injuries they incurred.

Today, thousands of soldiers and civilian laborers in war-torn areas suffer from Post-Traumatic Stress Disorder (PTSD) and from survivor guilt. War-related PTSD, I'm convinced, will affect our military personnel and their families for generations to come.

Yet the impact of survivor guilt is much more far-reaching than the military. I've seen it in survivors of accidents, terror attacks like 9/11, workplace violence, and a myriad of other traumatic incidents. If you are experiencing survivor guilt, I would remind you that if you are still alive and functional, it's for a reason. You have a new opportunity to make your life more productive than it could have ever have been had you not come face-to-face with the uncertainty and brevity of life.

As I worked with employees of organizations on the post-Katrina Gulf Coast, many confessed that they felt guilty because they didn't lose everything like their neighbors. I reminded them that this allowed them the privilege of rolling up their sleeves and concentrating on giving practical help and showing concern for their devastated neighbors.

That's the secret to surviving survivor guilt. The fact that you survived is a gift. You have the responsibility to pass that gift along to others by living life fully and productively, doing all you can to make this world a better place.

YOU HAVE A CHOICE: GUILT OR SELF-FORGIVENESS

Guilt can keep you forever tied to the situation from which you are trying to recover. Do what you need to do to legitimately resolve it and let it go, and you will pave the way for restoration in your life.

Drowning in Guilt

You can't breathe the oxygen for recovery when you're drowning in guilt. You sink deeper and deeper, with each gulp of the liquid poison stealing your life. Here are four reasons why.

1. *Guilt generates low self-esteem.* Chronic guilt erodes the healthy confidence you need. You see, your self-image is based on your comparison between what you believe you should be versus what you think you are. Destructive, lingering shame reminds you constantly of the conclusion you've drawn—that you did not, do not, and cannot measure up.

The longer you give yourself a derogatory label and assume that you are "less than," the stronger will be your prediction that you just can't do anything right. And guess what: your behavior will line up with that belief. After all, if you see yourself as a failure, you try fewer things. When you do get up the courage to try, your anxiety about your performance causes you to make more mistakes. The result? Diminished success. Your response? "See! I knew I was a failure!" This is a vicious cycle.

2. *Chronic self-criticism often leads to depression.* Depression is a second hidden cost of unhealthy guilt. When your mind becomes fixed on what you've done wrong, you ignore what you are doing right. This is a perfect recipe for depression.

Dr. Aaron Beck, a prominent researcher in cognitive psychology, describes the triad of negative thoughts leading to depression: an overly negative view of yourself, an exaggeration of the negatives of your situation, and a negative and hopeless view of your future.[2] Habitual self-criticism sets you up for all three.

Want to cook up a good case of clinical depression? Then make yourself responsible for things over which you have no control. Toss in a little wishful thinking that you should have had the supernatural ability to see the future and do something differently, though what you did was perfectly logical. Add some ongoing self-condemnation for your actual mistakes—after you've asked forgiveness and changed your behavior. Top off the mixture with the belief that you are a total screw-up. Do all this, and the results are virtually guaranteed!

3. You "hide" in relationships because you fear what they would think if they really knew you. Chronic guilt wreaks havoc with relationships because it sabotages true intimacy. Think about this. To form and maintain deep, genuine relationships, you have to be willing to "be known," you have to feel accepted for who you really are, and you deepen intimacy by sharing more of yourself.

When you see yourself as defective, you're afraid that if people really knew you, they would reject you. As a result, you wear a facade. You want to mask what you believe to be despicable. However, at the same time you create a wall that does not allow people to have the privilege (and it is!) of really knowing you, of appreciating the life experiences from which you have learned. They are robbed of the opportunity to give you acceptance as a normal human being, to affirm you for how far you've come, and to appreciate the life lessons that have shaped you into the person you are now. You miss out on the treasure of a true friend, one who knows the worst things you've ever done and loves you anyway!

A deep sense of shame and guilt can also affect your career, tempting you to act out what's been called "the imposter phenomenon."[3] You think, "Yes, I'm achieving certain things at work, but if people honestly knew me, they'd find out I'm really not capable." You discount the successful outcomes you've had, neither enjoying them nor being encouraged by them. You carry the burden of thinking that you are an imposter. As a result, you lack the confidence to take necessary risks to advance your career.

I hear you saying, "Now, wait a minute, are you saying that you go around telling everybody everything?" No way! But there is much healing in entrusting to those two or three most supportive, valuable friends (or a professional therapist) the things for which you are most self-condemning. I suspect that you will get a fresh perspective, and you'll probably find out that your prediction of others' reactions was way off base.

4. *You engage in self-sabotage because you feel you don't deserve success.* A final cost of guilt is that you may consciously or (more often) unconsciously sabotage yourself when you are on a pathway that can bring you good things. When you are on the verge of choosing to strike out in a more positive direction or actually achieve a long-hoped-for goal, you tell yourself you don't deserve it, that it's a pipe dream, that it's no use. What happens when you talk to yourself this way? You can derail—before you begin or before you finish.

Listen to Marilyn's description of her experience with this kind of guilt. "When my kids left home, I started thinking about school and a new career, which I couldn't do when the kids were home. But I kept telling myself, I should now be devoting myself to my parents. It was very traumatic for me when my parents divorced, and I felt pulled between them. I've always defined myself as a caretaker, and now I felt that I was supposed to devote myself to caring for my parents.

"To make matters worse, my mother lost everything she had in a hurricane, so she was going through a difficult personal adjustment. I felt compelled to rescue her emotionally. I felt that if I got a job or went to school, then I'd be abandoning her. My dad, who lived in another town, had his own set of issues. It felt like the ongoing battle between my parents was played out in how much time I spent with each of them, and I was responsible for keeping them both happy.

"Did I have a right to pursue something for myself? I knew that I would never desert my parents. Yet I struggled with the desires that wouldn't go away. Did I have a right to be selfish, go back to school, and finally have a career?"

Marilyn was on the cusp of a new phase of life when she could develop her talents and contribute to the world in a fresh way. Yet she believed she was being selfish to think about doing something for herself. Have you ever felt like that?

Like most people who are truly concerned about whether they are being selfish, Marilyn was anything but. (In fact, she chose to pursue a profession in which she would help many others, not just herself. She is currently enrolled in a graduate program in psychology.) Selfishness is not defined as "doing something for yourself." Rather, selfishness is the *consistent* pattern of focusing on yourself at the expense of others. Selfish people don't spend much time even considering whether they are doing enough for other people. If you, like Marilyn, are struggling with the fear of selfishness, I seriously doubt that you qualify!

> *Selfishness is not defined as "doing something for yourself." Rather, selfishness is the* consistent *pattern of focusing on yourself at the expense of others.*

Give yourself permission to learn, grow, and explore new ways to contribute. Don't let guilt or fear of selfishness prevent you from taking the opportunities placed before you. If you have a heartfelt desire to pursue a worthy purpose, don't discount it. Go for it!

Self-Forgiveness Restores

After you've asked for forgiveness from God and from anyone you feel you've injured, you must not refuse to extend to yourself the healing hand of self-forgiveness.

1. *You regain confidence.* Self-forgiveness releases you to believe

that you might actually be able to tackle new things and succeed at them. You're free to entertain your dreams. You gradually come to see yourself as a valuable person with the potential to make a difference in the world.

2. You are capable of greater intimacy in your relationships. It's been said that to love others, you have to be able to love yourself first. I don't completely agree with that. There are many who love others "too much," while not extending grace to themselves.

However, I do know that you are capable of much healthier, balanced, and loving relationships when you come to love and respect yourself despite your warts and your wonderful parts, your mistakes and your triumphs. You recognize that God loves you just as you are, and you choose to agree with Him on the matter! That life-changing decision frees you to take off the mask of perfection and be real.

Real relationships, the kind that last, are between real people. Authentic people have real issues and real struggles, and they are not afraid to acknowledge that. Without that honesty, true intimacy is not possible.

You may have heard the phrase, "Love your neighbor as yourself." In this case, "as" means "like." In other words, you're to love your neighbor *and* yourself. Have you been weighed down with guilt, trying to love others while condemning yourself? Then do yourself and those you love a big favor. Forgive yourself!

3. You have more compassion for others who have made mistakes. A beautiful by-product of self-forgiveness is that, after receiving forgiveness for a failure, you tend to have more empathy and less judgment for others. You realize that even "good" people make mistakes sometimes. As you experience the relief of forgiveness, you are motivated to share that same acceptance and encouragement with others.

The awareness of your fallibility inspires you to lift up others

172

who have fallen. If you are spiritually mature, when others make mistakes you'll reach out a gentle, helping hand to restore them. You do this because you realize that you may be the next person in need of restoration.

Learning from your mistakes can become one of your greatest assets when it comes to being a compassionate helper. People in need tend to listen more attentively to someone who's "been there."

4. *Self-forgiveness releases you to find peace.* Forgiving yourself will help you on the pathway to finding peace. However, keep in mind that peace is not the same thing as happiness. Happiness can be rather elusive because it's usually tied to your current situations. As you've learned the hard way, situations can turn your world upside down. When you are struggling with guilt and even after you forgive yourself, you may wonder, "Do I deserve happiness?" Well, the truth is, *none* of us deserves happiness. We've all veered off the ideal path. Are we perfect? No one is perfect! Yet no matter what has already happened to cause us unhappiness, we all have the responsibility and privilege of pressing on. One thing I know from years of trial and plenty of error is this: seeking divine wisdom and aligning our steps with a wiser course brings peace—peace with a loving and merciful God, peace with those around us, and, importantly, peace with ourselves, no matter what our circumstances.

BEGIN NOW TO CHOOSE SELF-FORGIVENESS

We've seen *why* it's best to reject lingering guilt and choose self-forgiveness. Now let's begin work on *how*.

The first step is to determine whether you are feeling the type of guilt that you should reject, or whether it is guilt that serves a useful purpose and requires a turn-around on your part.

Differentiate Between Constructive Guilt and Destructive Guilt

Some claim that all guilt is bad and that you should simply rid yourself of it. Well, when I perform forensic psychological evaluations of people charged with crimes, I occasionally get to meet some who have done just that. Believe me, you don't want to emulate them.

Healthy guilt is an essential part of the mature personality, serving the purpose of alerting you that something needs to change. Yet it's important to distinguish whether you are truly guilty or whether you are just feeling guilty. Is the guilt you are experiencing constructive, building your life, or is it destructive, tearing you down?

Here are four important questions to help you determine what type of guilt plagues you and what to do about it.

1. *Is your guilt unrealistic, or is it based in fact?* When you go through traumatic events, it's easy to slip into an unrealistic sense of failure. Reexamine the facts of your upsetting situation. What information is available to help you grasp what actually happened, along with the probable causes?

This is a good time to talk with various professionals about what has happened. Get the opinions of experts about any contributors to the traumatic event, including what, if anything, you could or should have done differently. Talking with a qualified therapist, skilled clergy, or even an expert in the technical aspects of the event can help you realistically assess what you could or could not have done more effectively in the process.

The goal here is to sort out how, if at all, you made mistakes with respect to your personal crisis. As we discussed earlier, in your search for answers, you often erroneously jump to the conclusion that there should have been "something" you could have done to stop it.

Consider, for example, the experience of Carol, the driver of a city transit bus, who made a left turn on the route she had traveled daily for two years. There he was, right in front of her.

Carol said, "I didn't see him in the crosswalk. The bus bumper kicked his legs out from under him and threw his body against the bus, landing his face against my windshield. It was awful. They called me the next day and told me that he had died of the injuries. I had so much guilt. I was driving the bus that killed that man, and he had a family. Everything changed for them because of me.

"To make matters worse, I was given specific instructions by my employer and the attorney not to have any contact with the victim's family. So I couldn't apologize to them, couldn't send them a card. That was really hard for me. Thankfully, I knew the pastor of the church the family attended. He told them that I was a young mother recently divorced, and how horrible I felt about what had happened. They told the pastor that they didn't harbor any hard feelings toward me. So I felt like they had forgiven me, but I was still struggling with forgiving myself. Why didn't I see him?

"Then the family sued me, the transit company, and the manufacturer of the vehicle. The suit was settled during jury selection for an undisclosed amount. But that suit actually turned out to help me with my lingering guilt. I found out from the experts hired to investigate that there were issues with the style of the bus, with the rate of speed the man was walking, and with the rate of speed I was moving. I was going slowly at the time. According to their findings, there was no way I could have seen him. The post created a pie-shaped barrier, a blind spot. The man was moving within that pie shape, and I couldn't see him. That's why as soon as I turned, I hit him. Those facts made me realize that it was an accident. This was beyond my control. I stopped hating myself and became able to sleep at night."

2. *Is your feeling of guilt general or specific?* Is your guilt focused on a specific, harmful behavior or attitude that needs to be changed

and you haven't done it? Then make that change! Build yourself a better life. That guilt that nudges you to correct a harmful behavior is very constructive guilt.

On the other hand, when you feel guilty, do you place a general, negative label on yourself, feeling somehow that rather than *doing* something bad, you *are* a bad person? Welcome to the world of destructive guilt and shame. You'll never feel that you're "worthy."

3. *Is your feeling of guilt long-lasting or time-limited?* Destructive guilt persists long after you have changed the behavior in question, have asked for forgiveness, and have made any possible restitution. It hangs on, nags at you, and drags you down.

Once you have made the needed changes, constructive guilt lifts (though it may take some healing time before the emotional relief occurs). Destructive, long-lasting guilt has outlived its purpose, which is to precipitate change. Turn your back on this type of guilt. Destructive guilt is not from God, and it has no place in a productive, abundant life.

4. *Does your feeling of guilt contain condemnation or hope?* Destructive guilt and shame whisper (or yell!) that, since you are a defective person, your future will only be a continuation of the negative past. That type of pessimism creates a self-fulfilling prophecy: your fears come true because you don't dare to take positive action. Why try when you have no hope?

On the other hand, constructive guilt has plenty of hope! It contains the idea that you can change, and that if you do, your life will improve. The positive seeds of the future lie in the things you learn from what you're going through today.

Reject Destructive Guilt

Next, choose to reject any destructive guilt you've identified. If you're being harassed, harmed, and held back by destructive shame, that confidence-robbing monster is probably not going to slink away on its own.

This guilt monster has intimidated you and reigned in your life too long. It's time to vanquish him with the truth—the facts about your situation, about your worth, and about God's grace and forgiveness. When you discover that your feelings are not based on objective facts, reject them. It's just that old guilt dragon trying to sneak his way back into your territory. Put up a "No Trespassing!" sign.

Ask for Forgiveness

Having sorted out true errors that are calling for action, you're in a position to do what's needed to get yourself back on track. Ask forgiveness from God and (if feasible) from those you believe you have injured.

God has promised to forgive you when you ask. You can rely on that.

Others may forgive you, or they may not. But in the heartfelt asking, you take a step forward in your own healing. What they do with your apology is not under your control or your responsibility. Your responsibility is to acknowledge your mistakes and to correct your part of the problems.

Trace the Sequence of Decisions That Led to Your Mistake

You can't change what you have done. So instead of dwelling on the past, focus on what you are going to do about it now. How will you live differently in the future?

To answer that question, first figure out what led to your unwise choice. Colossal mess-ups typically don't happen as a result of a one-time thought or action. A chain of little decisions loop together, taking you ever closer to that action that contributed to unwelcome consequences. Map out your own decision chain. What were those successive thoughts and behaviors that led to your trouble?

Second, think about what you will do differently in the future. The earlier in that sequence you correct your course, the greater your chances of resisting. It's much easier to nip something in the bud than to deal with a very compromising situation with all your passions, desires, and justifications in full swing. So make a plan for how you will keep yourself from heading down that destructive road.

When I conduct forensic psychological evaluations, I'm struck by some of the ways inmates describe their experiences. They often talk about the emotional traps that got them into trouble. They tell me things like, "In a jail? Me? Never in my wildest imagination. Drugs got me here. I experimented a little, telling myself I would never use regularly and that I'd never touch the 'real' drugs. Little by little, addiction took over my life. I started dealing to support my habit. I feel so guilty about all the people I hurt, especially my three kids."

"I'm clean here in prison, and I tell myself not to worry, that I'll never use again. But I know that I'd better do some planning. I know I have to stay away from temptations—certain people and places. I've learned that even the way I think can be a temptation to use again. So I know that I can't just tell myself everything will be Okay; I've got to do some real planning."

Planning, yes, and rehearsing. Any entertainer knows that rehearsal is essential to a good performance. Whenever there is the slightest opportunity, practice your intentions to create better habits. Do something—even just one little thing—differently than you might have done before. They say, "Practice makes perfect." But that's not true if you're practicing the wrong things! It's practice of the right thoughts and actions that will create a more positive outcome. That's how you'll form the new habits that work for you automatically.

Don't Feed the Monkeys!

I was delighted when I walked outside my flat in Durban, South Africa, on a speaking tour in that country. There were cute little monkeys playing up in the trees just outside my door! Wow! I talked to them, trying to coax them to come closer. They ignored me and jumped about limb to limb.

Bananas! I had some inside. Maybe if I held out some bananas I could get them to come nearer.

About that time my driver arrived, and I told him what I was about to do, pointing out the adorable little furry creatures.

"Don't feed the monkeys!" he exclaimed.

"Why not?" I asked. "They might be hungry, plus they'd probably come closer, and I could play with them."

"No way," he countered. "First of all, those cute little monkeys carry disease. Furthermore, if you feed them, the owner of this house will never forgive you. They will never leave, and soon they'll take over. In fact, if you feed them, they will begin to open the windows of the house and come inside to get food. We had a mango tree, and the monkeys were constantly eating all the mangoes. When we came out of our house, the monkeys would actually throw the mangoes and hit us in the head. So whatever you do, don't feed the monkeys!"

As I reflected on this experience, I couldn't help comparing those cute little monkeys to how we deal with temptations and to the formation of the bad habits we have trouble breaking.

Temptations by definition look good at first. The tempting activity looks like it will bring fun, stress relief, satisfaction, profit, and approval—whatever the appeal. In these initial stages, you don't really look at the possible consequences of going down this road. After all, nothing bad will happen, and you certainly won't let it get out of hand, right?

You begin to feed the monkeys. You think about the temptation, imagine what it would be like to do it, flirt with the possibilities. You take one little step forward (or actually backward), telling yourself, however, that you'd never take that *next* step. When you do take the next one, you reiterate to yourself that you will not move any further—while inching ever closer to full-fledged experimentation. Every movement makes the next easier.

"How did I get here?" you ask yourself. "How could I possibly have gotten entangled in this situation? How could I have acquired this bad habit, dare I say it, this addiction?"

The monkeys take over. Like the South African monkeys, the destructive habits in your life can begin to rule the "personal property" of your life. They begin to open windows and gain access to other important areas, affecting your relationships, your work, your spiritual life, your emotions, even your future. They come in and rob you of your "food," that which you need to sustain a healthy lifestyle. Those activities that seemed so appealing at first begin to "throw mangoes" and create big knots on your head.

You've already learned that. However, it's easy to slip back into the patterns by telling yourself things like:

- "Just this one time won't hurt."

- "I'm too smart to get caught."

- "Plenty of other people do it, and they seem to be doing Okay."

- "No one will ever know."

Yep, that's what everybody thinks. However, ultimately there are no free passes. Feed the disease-carrying, aggressive monkeys and you'll pay a price.

When you are flirting with the "cute little monkeys" in your life, remember this: almost anything in life is easier to get into than to get out of.

Decide to Forgive Yourself for Real or Imagined Wrongs

You've evaluated whether there is an objective reason to feel guilty. You've learned whether your guilty feelings are helping or hurting, whether they are helping you build a life or tear down your life. Where you've made mistakes, you've taken corrective action. So what's left to do? It's time to release yourself from self-condemnation and self-punishment.

Make a conscious decision to forgive yourself. Create an event out of it. Tell God, a trusted friend, and/or a therapist about this important happening. Date this decision, and document it in your journal. "Today, I'm choosing to forgive myself for . . ."

Ritualize the decision to let go of destructive guilt by writing on paper the wrong for which you are forgiving yourself and then (safely) burn that document or place it into a helium balloon and release it into the heavens. Such visual experiences are powerful in reminding you that you have made a decision to let it go.

Identify and Challenge Self-Demeaning Thoughts
That Trigger Unhealthy Guilt

Having worked on ways to address any true guilt and to prevent the reenactment of the mistakes of your past, and having chosen to forgive yourself, you now have some thought habits to fight. The kinds of thoughts that lead you down the dead-end street of destructive guilt and shame don't just disappear. You have to take charge of them. You have to replace them with thoughts more in line with the positive truths you're coming to embrace about yourself.

The first step in that process is to identify the kinds of thought habits that position you on a greased chute toward renewed shame and depression. How much time are you spending thinking and obsessing about the following:

- the actions you regret;

- being a failure;

- someone you feel you let down;

- being an unworthy and unlovable person;

- being stupid for doing what you did;

- the ways you think you compare unfavorably to others?

When you find yourself lingering on thoughts that trigger destructive guilt, challenge them with positive and accurate thoughts. Remind yourself of God's love and acceptance of you, of the steps you've taken toward forgiveness and restitution, or of the many examples from your life that contradict the negative labels you've assigned to yourself.

At times, it helps simply to distract yourself. Get busy doing something that engages your mind so that you aren't focusing on those depressing ideas. Call a friend, watch a funny movie, or read an inspirational book.

Will you have passing thoughts about your mistakes of the past? Yes, but the key word is passing. It's like Martin Luther once said, "You can't prevent a bird from flying over your head, but you can keep him from building a nest in your hair."

Change Self-Critical Thought Habits That Lead to Self-Sabotaging Behavior Habits

Thoughts, like behaviors, become habits. How? By repetition. You think them so often, they become automatic. Guilty thought habits equal chronic guilty feelings, and self-destructive actions tend to follow.

If you want to stop feeling guilty all the time, then you must stop assuming you are always to blame. I was reminded of this recently during a counseling session with a client I'll call Sheila. She had already told me about her husband's excessive drinking habits.

"Although my husband left me a few months ago, I didn't know where he was staying. People had told me they'd seen him out a lot in the bars, so I assumed he was spending plenty of time with his 'mistress,' alcohol. But last week I saw where he was living. I couldn't believe it. A little broken-down house in a bad neighborhood."

Through her tears, she asked, "Dr. Bev, please tell me, what about me was so undesirable that he would stoop to even this to avoid being with me?"

Do you habitually assume that you are responsible for others' problems? If so, you're set for a life of chronic guilt, shame, and pain. Challenge that thought! All people are responsible for their own choices.

Interestingly, a few months later, Sheila got a chance to apply a version of the "best friend" method in a real-life experience with her girlfriend, Evie. (I'll explain more about the best friend method in a moment.) Unexpectedly, Evie's husband left her, and his alcohol problem and infidelity appeared to be major contributors. Sheila told me, "I've watched Evie's love being consistently expressed toward her husband for all these years. She had a sweet, gentle spirit. She didn't nag. If anybody did everything possible, she did."

I responded, "So what you're telling me is that it is entirely possible that her husband is responsible for his own choices? And that no matter how hard she tried, he had the ability to persist in abusive drinking and running around on her? If that's possible in her case, why not yours?"

Sheila began to get the picture. Was she totally innocent, having made no mistakes in this relationship that went south? Of course not. But she began to free herself from bearing undeserved blame for another person's choices.

You can deliberately employ that best friend technique. Ask yourself honestly, "If my best friend had gone through this same experience and were engaged in self-blame for the very same things I'm condemning myself for, what would I say to that friend?"

First, let's listen to some of the ways you may be lecturing yourself:

- "How could you be so stupid?"

- "You are such a failure."

- "It's no use. You'll just never measure up."

- "How on earth could you do such a thing?"

- "You should have seen it coming."

If some of those self-berating remarks ring a bell, the best friend technique may be helpful for you. If your best friend had been through your exact circumstances and had behaved exactly as you did, would you respond to him or her with such judgmental statements? Would you put your friend down? I seriously doubt it. First of all, you'd recognize that these statements are distorted. Second, you'd want to encourage your buddy rather than tearing him or her down through criticism.

You'd probably tell your friend something like:

- "You had no way of knowing."

- "You did the best you could. Other people had choices too."

- "We're only human. We want to keep everyone happy and safe, but we live in a world where that's not always possible."

- "Don't keep beating yourself up for this. It certainly wasn't all your fault."

Yes, you know how to respond to a friend. Wanting to be constructive and lift your friend up, you'd say things that put mistakes into perspective, give hope, and offer acceptance and support.

So why not do the same for yourself? Why wouldn't those same statements be true and helpful for you? Could it be that there's no objective basis for your current guilt? You simply feel guilty, so you assume you are guilty? Feelings are not facts. Destructive guilt assumes the worst.

Refuse to Believe That Your Past Dictates Your Future

Listen up! This is important! Your past will dictate your future only if you let it.

You can challenge the thought habits that accuse and point fingers and predict the worst. With systematic, hard work on your part, supported by divine energy and (if available) encouragement from supportive friends, you can change the way you think about yourself.

Hear me, and hear me well. You are a valuable person, one with many talents and gifts. God has plans for you. You have hope and a future. If you've made mistakes in the past (and who hasn't?), you can walk more wisely in the future. With divine empowerment, you can elect to see that events that caused harm or that were even meant for harm are overturned and used for good.

You can learn from every experience you've had. Even your blunders can become key ingredients in the mix of your becoming all you are destined to be.

Enjoy Your Freedom!

Don't let negative, shame-based, guilt-ridden thoughts keep you from fulfilling your calling and using your gifts! When you begin to forgive yourself, you take in a deep breath of the pure emotional and spiritual oxygen you need to sustain life and to give you the energy to move forward.

The real or imagined mistakes in your past can't sabotage the fulfillment of your purpose without your permission. So be on about the business of living well today!

MY COMMITMENT TO *SELF-FORGIVENESS*

This day, I release myself from the burden of self-condemnation and destructive guilt. I am now free to be the person I was created to be—a unique, valuable, and worthwhile person. I say a resounding "no!" to the voices of people in my past who caused me to doubt that I could ever measure up. I withdraw from the internal conversations with the voice that reminds me of my shortcomings and past mistakes.

I choose to forgive myself for being imperfect and human, at the same time taking responsibility for turning away from the attitudes and actions that may have created problems for me. I recognize that my worth is not based on how I compare to others, my achievements, my material possessions, or the approval of others. Instead, I respect myself, even when I've lost status or failed to achieve what I thought I should.

I affirm the confidence that arises from that self-respect by trying new things and trying old things differently. I do not see myself as greater than others, nor as less than them. Today is a new day, for I choose self-forgiveness.

7

"Just Stay Away!"

CHOICE #7: ISOLATION OR CONNECTION

Cari had glanced into the backseat when her daughter had begun to cry. Though the other driver was clearly at fault, she felt responsible for the car accident that took the life of eleven-month-old Lindsey—and she assumed others must be judging her too.

She told me, "After the accident with an eighteen-wheeler in which my precious daughter Lindsey was killed, people came around, trying to offer sympathy and to help in practical ways. I was going through rehab because I had lost my foot, and the truth is, I could have used more help at the house. But I just couldn't stand to have people around. I felt that they were secretly judging me because I had not been looking at the road when the truck suddenly jackknifed in our pathway. Oh, they didn't say it, but I could tell they were thinking it."

Isn't it ironic? The presence of others can be comforting and healing, yet you may feel like isolating yourself at a time when you need support most. Even if previously you were an outgoing and friendly person, you may find yourself strangely withdrawn after you've gone through a life-shattering personal crisis. Having people around you can feel intrusive, irritating, and awkward.

In fact, others may feel awkward, too, wanting to help you, but not quite knowing what to say. At times you can bounce between "Come here, don't leave me!" and "Just stay away!" This can get confusing to those who want to help.

YOU DON'T HAVE TO BE ALONE TO BE ISOLATED

Isolation doesn't just happen when there's no one around. Clearly, you can be lonely in a crowd—though a crowd is probably about the last place you'd want to be. You can isolate yourself in at least three ways:

You Can Physically Withdraw from People

You may go out only when you have to. If you are working outside the home, you may eat alone, skip the early morning "catch-up" sessions, and communicate at the bare minimum to fulfill your job responsibilities.

You Can Withdraw Emotionally

You may sacrifice emotional intimacy with anyone, feeling unable to share what's happening inside of you because it feels as if no one could understand. You live alone in your private, torturous world.

You Can Numb Your Emotions

Numbing your emotions is a defense mechanism that provides a temporary escape from the pain so that you may interact, but not feel. That way, no one can get through to your heart, and you feel protected from further injury.

The problem is, the isolation itself injures you. Trying to go it alone is a recipe for depression and dysfunction, similar in a way to one part of the human body trying to function by itself. The heart, liver, arm, eye, and even the brain need the other parts of the system to live and do their jobs. Though your feelings may sometimes scream a different message, you need the nourishment of empathy and support.

WHY DOES ISOLATION HAPPEN?

I believe there are six main causes for the desire to isolate yourself after you've been blindsided with a life-altering event.

You Think No One Will Understand

You may have the feeling that this experience has so fundamentally changed you that there is no way people can understand what you've been through. And you would be right about one part of that. No one really does understand exactly what you've been through, even those who have had a similar experience. Lose a child and so did your friend? The knowledge of that commonality may make you feel closer, but the truth is, your responses are unique because your backgrounds, your spiritual and emotional resources, your relationship with your children, your relationships with significant others, and dozens of other factors come into play.

So the people you meet probably won't understand what you've been through. And guess what? You don't know what they've been through either. As a practicing psychologist, I learned a long time ago that people you see in the workplace or church or in the grocery store who seem to have it all together have actually experienced much more than you realize. You really never know the pain in people's lives, and you certainly can't tell from outside appearances what they've gone through. So in essence, they may understand more than you think.

Even if others can't relate exactly to what you've been through, that doesn't mean that they can't care about you and offer companionship and support. People who are very different can learn and grow together.

You Fear You'll Have an Embarrassing Reaction around Others

Donna, whose husband died of an aneurysm, was afraid of how she would respond to being around other people, so she stayed away. She said, "I just don't know what to expect from myself anymore. I tried to go to church last Sunday, but we were hardly into the singing when I began to feel like I couldn't breathe, and I wondered if I was going to faint. I sat down for a little bit and managed to get my breath. Then they began to sing one of my husband's favorite songs, and that's when I lost it. I felt the tears coming, and I knew I was about to make a fool of myself. I got up and ran out. Everybody was looking at me. I hurried to my car, and I sobbed and sobbed. When I finally was able to drive, I made it home. That was so embarrassing."

I know, you probably don't recognize your own reactions lately. You never know when the tears will spring out or when you'll feel like you can't get your breath.

However, anyone who knows you well will probably be aware of the fact that you are recovering from a really big deal. Most of them (the friends worth keeping!) will recognize that big deals often produce big emotions. You'll get their compassion, not their judgment.

Even those who don't know your situation are likely to be much less aware of your reactions than you are. It's easy to convince yourself that everyone is watching you. The truth is, on any given day, most people you'll meet in public are self-absorbed. I don't mean that critically. It's just human nature. Typically, people are more worried about what they have going on that day, how they look and feel, and yes, what people are thinking about them!

You Are Not Able to Tolerate Much Noise and Stimulation

Rachel, who was working full-time while taking chemo for breast cancer, recalls, "When I came home after work, my husband and kids wanted my attention. All I wanted was to be left alone. I had worked all day, felt awful, and just didn't have much to give. Noise jarred my nerves and made me irritable. I didn't want to snap at them, so I tried to keep to myself as much as possible. If someone was coming over, that made it worse. I felt the pressure to be 'on,' and I just didn't want them to be there."

Even normal interactions with family or friends can be emotionally draining and irritating during and after a traumatic experience. This is understandable since trauma can create a physiological reaction in which the sympathetic nervous system works overtime. Even though currently there is no real threat, your body remains on high alert. You have that jumpy, looking-over-your-shoulder feeling. Every little thing can get on your last nerve. You may find it difficult to tolerate noise and even laughter around you.

Talk to your family about this, explaining that right now you have to take noise and high activity in small doses. Let them know that you love them and that wanting to be alone does not indicate otherwise. It's not personal; it's just that your nervous system is hypersensitive right now. Tell them you're working on getting better, but you need their understanding right now.

When there are young children involved, whenever possible enlist the help of your spouse, supportive family members, or friends to help you deal with them when their emotions and energy levels are in high gear. However, if you are their parent, they do need attention and contact from you—or else they will probably act out to get more of it!

You Have Difficulty Trusting People

If the deliberate actions or negligence of a person or persons was at the root of, or at least contributed to, your heartache, you may have trouble trusting people again. In general, when there is a perceived perpetrator of disappointing and heartbreaking events, the kick in the gut is more powerful and the recovery more complicated. One reason for that is the loss of the ability to trust.

I'm not saying you should trust indiscriminately. Where you've been too gullible in the past, it's wise to learn legitimate lessons. If you've been naive in your approach to others, learn to look for true danger signs in people and take reasonable steps to make you and your loved ones safer.

However, you can become so sensitive to any sign of danger that you become paranoid. Given what you've been through, that may be a pretty natural reaction at first. However, your task in recovery is to balance that out—to take reasonable steps to prevent the problem from recurring, while not projecting onto every person you meet the assumption that he or she cannot be trusted.

You Want to Avoid Anyone Like the Person(s) Who Hurt You

After a traumatic event, you may have a particular aversion to a person with any characteristic in common with the person(s) who harmed you or the loved one(s) you lost.

For example, Gary sustained a severe head injury in an automobile accident in which two African-American men in the other vehicle were at fault. When these intoxicated men got out of their vehicle at the scene of the accident, Gary remembers seeing gold teeth flashing. "And they were laughing!" he told me. They had walked away from the accident unharmed, unlike Gary. He underwent several neurosurgeries, months of rehabilitation, separation from his family, and the inability to work.

Gary had never been a racially prejudiced person before, but when he finally started getting out again and went back to work part time, he experienced rage when he saw any African-American person or anything that reminded him of the men who caused his injuries. For instance, a man with a gold tooth made a service call to Gary's house. Gary became irate over a fairly innocuous exchange with the man, and he ordered the man off his property. Another example of this was the difficulty he had with a certain African-American female staff person who worked in the corporate human resources department. Because of his medical insurance and disability issues, he had to speak with her often. Though her role was to help him, which she apparently went out of her way to do, every conversation with her was infuriating to Gary, leaving him irritated for hours afterward. Gary's job involved serving customers. When working with African-American people, his tone of voice and obvious disdain began to endanger his job.

Gary reacted to people of the same ethnic background as the individuals responsible for the accident that caused his head injury. He had to learn to separate the specific people responsible for his life-threatening injuries from a general attitude toward African-Americans.

You, too, may find yourself overgeneralizing, tensing up, or becoming angry when you're around a person with any characteristic (such as eyes, body type, personality, occupation, even gender) that feels similar to the person you blame for your pain. You'll learn more about the whys of this when we deal with the avoidance/courage choice. For right now, however, just recognize that overgeneralization can contribute to unhealthy isolation.

You Crave Attention So Much That You Drive People Away

You can become so needy and smothering that you drive off the people you need so desperately. You may be particularly vulnerable to this if your current or past life experiences involved perceived abandonment.

The experience of abandonment is emotionally devastating, as Susan Anderson describes *in The Journey from Heartbreak to Connection.*[1] The emotional stages of abandonment involve feeling shattered, disconnected, and devastated, followed by withdrawals similar in craving and intense yearning to drug withdrawals. The painful longing for a "love fix" can manifest itself in clingy, don't-get-out-of-my-sight behavior. This style can wear out support people and sabotage your chances of future relationship success. Ironically, in your frantic efforts not to be alone, you ultimately create what you fear most—isolation. You can become so intent on preventing people from leaving you that you make them want to leave! If you're having these kinds of reactions, a caring and competent therapist can help you sort through your fears, become more secure, and make better decisions in your relationships.

YOU HAVE A CHOICE: ISOLATION OR CONNECTION

Jack, whose daughter had severe bipolar disorder beginning in her early teens, recalls, "We really just abandoned our social life when Nancy's acting out got so bad. We felt that nobody would understand. Also, we didn't want other people to have to hear it. By the time she was thirteen or so, her language and her behaviors were so atrocious, and they came out worse when we had company. It was just easier not to have friends."

Jack and his wife were under severe and unrelenting stress. They desperately needed time with adult friends to give them a break from the arduous tasks of parenting their daughter. Yet gradually, they withdrew onto their private deserted island.

Yes, you do need some time alone to think, rest, and process the enormity of the changes that have occurred. However, though at times you may find it difficult to grasp the hands reaching out to you, pushing past that initial discomfort allows you to avoid the costs of isolation and gain the benefits of connection.

Isolation Compounds Tribulation

You've already begun to see how withdrawal from human contact can rob you of needed emotional nourishment. When you're isolated, the costs don't end there.

1. *Your negative, intrusive thoughts gain credibility when you are alone.* Left "idle" and without distraction, your mind works overtime on replaying memories, worrying, and thinking about things that are wrong and could go wrong. When there's no one else around, you are left with your own ruminations and nothing to distract you from them. The more you think negatively without outside input, the more certain you'll become that your negative assumptions are accurate.

2. *You don't have help, encouragement, or support.* When you aren't connected to positive people, you block life-giving encouragement. Look at the root word and prefix of *encouragement.* You'll see that, in essence, encourage means "to infuse courage." Left alone in your pain, it's hard to muster up the courage to get up and face your anxieties and forge ahead into rebuilding and recreating a productive life.

We do need each other. King Solomon reminds us, "Two are better than one, because they have a good return for their work. If one falls down, his friend can help him up. But pity the man who falls and has no one to help him up! Also, if two lie down together, they will keep warm. But how can one keep warm alone? Though one may be overpowered, two can defend themselves. A cord of three strands is not quickly broken."[2]

When you are down, don't refuse the hand that is there to lift you up or the person who wants just to be there with you. You'll be surprised how much it will help when you begin to open yourself to the gentle encouragement or the practical help of a kindhearted and compassionate person.

3. *When you isolate yourself, your confidence in your ability to relate with people will diminish.* Muscles that aren't used begin to atrophy, and what's left is flab. When muscles are atrophied, it's harder to get out and start an exercise program because you don't feel as strong, and you don't like the way you look. You could do it, but you lack the confidence and the motivation to do it.

Something similar happens when you've been isolated. You feel that you may have forgotten how to relate or that you won't know what to say. Like exercise, getting back into relationships with people when you've been away from them for a while can be challenging, and the first steps are the hardest. If you jump right in and exercise as hard as you did when you were at your best, your muscles will become very sore and you may quit.

So in getting reconnected with others, start slowly. Begin to talk with people with whom you've had the most positive relationships in the past. As it happens in your physical fitness efforts, you'll gradually build up and regain your confidence and your comfort.

4. *Your risk for clinical depression is increased.* The connection between isolation and depression is well documented, and the relationship between the two is circular.[3] When you're isolated, you're more likely to become depressed, and when you're depressed, you're more likely to feel like withdrawing from the people around you. In fact, one of the risk factors for suicide is isolation and the lack of a support system.

In the next chapter, we will look at the downward spiral of depression and why you definitely want to stay out of it. Isolation positions you for descent on that slippery slope.

Connection Adds Protection

Human beings need one another. That's why we were given different talents, different personalities, and different motivations. Standing alone, no one has enough. Together, as we each contribute our unique gifts, we create a system in which we all have what we need. Connection with loving, supportive people nourishes our souls.

Empathy feels these thoughts: your hurt is in my heart, your loss is in my prayers, your sorrow is in my soul, and your tears are in my eyes.

—WILLIAM ARTHUR WARD

1. *Your physical health is improved by connection.* Many research studies document the physical health benefits of social support.[4] People who are isolated are more prone to heart attacks, cancer, and autoimmune diseases. Getting connected with others improves your immune function and can actually help you live longer when confronted with catastrophic illness.

2. *You have an improved prognosis for emotional recovery.* I've interviewed thousands of people over the years who have been through horrific experiences. Time and again, I've observed that those who get better faster and recover more fully are those who are not trying to go it alone.

Some of you have the luxury of an intact and positive family support system, and others of you live alone. If you are blessed with having folks around you who care and are willing to help, don't shut them out. Of course, you need some time to yourself. I'm not talking about never having a breather from them. But don't carve out a circle around you and mentally dare anyone to cross it.

If you live alone and/or don't have family nearby, you may have to garner a little more courage to reach out. If you are part of a church or synagogue, there are people there with good hearts who would welcome the opportunity to befriend and help someone—if they knew about the need. Contact your pastor, priest, or rabbi to explore that possibility. In many communities, there are support groups for practically every type of imaginable difficulty. Make a call and speak with one person in that group. That way, when you go for the first time, you won't feel like a total stranger.

You can also experience "connection" from a gentle, loving pet. The nonverbal support you get from an affectionate pet can be a comfort when you don't feel like talking.

Right after my mother died from Alzheimer's disease, I kept dreaming that I had a white cat similar to the one I had as a child. Even in the daytime, for some strange reason I seemed to have the urge to get a cat. Why was I dreaming this? I thought about the fact that when my daddy died of cancer, my loving white cat was always there to comfort me when I was upset. An only child, I could talk to my cat about what I felt. My mother was so sad, and I didn't want to upset her more by letting her know how I was feeling. It seemed my cat communicated with me through her soft touch and purrs.

Having had that insight about where these dreams and odd desires were originating, I told myself I should not act on impulse and should wait a couple of weeks. After all, I argued with myself, I travel in my speaking business. Who would take care of the cat while I was gone?

Two weeks passed, and I still wanted a cat. I began to watch the classifieds. Sure enough, that very week, the ad was right there: "Beautiful white, fuzzy kittens—free to a good home." The owner lived about two hours from my home, so my granddaughter, Scarlett, and I shared a wonderful trip to pick up our soft new friend, who we named Angel. I've never been sorry. In those times when I needed to grieve in private, she was there—unintrusive, accepting, and loving.

Feeling "understood" and accepted by an animal along with your connections with human friends can be a powerful aid to your recovery.

3. *Interaction creates distraction.* Communicating and relating with others gives you a break from the memories, anxieties, and depressing thoughts that plague your mind. When you do something outside your limited routine, talk with other people about their lives, or share a lunch with a friend in a quiet place, your negative thoughts get a rest (or at least a power nap).

You can't concentrate on two things at one time. Participating in conversation and activity with another person competes with the negative thoughts that close in when you are alone. The more you can focus on something or someone outside yourself, the less you will obsessively focus on your worries.

4. *You receive practical help, which brings psychological relief.* Trauma survivors have told me that one of the greatest benefits of social support is having some assistance with routine or out-of-ordinary tasks that suddenly seem overwhelming.

Abby Shields, whose foster daughter drowned in the family swimming pool, shared this: "I was ready to commit suicide. I called my friend Mary Ellen and said, 'I can't do this anymore. I'm ready to check out of here.' She said, 'Hold on, I'll be right over.'

"The laundry was piling up, the dishes were piling up. She said, 'Let's go into your bedroom. We'll take this pile of laundry with us, and we're going to sit down and watch television. We're going to cry, and I'm going to hold you and let you feel your feelings while the television show is on. And then we're going to fold laundry during the commercials. So I just would sob and sob and talk. Then when the commercials were on, we'd fold laundry. We did this for days. Mary Ellen didn't try to 'fix it.' That was the Holy Spirit's job. She just sacrificed her time."[5]

This example of kindness reminds me of the thoughtfulness of a woman who came to the home of my friend who had just lost her son. Knowing that guests would be coming into the home, she brought lots and lots of toilet paper. Now that's practical! In times when you are incapable of remembering those mundane things, it's invaluable to have the minds and hands of others.

5. *You can learn from others' successes and struggles.* A fifth benefit of connection is learning how others have dealt with struggles similar to yours. While no person has had your exact experience or responded in exactly the same way you have, there are many folks out there who understand adversity firsthand. A person who was raped has many things in common with another individual whose home was burglarized. Both people feel violated. Even if your experiences with adversity seem very different from those of another person, there is much you can share.

It is especially true that you can learn from people who have been through a similar experience. For instance, Compassionate Friends is a support group for parents who have lost children. In a support group related to your particular trauma, you can see that people like you can come through a personally catastrophic event and that the pain won't always be as intense as it is now. You regain hope, along with ideas about what helps at various stages in your recovery.

If you have developed a life-altering illness, many local hospitals sponsor related support groups. There you can educate yourself about your illness, gain courage to face it head-on, and build a quality lifestyle in spite of it. Sometimes it even helps to listen to people with victimlike, complaining attitudes. You can see how those habits limit their lives and irritate people around them. This can give you a strong determination not to be that way!

BEGIN NOW TO CHOOSE *CONNECTION*

I hope that I've been able to communicate to you how important it is to begin to relate with others again, though trust may be difficult. Now I want to share with you a baker's dozen of practical steps up the ladder of connection.

Don't Let Negative Past Experiences Keep You from Asking for Help

Are you finding it difficult to ask for help? Let's try to identify the source of your fear. Perhaps the answers lie in negative experiences in the past when you asked for help. For instance, maybe you turned to others at a time of need and one of the following occurred:

- You were not believed. ("You must have dreamed that. You know your grandfather would never do something like that.")

- Your feelings were discounted. ("You shouldn't be feeling that way. Just get over it!")

- You trusted someone who breached your confidentiality. ("You think I started those rumors? You know I wouldn't do that. You must have told other people about it too.")

It's true that people can disappoint you, and you may have learned that from hurtful experiences in the distant past or in more recent experiences. Some you thought would be there for you won't, but God will send others you never could have imagined would play such a significant role in your healing.

Michelle Nichols remembers a hurtful experience that made it difficult to trust others after her son's death. "About a month after my son died, my daddy called up in his sing-song voice and said, 'Hi, Michelle, how are you?' Well, the shock from the sudden death of my firstborn was starting to wear off. I said, 'Well, Dad, my son just died. How do you think I am?' And with that, my parents left and didn't come back again for a year and a half. They said, 'Let us know when you're normal.'"[6]

Alice's husband, a pastor, was caught cheating with a female parishioner. This resulted in his dismissal from the church and a very public scandal in that small town. Alice, who chose to stay with her husband, said, "It was awful. Even people who had been close friends just stopped calling. It was worse than a death, because at least if someone dies, people rally around you. People didn't know what to say, so they just avoided me completely. I also believe people thought, 'What if that happened to me?' The result? They just didn't want to hear about it or talk to me."

If you've had hurtful experiences in the past, don't let that prevent you from connecting with the people God sends your way today. Don't jump to the conclusion that because some of your previous attempts to seek support did not go well, it's just better to brave this storm alone in your own boat.

Identify "Triggers" That Are Creating Your Anxiety and Avoidance

Triggers are cues you encounter in your daily environment that remind you of your painful experiences. Become more aware of people-related triggers that make you want to stay away from an individual or group of people altogether, such as:

- Mannerisms that remind you of a person who harmed you or a person you lost

- The same ethnic background as someone you associate with your negative experiences

- A mistake similar to one made by you or someone else during your trauma

- A social activity that reminds you of something you lost (something you used to enjoy with a deceased loved one)

- A person biologically related to someone you perceive as dangerous

- A situation in which you feel similar emotions to those of a past hurtful experience

Are any of these people-related cues hindering your relationships now? If so, be aware of them so you can take necessary steps to overcome these hindrances to relationships.

Challenge the Mental Error of Overgeneralizing

Once you've identified the human triggers that create anxiety for you, you can begin to battle the thinking errors that are causing you to detach or overreact. Trauma can change the way you think and process information. You feel vulnerable as never before, and you determine never to let something like this happen to you or yours again. Therefore, you become highly sensitive, so intent on avoiding danger that you "overgeneralize" and cut yourself off from people and situations that are either neutral or could be positive in your life.

Overgeneralization is taking some aspect of your traumatic situation and drawing general conclusions from it, assuming it applies in all situations. Do you find yourself saying things like these?

- "Men are all alike; they want one thing."

- "You can't trust bosses; they always put profits over people."

- "Nobody could possibly understand."

- "I'm just not able to relate to anybody anymore."

- "I could never have a serious relationship again."

Do you notice the absolute words in these statements? *All, always, nobody, anybody, never*—these indicate that you're over-generalizing.

The cure? Be specific. Narrow your thoughts and observations to the unique situation you're dealing with now.

One technique that can be helpful is to challenge the over-generalization in writing. Draw a line down the center of a page in your journal. On the left side, write the absolute statements you make to yourself such as the examples above. On the right side of the sheet, challenge each absolute thought with a more accurate statement, such as:

- "Some men are abusive, but others are not. I just need to make better choices."

- "Not every boss is like the boss who fired me without cause. In fact, the most successful companies realize that profits come from treating their people well. I'm going to look for a job where the leader really gets that."

- "It's true that some people won't understand. However, there are others who have been through hard times who not only can understand, but they care."

- "I'm having some difficulty right now in relationships. However, I have made a little progress in relating better with my kids and spouse. I'm going to call my friend Betty next week. She's always been easy to talk to. Gradually, I'll regain my ability to relate."

- "Right now I'm feeling very hurt after my husband cheated on me with my best friend. After I've had some time to heal, I may be able to enjoy some time with men. I don't have to figure all of that out now."

Combat "All-or-Nothing Thinking" and the Requirement of Perfection

"All-or-nothing" thinking is another cognitive error. Do you think in extremes? Do you see yourself or the other people in your life as either great or terrible? Is there no middle ground for you, no partial credit?

The tendency to think that you must be able to trust a person 100 percent, or not at all, can be more pronounced after a traumatic experience (though you may have already had a tendency to be a perfectionist). Because you want to stay safe, you try to reduce your anxiety by not tolerating any less-than-perfect behavior in yourself or others. This can be deadly to your relationships.

The truth is, we're all human, and all humans make mistakes sometimes. People are a combination of good and bad characteristics. We are all at various stages of maturity. That's just how it is.

Practice thinking of performance in degrees rather than extremes. For instance, rather than rating a conversation as "great" or "terrible," ask yourself, "What did I like about that conversation? What did I do well? What would I like to do better next time?" Or you might say to yourself, "In that visit, Sue seemed to be really listening to me about 80 percent of the time I was sharing with her." (This rather than concluding from the moments she was distracted by a phone call, "She didn't listen at all to me. She doesn't care.")

All-or-nothing thinking can also apply to your view of your relationships before and after the trauma. It reminds me of a conversation I had with Lanny, who was disabled in an offshore accident. He told me, "When I got hurt and had to come home from the rig, that changed everything. My wife and I had no problems before that. We got along great. Now we never say a kind word to each other."

Oh, really? He and his wife had "no problems" at all? I've never seen a marriage like that, and I suspect Lanny hasn't either.

Recognize That Feelings Are Not Facts

Your feelings can insist to you that they represent reality, but this may not be the case at all. Just because you think others look at you critically when you are around them doesn't make it so. That look you noticed on their faces could be because of concern, deep thought, or their own anxieties. Even though your gut tells you that individuals similar in some way to the perpetrator are dangerous, you may simply be experiencing an anxiety trigger. Do you feel like your coworkers see you as a wimp for having emotional reactions to the tragedy you've been through? I doubt that's true. You cannot read their minds.

Your emotions have undergone a significant injury, and it's going to take awhile for them to heal. So right now (or ever, for that matter!) you can't trust your feelings to give you completely accurate information. I'm not telling you never to pay attention to your gut. I'm just saying, don't assume that what your emotions are telling you is correct without examining the evidence.

Review Your Experiences to Discover Any Blind Spots about Unsafe People

We've been talking about possible overreactions that cause you to unnecessarily close yourself off from relationships. However, I caution you not to fall back into any patterns of gravitating to the people who prey on your areas of vulnerability, people who are irresponsible and ripe for your unhealthy caretaking, or those who take advantage of your good nature.

We've all heard someone who seemed stuck on the same song, second (or third or fourth) verse. Listen to the danger signs in Angela's description of her current relationship: "My new boyfriend Charlie is nothing like my ex. He doesn't drink every day like Austin did; he only drinks with his friends on weekends. And Charlie doesn't get mean when he drinks. I'm so lucky to have found someone who really cares about me. Finally, I'm ready for a fresh start."

If you contributed to the life-robbing events in your life by being gullible or too trusting, take a good look at that. Acknowledge how your tendency to see the best in people could have been out of balance and then learn to set better boundaries. If you've allowed a long-term pattern of abusive relationships, get yourself some help to change that. It's time to become wiser in your choices of folks to hang out with.

Calculate the Risk of Trusting

Don't trust people indiscriminately; instead, pay attention and identify actual red flags in people. Then take small leaps of faith with reasonably "safe" people.

Some types of traumatic experiences make you extremely cautious about your physical safety. There's no shortage of information on this topic in today's world where crime, terrorism, and natural disasters loom as possibilities. Inform yourself about what to look for, what to do, and how to physically protect yourself in these situations. There are plenty of books and news show interviews with the experts to help you with that.

Protecting yourself at an emotional level is not so straightforward. If you are considering a business or personal relationship with a person and your emotions seem to be flying those red flags, test it out.

1. *Clarify what type of relationship you will have with this person.* What will be required in your interactions with this individual? In what areas will you need to trust this person? What are the consequences if he/she is not trustworthy?

A different level of trust is required to become a partner in a class assignment versus a partner in a business venture. Meeting someone in a restaurant for lunch is less risky than having a person you met on the Internet pick you up for an outing. Sharing parts of your story with a friend is less risky than a tell-all conversation with someone at work.

2. *Form a hypothesis about this person and test it out.* Ask yourself, "What evidence do I have at this time that this person is or is not trustworthy? What are my areas of uncertainty? Based on what I know at this point, what's my best guess about it?" Write out your responses.

3. *Test your hypothesis.* Gather some information to add to the knowledge on which you will base your decision about whether to engage with this person. Talk with people who know the individual, check out written records, and talk with past clients (in a business situation). Arrange for some low-risk, experimental time with this individual to observe more closely how he or she behaves. Talk with the individual, asking questions and both watching and listening to responses. Incorporate what you learn into your decision about a possible relationship.

The question you're trying to answer is, to what extent can I trust this individual within the context of what I will be doing with him or her? Notice this is not an all-or-nothing, do-I-trust-him-with-my-life? sort of answer. Your conclusion should be specific to what you are considering doing now. If you decide to go farther in your relationship and the level of your involvement, you can recalculate.

Based on what you know now, you can decide to:

a. proceed with little reservation;

b. run far and fast the other direction;

c. gather additional information before making a decision;

d. build in safeguards.

You're now developing the skill to be open to the positive possibilities of healthy relationships with trustworthy, caring people—yet wise in your attention to real evidence when danger lurks ahead.

Deepen Your Connections with "Safe" People

Think about the people in your life who, historically, have been the most dependable, the most caring, and the most understanding. These may be folks you have known for a long time, or they may be new friends you've met in the course of dealing with the sad events in your life. But you know who they are.

Wait! Don't start protesting to yourself about all the reasons you don't want to connect with them now, such as you don't want to burden them, you don't want them to see you this way, they wouldn't understand, and so on. Just identify who they are as a first step.

Make a list of people who seem to fall into the category of a "safe person," such as:

- a loving family member;

- an old friend;

- a friendly acquaintance who has indicated an interest in sharing some time with you;

- your minister;

- a person to whom you've related well in a support group;

- someone who went through a similar experience and who seems to have come a long way in recovery;

- a person in your church or community who seems to have a calling to reach out to people in emotional pain;

- a therapist or professional who has been recommended to you;

- people you can hire to do those jobs you just don't feel up to doing right now (such as housework, yard work).

Begin Where You Are, and Take Small Steps toward Greater Connection

Take a look at the people on your list. Are there some there who may have been just waiting for an opening to relate with you, but they didn't want to intrude? Though they have wanted to be respectful of your desire for privacy and solitude, they would be delighted to have a phone call from you. You don't have to call them and tell them everything. Just a brief conversation to say hi and to ask about their lives would be a step in the right direction.

As your comfort level increases, you can share more about what you are going through—or not. The conversations do not have to focus on you. You can have great interactions by being an active listener, asking good questions, and reflecting back your understanding and empathy for what the other person is sharing with you.

As you become more at ease, you will probably feel more like opening up yourself. However, just getting the communication going, whatever form that takes, is a step out of life-sapping isolation.

Barbara Glanz's book *What Can I Do? Ideas to Help Those Who Have Experienced Loss* is a treasure trove of strategies for people who want to help those who are grieving.[7] However, because most of these ideas were from survivors who shared what helped them most, it can also be a great resource for you as a survivor, giving you creative ideas about how to engage with others in ways that help you continue to heal.

You may just want to begin by doing something simple with someone on your list. Having a companion to go for coffee, shop for groceries, or take in a movie makes getting out of the house so much easier. The anxiety of attending that first support group meeting is diminished if you can walk in with someone you've already talked with or that you know. (Call ahead and "meet" someone, even if it's just by phone.)

Others on your list are those who have the gift of serving in practical ways. If they only knew what to do, they'd be glad to do it. At our church, we have a bulletin board called "Duo," which stands for "Do unto others." There volunteers post their willing-ness to perform services like transportation for people unable to drive, house repairs, and sitting with shut-ins for their loved ones to take a break. If you are fortunate enough to be in a church that expresses love for people in practical ways, don't be afraid to access that help. The outcome will be double blessings—for you and for the person who has the privilege of serving.

Tell Your Story—Wisely

Most of us have an urge down deep to have our story be heard, and be heard, and be heard. Even if you're scared to do it, that desire likely lives somewhere in your heart. Putting words to your story and your emotions speeds emotional healing.

However, some spill it to anyone who will listen. That's dan-gerous. Telling your story to a nonsupportive listener can be very damaging, and the words of a judgmental person can cause you to shut up and back up from everyone.

So I advise you to be wise. Pick carefully the few first people with whom you verbally share your experience. Even then, you may want to share only parts of your experience at a time for two reasons. First, you're less likely to get emotionally overwhelmed yourself with the stressful process of telling the story. Second, you can gauge your friends' reactions and test whether these are people with whom you want to divulge the most intimate details. Beware if the person begins to make comments like, "You should have known . . ." or "You've got to be exaggerating. Are you sure you're not just being a drama queen?" or "That would have never happened to me. I'd just have . . ." You can give the person feedback that these kinds of responses are not what you need; you just need to be heard and supported. Or you can change the subject and recognize that this is not a person with whom to share this sensitive material.

Telling your story is a way to acknowledge the realities to yourself, a way to desensitize yourself to the overwhelming emotions, and an opportunity to receive affirmation and support. Though you may feel somewhat out of control as you fight the feelings that initially flood you when you talk about it, you will have taken a giant step toward gaining control. The more you avoid talking about it, the greater the internal turmoil that churns. The more you tell it, the less power over your emotions the story will have. We're going to address this phenomenon more specifically in chapter 9.

Work toward Balancing Reasonable Caution without Overprotectiveness

It's normal to be frightened after the unexpected unthinkable happens. However, if you allow your anxiety to cause you to become too worrisome and overprotective, you can unintentionally create tension and disconnection with your loved ones. For example, if you expect your spouse to report every move and answer dozens of questions throughout the day, resentment and defensiveness can grow.

When your fear-based protectiveness causes others to become defensive, connection is blocked. Figuratively, the defensive person draws arms up in front of the face, blocking out potential "blows." This emotional barrier inhibits communication and caring expressions. Ultimately, defensiveness grows into irritation, and irritation evolves into anger. Emotional and physical intimacy wither in an angry emotional environment.

I know you may be trying to reassure yourself that everything is okay by your constant checking and questioning. However, those behaviors tend to have the opposite effect. By anxiously watching every move and trying to remove any possibility of danger, you make everything "not Okay."

A parent who is overprotective of a young child (constantly warning of potential danger, preventing the child from normal experimentation with independence) sets that child up for a lifetime of anxiety and fear. As the saying goes, we learn what we live. That's not the legacy you want to pass on to your child.

And then there are the adolescents. They already don't like you tracking them closely because they are trying to establish independence from their parents. And yet (though it sometimes doesn't look or sound like it) they want the security of being attached to their families.

Every caring parent struggles with how much to control and how much freedom to give when trying to raise healthy teens. When you are a survivor of trauma, your anxieties are likely to make that task even more daunting. The truth is, there are many dangers out there, and you may find it nigh to impossible to just relax and go with the flow. (You shouldn't even do that in normal circumstances.)

So how do you prevent your teenager or any other members of your family from becoming an unnecessary prisoner of your worries? How can you know when you are just being conscientious and when your protectiveness is over the line?

First, ask your family members what they see as overprotective, asking for specific examples. Then honestly evaluate each behavior they mention, using questions like these to help you:

- In what specific ways does this behavior promote the health and safety of my loved ones?

- Are there any ways in which the behavior works against their making good choices or significantly interferes with our relationship?

- Based on what you know and what objective experts might say, are your instructions exaggerating the danger?

- How does the danger in the situation in question compare to the danger you experienced during your traumatic event? Are you mixing these up?

Let's consider the example of Jean, who had stopped at a convenience store one evening when robbers came in, held her and three other customers at gunpoint, then shot and injured the clerk before getting away.

Understandably, Jean had some trouble at first going into convenience stores. Then she noticed she was feeling anxious when she had to go into banks or other establishments where robberies were more likely to occur.

When her teenage son started out the door with his friends, she'd warn him, "Don't you dare stop to get a Coke while you're out, especially with it being nighttime."

He'd protest, "Aw, Mom, that's ridiculous. They'd laugh me down if I said, 'My mom won't let me stop at a convenience store for a soft drink.' I'm sorry that happened to you, but you just can't make me a prisoner because of it!"

So the question for Jean was, what's the real danger in going into a convenience store or a bank? How many times do people go there and absolutely nothing happens? Sure, anything is possible. But what is the probability? Okay, so you may be justified in keeping your kids away from convenience stores in high-crime neighborhoods. Most frequently, however, the safety statistics are on the side of the customer.

Despite your own personal post-trauma nervousness, don't restrict your loved ones from living a normal life. You can't ex out every possibility of danger. Trying to keep yourself and those you love in a protective bubble is an unhealthy option.

Consider Joining a Support Group

I can't tell you how valuable it is to be a part of a support network of people who have had similar experiences to yours. Check with your local library, community mental health center, crisis help line, mental health professional, hospital education department, newspaper community listings, or church staff to learn what groups are available in your local or neighboring communities and when they meet.

If appropriate support groups are not available locally, look for respected national associations via the Internet. These associations can provide valuable information on the issue with which you are struggling and, when you are feeling a little stronger, you may want to get their help in founding a local chapter.

Speaking of the Internet, there are many electronic support groups of which you can become a part. My bias is that face-to-face meetings are more powerful, but electronic groups can be a great first step in "meeting" people who have experiences similar to yours and feeling that you are not crazy and you are not alone.

Work with Others to Make a Difference to Other Hurting People

I'm getting a little ahead of myself, because we're going to talk about this subject in detail in chapter 10. However, allow me to mention now that one of the best ways to get connected is to get out and do something meaningful with other people.

An example of helping others that I experienced recently was the collective post-Katrina experience in my home state of Mississippi. Katrina has become a time marker for us—we talk about life "before the storm" and "after the storm." (This may be the case for you, too, as you think about your own life "hurricane.") Almost immediately, people who had been living next to each other in anonymity became true neighbors. They pitched in, removed trees from houses, cleaned up debris, replaced roofs, and shared food and ice. Many who had nothing but a concrete foundation left of their own homes were out trying to make a difference to others who had the chance to salvage something. Soon, people from all over the country were arriving with a zeal and a compassion that is unparalleled in my memory. The physical community was virtually demolished, but the emotional community was solidified and made unbelievably stronger. Connected? In the midst of horrific circumstances, you bet we were!

A Harvard-led study of Hurricane Katrina survivors was released via Reuters news service in August 2006.[8] Lead researcher Dr. Ronald Kessler announced that five to eight months after the storm, about 15 percent of survivors were found to have serious psychological difficulties, including Post-Traumatic Stress Disorder and depression—double the normal rates for these problems. Nearly 85 percent of these survivors had suffered major financial, income, or housing loss.

Despite all this, this study found that the urge to commit suicide actually fell! Dr. Kessler said that the reason for this unpredicted finding was that many survivors had found greater meaning in life by forging stronger ties with their loved ones and communities. He reported that an extraordinarily high proportion of the respondents said that despite their sadness and anxieties about the future, they felt closer to their loved ones, and they felt more closely connected to their community. They felt much more religious. They felt that they had more purpose and meaning in their lives. These were the people where suicidal tendencies decreased.

This study reveals what many of us have personally found to be true: even in the worst of adversity, bearing one another's burdens lightens the load for everyone.

MY COMMITMENT TO *CONNECTION*

I choose connection, drawing on the positive power of caring and encouraging people to help me along in my journey and speed my recovery. Though I may have been injured in the past by the unthinking or willful acts of others, I choose not to draw negative conclusions about the human race because of it.

Where I have made mistakes in judging character, I do not totally withdraw out of fear that I will endanger myself again. Rather, I choose to take a careful look at my choices and learn specific lessons to improve my decision-making skills. I recognize that isolation that I think will bring me relief actually leaves me alone with the thoughts that torture me, and it hurts those who love me.

I make the decision now to begin to connect, first with one and then another, sharing what I think and how I feel. I will take small steps across the bridge of trust to access the support of others who have walked this path before me. I want to be healthy in my mind and in my body, and I acknowledge that strong, positive relationships boost my immunity to all kinds of emotional and physical threats.

I affirm the wisdom of the principle demonstrated over and over since the beginning of time: it is not good that a person should be alone. Therefore, I challenge my anxiety and reach for the blessings of nourishing relationships. I commit to connection.

8

"My Dreams Have Turned into Nightmares"

CHOICE #8: DEPRESSION OR GRIEF

John lost his beloved wife in an automobile accident. When I interviewed John, he described how his grief edged over into depression. He told me, "I lost hope of things getting any better. My wife was my best friend. I just didn't see how I was going to get through it. My thoughts were so out of character. I didn't recognize it was grief. I thought it just had to be something else, that I was really sick or had gone crazy.

"Day after day I'd head home as the sun was going down. The closer I got to the home we had shared, my heart would scream, 'God, I just can't do this!' I actually reached a point where I said, 'The quality of life that I have is just not worth it.'

"You know what? Before this, I never had understood how anyone could even contemplate suicide. But suicide became a seductive option. Going through something like this lets you know that you are not immune from anything—even thoughts of killing yourself."

John's words are yet another example of how a traumatic experience gives you a new appreciation for what you may have judged in others before. You come to understand firsthand that you should "never say never" or consider yourself above those "crazy" reactions others have. Fact is, you don't know what you will feel and do, given the right (or wrong!) set of circumstances.

Was John experiencing just plain grief, or was it depression? After all, grief can feel so gut-wrenchingly awful that you just don't believe you can stand it and you wonder if you'll ever feel better. Sounds pretty depressing, doesn't it? The distinction between the two can be a little cloudy, so I'm going to try to make that clearer momentarily. First, though, let's talk about grief and the role it plays in your healing.

YOU HAVE TO FEEL WORSE TO FEEL BETTER

Grief is nature's way of moving you through the dark tunnel of the experience of significant loss. Though grief can seem like a curse, it is actually a blessing. Grief is a God-given emotional tool to help you live again after those inevitable times when your expectations, dreams, and plans have derailed.

Grief helps you absorb information that initially "just can't be true." It allows you to identify the losses brought on by a personally catastrophic event and gradually, painfully, come to terms with those losses. The grief process finally transports you to a place of acceptance of the reality of what's happened and its impact on your life. (By the way, accepting the reality doesn't mean liking it!)

When you are grieving, you long for what you previously had. From an emotional standpoint, you go through withdrawal from things you valued. They're gone, at least in their previous form, and the pain can be excruciating.

I once heard Bishop T. D. Jakes say that life sometimes writes a check your soul can't cash. You get blindsided with something that feels so terrible that at first you just can't take it in and comprehend it. Though heartbreaking, grief is the emotional pathway through and out of those barren places.

Of course, people in their right minds would prefer to be able to go around grief rather than through it. Who wants to feel pain? But that's not the way it works. You can run from it, stay frenetically busy, or try to escape in myriad ways. Though you may escape it temporarily, grief is patient. Ultimately, it comes to collect.

The day Joseph first showed up in my office, he was a mess. He told me, "You've got to help me, Dr. Bev. I think I've really lost it."

"What's going on, Joseph?" I asked.

"I haven't been to work in three days. I can't eat, I can't sleep. I'm crying all the time. I've even been throwing up."

"Wow, what happened?" I questioned.

"Well, my girlfriend's dog died," he said sheepishly.

Somewhat taken aback, I explored further. "Were you really close to this dog?"

"No!" he sobbed. "That's why I think I'm going crazy!"

As we explored what could be going on, I found out that Joseph's father had died suddenly some four years before. Joseph had stayed strong for everyone else during the crisis time and during the funeral. Afterward, he threw himself obsessively into his demanding job, then hit happy hour at the local bars when the long day ended. He had worked hard not to feel and had managed to do so . . . until this. His girlfriend's grief over her lost pet was a catalyst for Joseph's unresolved grief to come out with a vengeance.

Grief is insistent. If you try to ignore it at first, it will knock loudly on your door later.

HOW LONG DOES IT TAKE?

How long does the grief process take? As long as it takes.

My clients often press me for an approximate timeline,

desperately reaching for an anticipated end to their pain. Yet your own unique reactions and time frames depend on a constellation of factors such as your personal history, the degree of your perceived loss, your history with other losses, your resources for coping, your relationships, your faith, and your sense of self-worth.

> *I have been trying to make the best of grief and am just beginning to learn to allow it to make the best of me.*
> —BARBARA LAZEAR ASCHER

Your history helps to determine your feelings and the reactions that "seem natural" to you. But what you can work on are the choices of thought and action that you make in the midst of your grief now. These choices determine whether your grief will lead you into debilitating depression or whether it is "good grief." In just a little while, I'm going to show you how to stay out of depression and remain in productive grief until the necessary healing has taken place.

SO WHAT IS GRIEF REALLY, AND WHAT CAN I EXPECT?

For our purposes here, we'll define *grief* as the healing process of fully experiencing the perception of loss. Let's take a closer look at each of the four components of our definition: healing, process, fully experiencing, and perception of loss.

Healing

Like many medical interventions, grief requires pain as a necessary part of healing. If you had a malignant tumor, the surgery to remove it would be painful. You'd be incapacitated for a while, but the pain of surgery would be a necessary component of your treatment. Grief is a lot like that—the process is certainly not pleasant, but it is essential to recovery.

Process

Grief is not a state; it is a process. First, you have to deal with letting go of what was. Gradually, you have to come to grips with the reality of the loss, recognizing that what you had in its past form is truly, irrevocably gone. You have to find ways to deal with your emotional reactions to the agonizing realization that life as you knew it has changed. When grief successfully accomplishes its assignment, you find a meaningful and productive way of living in your new reality.

Maybe you've heard of the five stages of grief attributed to Dr. Elisabeth Kübler-Ross: denial, anger, bargaining, depression, and acceptance. Incidentally, Dr. Kübler-Ross actually called these the five reactions to receiving catastrophic news, and others began calling them the five stages of grief.[1]

In my opinion, a simpler and more helpful model for understanding the overall process of grief comes from Dr. Therese Rando, author of several books on grief, death, and dying. In *Treatment of Complicated Mourning*, Dr. Rando described three common responses to major losses over time.[2]

1. *Avoidance phase.* The avoidance phase is the period when you are reeling from the shock of the news of your loss. You may feel confused, numb, disoriented, and mentally disorganized. Things around you may feel unreal.

As the reality of what has happened sinks in, denial steps up to the plate to protect you. (Remember, we talked about this in chapter 1.) Denial can serve as a temporary buffer, a type of emotional anesthesia to keep you from being overwhelmed by your loss. But denial that persists blocks your recovery.

2. *Confrontation phase.* The confrontation phase is the most

acutely painful phase. The pangs of grief are extremely intense because of pining, yearning, and searching for the lost experience. You confront the reality of the loss and are repeatedly stabbed in the heart as you experience seemingly endless reminders that the loss is real. Your emotions are all over the map. You alternately avoid and confront the distressing material as you attempt to work it through.

3. *Accommodation phase.* In this phase, the raging emotional storm begins to subside, and you begin to reenter the everyday world. It's not that you forget about who or what you lost. Far from it. But you are finding ways to deal with the scars of your loss in a way that does not prevent you from learning, growing, and living purposefully again. You "accommodate" your loss by redefining your roles and relationships and developing the new skills and habits that allow you to be successful again.

Yes, you're right. Mourning is very hard work.

Fully Experiencing

This third major component of our grief definition refers to the fact that deep grief affects you at all levels—emotionally, mentally, behaviorally, socially, physically, and spiritually.

Emotionally, your feelings are topsy-turvy, bouncing around from sorrow to anger to anxiety to helplessness to loneliness to . . . you name it.

Mentally, you have trouble thinking because your mind is consumed with repetitive thoughts about the details of the traumatic event. You struggle with a lack of focus and concentration, mental disorganization, and trouble making decisions.

Behaviorally, you may find yourself doing things you would not normally do (such as being late for work, drinking too much), or find it excruciatingly difficult to do your regular routine (such as getting dressed, washing clothes).

Socially, you may find yourself so preoccupied that you have no interest in other people, and you withdraw from the very people who could offer support to you. On the other hand, you may become dependent and clingy. Your relationships may suffer because you are angry, irritable, and critical.

Physically, you may find yourself unable to eat or eating everything in sight, sleeping too much or too little, being physically exhausted and depleted of energy, or being hyped-up, sighing, and crying.

Spiritually, you may feel that God has let you down, and you may question your spiritual beliefs. Or your faith walk may be deepened as you draw closer to God for comfort.

You see what I mean by "fully experiencing" your grief? It's no wonder all this can make you think you've lost it! Yet every one of these symptoms is within the range of "normal" when you're grieving.

Perception of Loss

It's not just what you obviously lost (a person, a job, an opportunity, etc.). More importantly, it's your perception of the loss, what that loss means to you, that really affects your life. When you least expect it, you can be bowled over by a song, a smell, a scene in a TV show, the beginning of the season in which your life changed. Such experiences stimulate thoughts about your perceived losses and thus have the power to trigger your grief anew.

A SPECIAL HEARTACHE: THE LOSS OF YOUR DREAM

Life often takes cruel turns. After spending more than a year of helping me schedule and organize interviews for this book and of sharing the vision for helping others in their times of loss, my wonderful assistant, Deana, experienced the tragic loss of her twenty-year-old son, Nick, in a motorcycle accident. Ironically, she became an interviewee.

Deana talked a great deal about the loss of her dreams, of all the things she would never be allowed to experience with the older of her two sons. In my own personal experience with loss, and in my work with thousands of survivors, I've noticed that some of the deepest pain is brought on when you try to let go of those fantasies and mental pictures of events that you erroneously assumed would be yours to experience—such as a child's wedding or successful future, growing old together with your spouse, or the satisfaction of seeing results from projects you are now unable to complete.

One of the toughest parts of grief is to let go of what you thought you would have and to grieve what now can never be.

GRIEF AND DEPRESSION ARE COUSINS, NOT TWINS

It's been my intent so far to help you know what to expect from grief so that you don't feel as if you are going crazy. I've also strongly hinted that you can make choices that make it less likely that you will fall into clinical depression.

Many people use the terms *grief* and *depression* interchangeably. And in fact, there are some similarities in the two. However, there are also notable differences.

Both grief and depression affect your emotions, your behavior, and your body. In both depression and grief, you may feel sad or anxious, cry, sleep too little or too much, eat too little or too much, feel bone-tired, have difficulty finding pleasure in things you used to enjoy, and have repetitive thoughts about what you've been through and the losses that resulted from it.

However, there are subtle but significant differences between depression and grief, and most of it happens between your two ears. The deciding factor is how you talk to yourself about the negative events in your life. To illustrate that, let me tell you a story I once heard.

Two brothers grew up together on a farm. One moved to the city; the other stayed behind to till the soil. Each time the city sibling would visit, his farmer brother was complaining—it was too hot, too cold, too wet, too dry, crops were failing, prices were low.

On one visit, the city brother observed that the crops were looking great. He thought, "Finally, my brother will be happy." When he got to the farm, his brother was sitting in the porch rocker with his usual depressed look on his face. "Why are you looking so sad?" he asked. "The weather's been perfect, the prices are at an all-time high, and you have an abundant crop."

His farmer brother shook his head slowly and said, "Do you know what a crop like this takes out of the soil?"

Notice the country brother's negative, pessimistic thought patterns. I can assure you that he was depressed. When you get depressed, even positives feel negative. If you think this way long enough, depression will be your inevitable destination.

YOU HAVE A CHOICE: DEPRESSION OR GRIEF

Depression and grief: what comes with the packages? The two may look alike, but they deliver very different results.

Depression is just plain depressing! Depression compounds your losses because if you don't do the work to change that debilitating negativity, you will stay in the misery much longer than you would in healthy mourning.

Shannon's husband of only two-and-a-half years packed up and left without warning. When the shock wore off and the agony set in, Shannon tried to talk with him. "I'm just not happy," he explained. "Maybe I'm just not cut out for marriage." Jason's abandonment was particularly painful because Shannon had been five when her father left her mother and her, eventually marrying "the other woman." Shannon became depressed and anxious, finding it hard to function at work.

She recalls, "I lost sight of any positives in my life. Nothing seemed to be right; everything was wrong. I was so down on myself. Why wasn't I enough for Jason? People would tell me, 'You have so much going for you. You'll find someone to love who deserves you.' But I couldn't hear it. All I could see were my flaws. Not only did I lose confidence in my ability to be in a relationship, it affected my confidence at work too. I was always thinking, 'Nothing good ever happens to me.' I put plenty of distance between me and other people. I had learned a big lesson: don't get close, because people always leave."

Sadly, that depressed way of thinking can become a self-fulfilling prophecy. If you believe you "can't" and that nothing will turn out well, you drop out of life. If you never get close to anyone, you continue to believe people can't be trusted.

Though the pain of healthy grieving can be excruciating and its sadness deep, you are less likely to get stuck in your sadness than if you have clinical depression. In healthy grief, you focus on your actual or perceived losses *without* exaggerating them by believing all is lost or no one cares or you'll never have a future. You fully experience the awareness of your losses and let it hurt. The grief process done diligently allows you to evolve and experiment with ways to adapt and adjust.

Your challenge, then, is to do the difficult emotional and spiritual work of grieving and mourning without allowing yourself to sink into clinical depression. First, I'm going to show you how to stay out of depression. Then we'll talk about how to face your grief and let it perform its healing work.

Reduce Your Risk of Depression

Take this ten-question true-false quiz to help you determine your risk for depression. Before we start, let me add the caveat that this quiz may not be as helpful if you have only recently been hit with a personal shock and are in the throes of initial crisis. At that time, your responses will be bouncing all over the place. However, even at that stage, you can learn more about the danger zones for depression and how to stay out of them. This is not a formal psychological test, but simply a tool to point you to some action steps that will help you climb out of the pit of depression. Also refer back to the chapters on victimhood, bitterness, doubt, guilt, and isolation for additional pointers, as each of these negative choices also places you at risk.

OK, ready? Decide if each of these statements are *more true* of you or *more false.*

_____ 1. *When I am sad, I think about my situation and my life in absolute terms like "everything," "nothing," "always," "never," "nobody," and "everybody."*

When you think that way, it gets overwhelming. If you convince yourself that everything is destroyed, nothing is going right, bad things always happen to you, you never get the breaks, nobody cares, and everybody has it better than you—of course you'll be depressed!

Action steps: Challenge your all-or-nothing thinking. Are there *any* exceptions to what you've said? Is it *always* that way? Is there *anyone* who cares? On paper (better) or at least in your mind, list as many examples as you can think of to prove your absolute statements wrong. Then, you can focus your thoughts and feelings about the specific issues that are bothering you—grieving each loss and working on problem solving.

_____ 2. *I am struggling with hopelessness because it seems like this pain will never get better.*

A sense of hopelessness—the belief that your life cannot and will not improve over time—is one of the hallmarks of depression. While it's true that you can't undo what's happened and put your life back just as it was, that doesn't mean your life is hopeless.

So listen up! Your life isn't over and there are brighter days ahead—*if* you create them by following God's principles and by making the healing choices we're exploring in this book.

Action steps: Choose to keep hope at the forefront of your awareness. When things are so dark you can't see your way through them and you don't know how things could possibly work out, know that there is hope. Our heavenly Father was not caught off guard by your crisis, and He still has a wonderful plan for your life. Grasp hope, and never let it go.

> *I know what I have to do now: gotta keep breathing, because tomorrow the sun will rise and who knows what the tide could bring?*
> —TOM HANKS'S CHARACTER IN *CASTAWAY*

_____ 3. *I minimize the positives about myself and my life, focusing instead on my weaknesses and my problems.*

If you maximize your weaknesses and discount the talents and strengths God has given you, you'll quickly get discouraged and lose the will to keep going.

Got weaknesses? Of course you do! I have gaboodles of them. Knowing that, I realize just how much I need God's help, strength, and empowerment. However, the more you focus on and obsess about your weaknesses, the stronger they become and the greater is their impact on your life. I don't know about you, but I don't care to have strong weaknesses!

Action steps: Remind yourself that God knew in advance all you would be facing in your life, all the things you'd be called upon to do. He placed within you all the abilities you'd need for your unique challenges. Don't discount your unique abilities and talents, comparing yourself to others. You have what you need. God's power operating through the special individual named you is more than enough.

_____ 4. *I think so much about "unfinished business," things I wish I had done or said before it was too late.*

My, don't our tragedies teach us lessons about what's important! How many have said, "If I had only known . . ." Maybe you wish you'd told a loved one more often about your love and appreciation. Perhaps you wish you'd invested more time, but you thought you had all the time in the world. Maybe there are things you needed to accomplish, but now your health condition won't permit it.

Many people become depressed because they had always believed that someday they'd have their mother's approval, their perseverance in a relationship would pay off, or their daughter would get back on course. But now that the dream is gone, the possibility has passed. Deep discouragement and hopelessness try to overtake their hearts.

Action steps: Unfinished business doesn't have to doom you to depression. The perception of lost opportunities is at the root of some of the deepest of grief. Acknowledge to yourself that it's true: some opportunities have passed. Feel the sadness of that. Write about it. Talk with a trusted friend about it. Then ask yourself, "What have I learned? And what are the implications of that for my

> *Don't let yesterday's regrets keep you from today's possibilities.*

life today? Are there people in my life now who need what I have to give?"

Grieving about missed opportunities? Open your eyes. What opportunities for service and love are available today? Look back, grieve when you need to, learn the lesson, and do it differently now. Don't let yesterday's regrets keep you from today's possibilities.

_____ 5. *I'm a chronic worrier.*

Worrying about the details of your saga is almost inevitable right after the heartbreak occurs and for some time afterward. Thinking and talking about the details can help you process the events and release their hold on your psyche. However, as more time goes on, if you're spending most of your waking hours in obsessive, worrisome, negative thought patterns, you could be in trouble. Rumination can be your ruination.

Repetitive negative thoughts become habits. Like drops of rain that head for the crevices, negative beliefs are attracted to the crevices of depressive thought habits. The more you think about distrust, inadequacy, and hopelessness, the more likely it is that your future thoughts will return there.

Action steps: Use a technique called the "worry chair" to limit the times and places in which you allow yourself to dwell on negative thoughts about yourself, your situation, and your future. If you find that such thoughts are constant and intrusive, set aside no more than (preferably less than) two, one-hour periods each day to sit in a special place (like a chair in another room where you usually don't sit) and think negatively to your heart's content. At the end of that hour, get up, leave that place, and get busy with an activity that occupies your mind. When your mind wants to visit the worst possible interpretations of your troubles throughout

> *Rumination can be your ruination.*

your day, postpone those thoughts until your designated "worry chair" time.

I know. That sounds weird. But psychological research has shown that this odd-sounding temporary practice helps you to break the constant habit of rumination. It frees you to do more productive things throughout the day. Many people complain that after a time, it's hard to spend even an entire hour in deliberate negative thinking! (Hey, that's good!)

I should add that there are also some medications designed for people who have a biological tendency to think obsessively and worry compulsively. If constant rumination has always been a problem for you, talk with your family doctor about the possibility of using nonaddictive medicines to supplement your efforts.

____ 6. *I believe what has happened has fundamentally changed me in a negative way; I'll never again be the person I was.*

Going through personal catastrophe does change you; there's no question about that. But how it changes you is up to you. You can come out of it fragile and vulnerable, or you can emerge with greater strength of character. You can give up, believing that you are permanently shipwrecked, or you can pick up the pieces and build an even stronger ship. The choice is yours.

Action steps: Remind yourself that the trauma you've been through has *temporarily* made it more difficult for you to function, even to do those routine things you previously did without

233

thinking. This is normal, and your ability to perform your responsibilities and to experience pleasurable activities will return as you heal. It's similar to what would happen if you sustained broken bones from a fall. You'd be temporarily sore and incapacitated. However, with rehabilitation, you'd be able to walk again.

Fight the temptation to believe that you are damaged goods. The apostle Paul wrote to the Romans, "For God's gifts and his call are irrevocable."[3] Yes, you've been injured; maybe yes, you've made some mistakes. But you still have the same DNA, the same God-given talents, the same spirit, the same inner core, and the same life purpose. The very good news is, God is in the restoration business. Give yourself into His care and follow His loving principles, and you'll once again find peace, productivity, and an unprecedented power to live and serve.

_____ 7. *I have become a couch potato, inactive and sedentary.*

After your difficult experience, you may have no energy. Even getting up and walking across the room takes a lot of effort. Or maybe you go to work and do what you just have to do, then totally crash the minute you walk in the door.

The last thing you feel like doing is exercising. Yet even a moderate amount of exercise generates energy and stimulates the production of serotonin, the brain chemical that fights depression. Further, just getting out and doing something—going outside for a walk and breathing—can be a welcome distraction that gives your tired mind and body a rest. It's kind of strange, but it's true: when you have no energy, exerting energy through exercise produces more energy!

Action steps: Start small. Take a five-minute walk in your driveway today. Do the same thing tomorrow. This is a huge accomplishment, because it's that first step that's the most difficult. Enlist a family member or friend to do it with you, and schedule an appointment. Having an exercise buddy makes it much more likely that you won't give yourself excuses, procrastinate, or back out. Add three to five minutes a day to your routine. Work your way up to twenty to thirty minutes a day of brisk walking. (You can choose another form of exercise if you like, but walking is a great one. It's available, simple, and invigorating.)

As time goes on and you are becoming physically and emotionally stronger, you might consider joining a gym. I love working with a personal trainer for strength training, which is one more way to encourage yourself to stay with it. Exercise classes provide additional support. Your fellow classmates let you know that they miss you when you're not there, encourage you when you're pooped out, and don't pressure you to talk about your personal business if you don't want to. That's a pretty good combo!

_____ 8. *I totally focus on taking care of others, which leaves me little to no time to take care of myself.*

Maybe you're a caretaker and nurturer by nature. I relate to that. You would be miserable if you felt that you were being "totally selfish" and looking out for yourself at the expense of others. I get that too. However, as we discussed previously, selfishness is *habitually* looking out for yourself while ignoring the rights, needs, and wants of others. I really doubt that being selfish is your problem, if you endorsed this item.

As a matter of fact, sometimes taking care of yourself is the most unselfish thing you can do. Even Jesus left multitudes on the banks of the lake with needs unmet while He withdrew to pray and replenish His spirit. He knew that if He didn't take care of Himself, He'd have nothing to give to others.

If you continue to ignore your own needs, you could be headed for a crash. Who are you going to be able to help when you're physically, emotionally, and spiritually exhausted? The depression that follows closely on the heels of such exhaustion can be incapacitating.

Action steps: A powerful admonition is to love your neighbor *as* yourself. Taking care of yourself (while also caring for others) is a godly act. During this time of intense pressure, it really is okay for you to focus more on yourself, doing what it takes to heal and become stronger so that you can rejoin life.

Enlist the help of others in your household or in your circle of friends, or even hire some help. This may be a little out of your comfort zone, but actually it's great practice for the rest of life. After all, a family is a team project!

I'll bet there are people in your life who would love to do some practical tasks to take some of the load off you—if they just knew what would be helpful. You know you would do it for them. Why deprive them of the blessing of giving to you in your time of need?

_____ 9. *I am not taking care of my personal hygiene—such as bathing regularly, brushing my teeth, washing/combing my hair.*

Neglect of hygiene habits is both a symptom of depression and a catalyst for more depression. Take a look at how Nancy described her hygiene habits after 9/11: "I didn't care if I combed my hair or brushed my teeth, and makeup was out of the question. I actually had to fight with myself to get in the shower. I slept a lot. I wasn't suicidal, but nothing excited me anymore. I didn't care if I left the bed or not, didn't care if the house got dirty, didn't care how I looked."

Imagine how Nancy might have felt when she passed by a mirror. Her disheveled image looking back at her would have only been more "evidence" that she was a mess and the world was a mess. Depressing!

Action steps: Whether or not you care how you look, whether or not you will see other people that day, and even if it doesn't seem worth it—will yourself to bathe, shampoo regularly, and ladies, don't neglect your customary makeup. There are times when depression is so severe that you have to schedule tasks like this one hour at a time because that's all you can manage. So if you need to take a bath one hour, comb your hair the next, put on a little makeup the next, that's just fine. In general, choosing to do constructive things before you feel like it is a key to battling depression.

_____ 10. *I am having persistent thoughts of suicide, including making a plan.*

Thoughts of suicide are directly tied to a sense of hopelessness—incredible pain coupled with the belief that it won't get better. Your judgment can become so clouded that you view suicide as the only out.

Here's how Angela described it: "I have been at the lowest of the low, to the point that I contemplated suicide and could have done it if I could have mustered the energy. I had lost my sight from sickle cell anemia. My husband became physically abusive, and I had to get out of that relationship. My visual impairment meant that I could no longer do my clinical work as a dietician. Then I had to have hip replacement surgery. I was lying flat on my back in the hospital, and I just knew that my life was completely over. I did not know it was possible to function independently as a blind person. I thought, 'My God, I'm going to have to rely on my mother the rest of my life, and then I'm going to end up in a nursing home.' I simply had no hope."

By the way, Angela is now finishing her Ph.D. in adult education. She went away for life skills training at a school for the blind and functions quite independently. She's an admired, active member of her church. She has plenty of friends. Angela is a testament to the fact that, no matter how bleak the future seems, there is always hope.

Fleeting thoughts of suicide are not unusual after you've been through severe trauma. However, if you find yourself dwelling on those thoughts, even making a plan and acquiring the means to carry it out—*stop!* Your risk level is getting higher and higher, and you need to get professional help right away.

People who are considering suicide often believe the myth that everyone would be better off without them. I wish you could listen in on my counseling sessions with people experiencing every imaginable negative emotion in the wake of suicide. After suicide, loved ones feel:

- abandoned, because the person who committed suicide chose to leave;

- grief-stricken, because of missing the person they loved;

- angry, because they wonder how their loved one could have done this *to them;*

- guilty, because they believe they should have been able to see it coming and prevented it;

- unworthy, because they think that if they'd somehow been good enough, the person would not have wanted to leave;

- anxious, because they fear losing others, they associate everyday experiences with the suicide, and they don't know how they will make it now.

Better off without you? Hardly.

Action steps: Don't tell yourself that no one will be harmed by your decision to "end it all." Unfortunately, for those you love, the agony would just be beginning. The people you care about will be deeply injured if you make that no-turning-back choice.

Though you cannot see your way through this painful maze right now, there is a way. God sees the beginning from the end, and He will lead you through each day, moving ever so slowly into the light. Today, you only need to get through today.

If you are feeling suicidal, seek professional help immediately. Don't compound the losses you've already experienced by leaving a lasting legacy of pain and heartache.

A WORD ABOUT MEDICATION

We've been talking about some of the cognitive (thought) and behavioral (action) components of depression. However, I must tell you that clinical depression also involves changes in brain chemistry. Because of this, the body's ability to think, to feel positive emotions, and even to move is literally depressed. Low levels of serotonin and norepinephrine—chemical messengers that allow us to respond to and transmit neural information—slow the body down, creating an exhausting emotional heaviness.

Antidepressant medication is often a helpful adjunct to the strategies I'm giving you in this book and/or working with a therapist. If depression is persistent, if it runs in your family, if you're having increasing difficulty just doing routine tasks, or if you have had more than one significant episode, talk with your family physician or mental health professional about the possibility of antidepressant medications.

BEGIN NOW TO CHOOSE *GRIEF*

We've been talking about how to reject depression and deal with the risky thoughts and behaviors that lead you down that dark path. Now let's discuss how deliberately to do the work of grief and mourning.

Determine to Go through Grief, Understanding That It's a Process, Not an Event

Throw away your expectation that after (fill in the blank) amount of time, you should be back to normal. As we've discussed, your recovery time depends on the nature of your losses, how significant they were, and what meaning you attached to them. And, of course, it depends on how you choose to deal with those losses.

Further, don't let anybody else pressure you to hurry up by saying things like, "What's wrong with you? Are you just having a pity party? You've got to get up and move. You've got to get back into life." Sounds like great advice, and it is—over time. But don't put an artificial time frame on it. A month or two probably isn't going to do it.

> *Mourning is not forgetting. It is an undoing. Every minute tie has to be untied and something permanent and valuable recovered and assimilated from the dust.*
> —MARGERY ALLINGHAM

Barbara Glanz, speaker and author of many books, experienced this secondary wounding only a little over a month after the death of her son. Her associate pastor paid her a visit—to comfort her? Unfortunately, no. He gave her a lecture. He said, "OK, Barbara, it's been almost six weeks. It's time for you to get back into life. You can have another baby."[4]

Barbara was in deep grief about the child she had wanted so desperately, the son she would never come to know. The last thing she needed was judgment in the form of a pep talk.

Set Aside Specific Quiet Times to Think About and Feel Your Losses

This step is especially helpful if you've been trying to stay so busy or otherwise distracted that you don't think about your pain. Stop running, pause, and focus to do some grief work. This doesn't mean that you're going to shut everything down and do nothing but sit and feel sorry for yourself. It means that you will schedule some "work appointments" between yourself and God, time to identify and focus on your losses and let them hurt.

Unfortunately, I must add that your work appointments will be accompanied by many intrusions of grief on the rest of your schedule. Grief has a way of happening when it wants to happen.

The strangest things can trigger sorrow—the smell of a certain cologne, a sunset similar to the one you shared, a television program that includes a detail or a theme that brings it all back. I remember one time my cat looked at me with those big green eyes and swallowed twice. Oddly, this reminded me of my mother, who in her latter days of Alzheimer's apparently did something similar. My tears began to flow. I know, it doesn't make much sense. But sometimes grief doesn't.

So despite the fact that the sadness can overwhelm you, any time, any place—setting aside these specific work times can help to make your mourning a little less likely to overwhelm you at unexpected and inopportune times.

List Your Losses, Both Tangible and Emotional

In facing your losses, you have to learn that then is then, and now is now. Listing your losses enables you to come to terms with that, helping you in at least three ways. First, it makes you think, which exercises the problem-solving part of your brain. Second, it helps you fight the tendency to believe "all is lost," which is a sure trigger for depression. A third benefit is that listing your losses provides you with a roadmap for both grieving and rebuilding. More about that in a moment.

> *Then is then,*
> *and now is now.*

First, list the tangible losses; those are a little easier to identify. These may include things like the physical presence of a person, your house, or your paycheck. However, these physical losses are usually not the direct source of your most significant grief. What those tangible losses *mean* to you, their psychological impact, and the emotional holes they left in your psyche—those are the real challenges.

Next, list the emotional losses you've experienced. Not sure how to identify those? Let me share an example.

Jack got laid off from his job as a foreman in a chemical plant after thirty-two years. He told me, "I believe what I heard someone at the plant say: 'First we downsized, then we rightsized. Now I think we've just capsized!'"

As Jack worked through this "listing" task in therapy, he wrote this:

Tangible Losses
- paycheck

- possibly the house and the car

Psychological/Emotional Losses

- security (What does the future hold? Will I be able to provide for my family?);

- identity (What do I say when people ask me that common question, "What do you do?" Who am I, anyway?);

- social relationships (I miss my buddies at work. We did so many things together. Where do I fit now?);

- routine (All those mornings I hated when the alarm went off. Now I'd love to have the need to set that alarm so early. I try to work on looking for a job, but it's so hard when you just kind of wander around, trying to figure out what to do next.);

- sense of purpose and accomplishment (I can't believe they let me go. I gave my heart and soul to that place. It hurts so badly to think that what I worked so hard to accomplish apparently wasn't worth much to them. Now what?);

- self-worth (I feel so embarrassed about being let go. I'm trying not to feel like a failure, but it's kind of hard. I took so much pride in my work.)

Jack's life situation may be different from yours, but maybe what he wrote will give you some ideas about how to do this step. List and describe the types of losses you have felt.

Spend Time Thinking through Each of These Losses

OK, now it's time to take these losses one by one, focusing on the ways you feel about each one of them. Think about some examples of each, some times in which you felt that particular type of pain, embarrassment, or heartache. Feel the sadness as you allow your mind to review those situations, thoughts, and events.

Now express those feelings in some way. Talk about them with a trusted friend or a mental health professional. Don't hold back, thinking that your reactions are dumb, that you should be "stronger," or that you should be better by now. You are where you are. Be honest with yourself and a few trusted others about those feelings. The process of going over the details again and again in a variety of ways can help to desensitize you so that you don't have a horrible physical and emotional reaction every time you think or talk about what happened.

Also, look for "nontalking" ways to express your grief. Write, write, write about it. Don't edit or think you need to create a composition ready for grading. That's not important. What's important is to get your thoughts and feelings out of you and on paper. Push "Record" on your mind's Dictaphone and then transcribe your thoughts. Don't judge them. Writing helps you to gain perspective and distance. When a difficult emotion is expressed on paper, it's not as likely to feel as if it's bursting inside you.

Another excellent way to work through grief is through artistic expression. I'm a musician, and I can attest to the powerful healing effect of sitting down at the piano or organ and letting it all out through my fingers. Some love to draw, and that's a great outlet. You don't have to be a talented musician or artist to express your feelings artistically. Get paper and color pencils, crayons, or chalk. Create patterns and colors that reflect your mood. Can you express your thoughts through poetry? Do it. Can you create a handicraft that reflects your feelings or commemorates something positive about the person or other valuable things you lost? How about a scrapbook?

Ironically, sometimes you can creatively express grief through celebration. My granddaughter, Scarlett, inspired me to use this method.

Scarlett was six when the first anniversary of my mother's death rolled around. She caught me wiping a tear and asked, "What's wrong, BeBe?"

I told her, "It's been one whole year since Nannie went to live with Jesus in heaven."

"Wow!" the child marveled. "She's been enjoying heaven one whole year. Can we have a celebration?"

Taken aback, I answered, "You bet we can!" She and I set off to the store and bought party hats and whistles. We purchased the ingredients to bake and frost a cake. Then we invited Scarlett's dad, Greg, her Aunt Amy, and my grandsons, Joseph, Ethan, and Eli, to a wonderful celebration of my mother's first birthday in heaven!

That spirit of celebration, seen through the eyes of a child, totally changed my perspective on what could have been a very sad day.

Cry If You Want to—and Even If You Don't!

Tears are especially healing, and in many cases they accelerate your recovery. Fighting tears that are pushing on your eyelids can be counterproductive. Tears have a purpose. They are a God-given physical way of letting off that intense pressure and pain.

Don Medley, attorney and author of the legal thriller *The Book of Luke*,[5] lost both his son and his sister in a plane crash as they returned from a weekend visit to his home.

Don told me, "There are times when the loss just overtakes me. When that happens, I just let myself go with it. If I feel like getting in a pile on the floor and just letting the tears go, I do it. I don't try to hold it in. I feel that God gave us tears as a mechanism to deal with grief. So I don't listen to those crazy ideas about how crying isn't manly. In my profession, I have to be strong, and I am. But I also don't have any qualms about weeping. Being able to let it go has helped me deal with the loss of George and Paula."

Macho does not prove mucho.
—ZSA ZSA GABOR

Are you one of those people who fights tears or denies their existence? ("My eyeballs are just sweating!") Do you see crying as a sign of weakness? It's not. In fact, the strongest people are not afraid to feel and deal with their grief. Are you afraid that if you let go, you'll totally lose control and not be able to regain it? If you've been holding back, your emotions may be a little intense at first. But don't worry, you won't go so far out you can't find your way back.

So when you think about what you've lost, cry if you can. As I've mentioned previously, there's a good reason they call it a "good cry."

Make a Habit of Noticing Small Changes and Improvements

After you've spent time (no, I can't say exactly how much) in the grief process, you should begin to feel the pain diminishing slightly. However, because the changes happen so gradually, you may not even notice them. The periods of excruciating pain may come a little less often, may be a little less intense, or may not last as long. However, you may perceive, "Everything's still the same."

One of the many reasons I highly recommend journaling throughout the grief process is that when you're feeling that nothing has changed, you can look back at your journal entries two weeks ago or a month ago. Then you realize you are not in the same place emotionally. Your personal notes help you see that you are taking tiny steps forward.

Use Your List of Losses as a Tool for Re-creating Your Vision of the Future

After you've devoted a significant amount of mourning time to each of the important losses you listed, along with all their "personal subcategories" and plenty of others you didn't think to list, begin to think about how you will now get those same needs met in your new world.

Did you lose companionship? Darla did.

Darla's husband of nineteen years came home and announced that he had "fallen out of love with her" and was leaving. They did everything together, she told me. After weeks of shock, anger, and depression over the rumors of his new "friend," and failed attempts to persuade him to go to marriage counseling, Darla asked me through her tears, "What do I do now?"

We explored ways she could reconnect with friends so that she would not feel as alone as she worked through the feelings of separation and abandonment. In the worst of timing, the one friend she had kept during her marriage to her possessive husband had gone to visit relatives in England. Darla tried joining some "friendly acquaintances" for golf, but she found it painful because she and her husband had played golf together. She began to open her eyes to notice people at work and church with whom she'd had friendly conversations in the past. She asked one woman to lunch and another to a movie. (I cautioned her to stay away from romantic comedies or love stories right now.) She joined a divorce recovery group, where she shared her experiences with others in her predicament.

Did these new companions replace Darla's husband? No. But they nudged her to get out of the house, where she was left with only her memories and her grief. They gave her a glimpse of the fact that she could enjoy the company of family, friends, and friendly acquaintances.

What about you? What are you going to do now to express yourself, establish new roles, and feel good about who you are and what you do? Are you feeling a loss of goals and dreams? Given your world as it exists now, what would you like to see happen in the future? What will you begin doing now to head in that direction?

We're going to talk in depth about the rediscovery of vision and purpose in chapter 10. Right now, however, I just want you to see that the very sources of your emotional pain can be clues to what's important to you in the rebuilding of a quality life. The psychological elements that you listed as meaningful losses become "rooms" in your reconstruction plan. Then you can begin to hammer one nail at a time, which may not seem like much. However, one nail after another becomes one beam after another, one room after another, coming together ultimately to make a beautiful home.

MY COMMITMENT TO *GRIEF*

I really don't want to go through this, but I know that I must if I am to heal. So I commit myself to doing the tough emotional work of grief. I resist the temptation to simply give grief a polite nod or a disdainful snub. I reject the false idea that strength is shown in stoicism, or that tears are a sign of weakness. Instead, I give myself permission to feel and to express those sad feelings, knowing that emotional honesty ultimately helps me to regain my strength and to grow.

I identify my tangible and emotional losses and spend time with them, acknowledging them, protesting them, feeling them, and grieving them. I guard my mind, diligently and courageously challenging the thoughts that discourage and taunt me by whispering that all is lost, that my life will never be better, and that I'm a failure. I replace them with the confidence that I have a valuable life left to live and the faith that I can live it. I choose hope, not despair.

I choose to believe the best, not the worst. I accept that not all of my pain will go away forever, but I do plan to live again, to create a meaningful life. But first, I commit to do the difficult work of grief.

9

"I Can't Go There—It'll Start All Over Again"

CHOICE #9: AVOIDANCE OR COURAGE

After the accident with the eighteen-wheeler in which Julie was driving and her friend was killed, Julie told me, "It took several weeks before I could even sit in a car and look out the windows. The anxiety was overwhelming. Then, no way did I want to get behind the wheel. At first, I just drove to the end of the driveway, then just around the block. I felt I couldn't breathe; it was so scary. Every time I'd hear about an accident on the local news, it would set me back. I decided it was just best to stay home. I was afraid I would hurt somebody else."

It is easy to understand why you might want to avoid the people, places, and conversations that remind you of hurtful events that have occurred in your life. After all, it's normal to want to avoid painful things. However, avoidance—a choice that would seem to make you feel better—can actually make you worse. We'll explore that paradox as this chapter goes on.

One of the reasons it's so tempting to try to stay away from any reminders of the trauma is that these reminders can unexpectedly trigger painful and distressing memories, flashbacks, intrusive and obsessive thoughts, nightmares, and physical anxiety reactions. Who wouldn't want to avoid those?

DO YOU HAVE POST-TRAUMATIC STRESS DISORDER?

There is a constellation of symptoms called Post-Traumatic Stress Disorder that has become widely discussed lately because of the many tragedies in the news that have the potential of producing this anxiety disorder (such as 9/11, the war in Iraq, and school shootings).

Maybe you've wondered what PTSD is and whether you have it. If you do (and even if you don't), understanding what is happening to you can help you muster up the courage to face down your fears.

According to the standard diagnostic manual used by mental health professionals, PTSD may be diagnosed when certain symptoms are present after you've been confronted with a life event that involved actual or threatened serious injury or death for yourself or someone else, and during which you felt frightened, horrified, or helpless.[1] People who have PTSD re-experience the traumatic event through intrusive memories, recurrent dreams, flashbacks, and emotional and physical stress reactions when they encounter a reminder of the trauma. As a result, they avoid stimuli that they associate with the trauma. They also feel numb and generally less responsive to people and their environment. In other words, they may feel detached or separate from others. They may have difficulty visualizing any kind of positive future. In addition, people with PTSD are persistently more aroused than they were before the trauma; for example, they may not sleep well, may be more irritable, or may startle easily. For a diagnosis of PTSD to be made, the symptoms must have persisted for at least one month and must significantly interfere with the person's life.

Whether or not you have been officially diagnosed with Post-Traumatic Stress Disorder, you probably have had at least some of these symptoms if you've encountered a major life crisis. While true PTSD theoretically happens only from exposure to death, physical injury, or the witnessing of it, you may have had experiences that broke your heart rather than injuring your body. Sometimes these "internal injuries" are even more serious than the physical ones. Violations of your trust, your plans, your dreams, your view of the world, and your life can also result in re-experiencing, avoidance, hyperarousal, and numbing. Certainly those nonphysical injuries also hurt like crazy, and the decision to withdraw and avoid facing reminders can be very tempting.

WHY DO POST-TRAUMATIC SYMPTOMS HAPPEN?

The reasons for the development of post-trauma symptoms after experiencing severe traumatic events are both biological and psychological. I think it may be helpful for you to understand these factors so that you won't jump to the conclusion that you've simply gone crazy or had that long-anticipated "nervous breakdown."

Biological Reasons

I am not about to give you a technical treatise on all the medical aspects of post-traumatic disturbance. (Probably couldn't if I tried!) Instead, I'm going to break it down into language so simple that even I can understand it.

Within your body are two systems that normally complement and balance each other. First, there is the sympathetic nervous system (also called the adrenergic system), which produces the classic fight-or-flight response. In other words, when you are feeling threatened or are under stress, the brain gives the orders to release the chemicals that get you aroused and ready to deal with the perceived threat by fighting or running.

Under normal circumstances, when the threat is over, the sympathetic nervous system returns to its baseline state, in part because of the balancing work of other hormones. The adrenal glands release cortisol and other compounds. Cortisol is a hormone that, among its other contributions, helps to regulate the typical stress response. In other words, these hormones bring you back to normal.

Sometimes, however, the stress is so high that this regulatory system becomes overwhelmed and overloaded. It cannot do the job of bringing down your body's arousal. Thus, when you encounter an overwhelming event, one that is over the top in terms of your ability to process it mentally and emotionally and your body's ability to accommodate it, you have a dual problem. You have a huge surge of adrenal activity, and the body's natural regulators have taken a punch that renders them incapable of handling the load. As a result, you stay on red alert and remain in an intensely aroused state.

When that occurs, you vividly encode into your memory every tiny detail of what is happening (though occasionally you have amnesia for some things). Because afterward you stay in a somewhat "hyper" condition, those memories tend to replay themselves, unwelcome intruders into your thoughts. The images and other sensory experiences that were burned into your psyche are then easily activated. They are powerful, and they can bring with them all the feelings you had when you were first traumatized.

So, no, you're not bonkers. Whether or not your trauma involved direct physical injury, it did have physical repercussions—and those also show up in your psychological reactions.

Psychological Reasons

Re-experiencing can also be a natural way to begin to heal from your psychological injury, a built-in method for processing the trauma in an attempt to come to grips with it. The mind repeatedly presents the unbelievable information to itself through flashbacks, nightmares, or intrusive memories as a way of getting used to the idea and getting a handle on the piercing emotions. As you go over the event repeatedly, you can start to become more desensitized to those horrible feelings and therefore more able to think rationally and to solve problems.

I've observed that many of my clients seem to be replaying the events in the futile attempt to rewrite the ending, to change the outcome. They semiconsciously believe that if they go over it enough times, maybe somehow things will turn out differently. Unfortunately, my friend, that story has already been written. No matter how many times you revisit it, what happened, happened. Acknowledge that now. You can emotionally accept it later.

AVOIDANCE TAKES MANY FORMS

Peggy shared with me a few observations of how her husband, Jess, was experiencing avoidance after the murder of his brother. She recalls, "Jess withdrew from his extended family because William's death was what they wanted to talk about. Also, he can't go near the graveyard, which happens to be right across from our house. His mom has to cut the grass around William's grave. He stopped going to the town where the crime occurred because he didn't want to be around anyone who would ask questions. He didn't want to go back over it and relive it.

"Before the murder happened, my husband was a voracious reader, making at least one trip each week to the library to get a fresh supply of Civil War books. He happened to be reading the night the news came about the murder. He hasn't picked up a book since."

When the re-experiencing process becomes more than you feel you can handle, you understandably try to shut it off. You want to avoid anything that will trigger those reactions. You may be more prone to avoidance if your experiences were particularly horrific, if they took place over time, if you previously had other problems like clinical depression or an anxiety disorder, or if you have always had trouble managing your emotions.

Some avoidance can be adaptive, especially early on. Remember in chapter 1 when I mentioned that denial can sometimes be healthy? That's when it acts like an emotional circuit breaker to protect your psyche from overload. In some cases, avoidance can serve that same function. You just can't deal with it all at once. You don't want to make things worse by placing an unreasonable demand on your emotional and physical resources. They've been through a lot already, that's for sure. But you do want to (well, maybe you don't *want* to, but it's wise to) face as many things as you are able to so that they don't gain an even tighter grip on your emotions.

The natural inclination to stay away from pain can lead you into avoidance in several forms—any one of which can ultimately strengthen the hold that anxiety and fear have on you. You may hope against hope that if you can keep yourself from any reminders, the emotional pain will simply go away. True, it's not good to dive headlong into more exposure than you can handle. However, totally trying to remove yourself from any contact with what we psychologists call "triggers" (situations or thoughts that bring it all back) is seductive, but unwise in the long run.

Let's talk about some of the ways you can try to dodge reality and therefore unintentionally sabotage your recovery.

You Avoid Places, People, and Activities That Remind You of the Distressing Experiences

Deana's son, Nick, was killed in a motorcycle accident. This natural tendency for avoidance was causing her some spiritual confusion. Deana told me, "I can't believe I've turned against my faith. I never thought I would. But since Nick was killed, I've had trouble praying. I feel so guilty. Before the motorcycle accident, I was constantly praying for him. He was having problems, and I was on my knees all the time, asking God to bring him through it."

I explored with Deana whether her resistance to praying came from anger toward God (it didn't), or whether prayer had actually become a trigger activity for her, one that caused anxiety because she strongly associated it with her deceased son. When she tried to pray now, she felt the pain of that loss. This insight was a relief as Deana realized that she had not lost her faith—no way. She was simply having difficulty with a normally comforting activity (prayer) that had become painful because of its mental association with the tragic loss of her son.

You Refuse to Talk about It

If you don't talk about it, it doesn't exist, right? Of course, that isn't true. But your desire for avoidance can convincingly whisper what you know to be illogical, and you buy into it because you want to believe it.

Maybe you are a person who typically isn't a big talker anyway. You prefer to mull things over, make sense of it, and figure out what to do. That's fine—up to a point. If you are typically analytical and introspective, talking about what happened may not be easy for you. But the fact remains that talking about your experiences does help to diminish the emotional intensity of them over time, while ruminating about and mentally replaying them can tighten their hold on you. This is a time when, for your own good, you may need to step out of your comfort zone and talk with one or two understanding, trustworthy individuals.

You Engage in Unhealthy Escapes

Escapes are another form of avoidance. If you've previously been dependent on an activity or substance to deal with anxiety or depression, or even if you haven't, you could fall into that trap when you go through a significant trauma. Do you recognize personal danger in any of these?

1. *You sleep too much.* This can be a sign of depression, but it can also simply be a handy tool not to have to think (or both!). Just snooze away, and you can escape your world as it has become. Problem is, you can't really.

When the conscious mind is asleep, the subconscious is still at work. You may have nightmares about the traumatic events, replaying them and feeling them—awakening perspiring and exhausted. Or you may dream crazy dreams and wonder, "Why on earth would I dream *that*?" Yet, when you really think about it, the theme of that dream was something you felt during the trauma or since—powerlessness, anger, trying to run away, feeling exposed or unprepared. While not every dream is significant and some goofy dreams occur simply because you ate too much pizza before you went to bed—some dreams can be very instructive, giving you insight about issues that you need to face rather than avoiding them.

2. *You stay very, very busy.* Busy is good, right? Well, compared to being lethargic, I would say it is. Forcing yourself to move about and take care of no-brainer, routine activities is good preventative medicine against depression. (I do acknowledge that at this time in your life, even no-brainer actions may seem to require more brainpower than you can conjure up). However, rushing about trying to stay so busy you don't have time to think is counterproductive.

The thoughts you are feverishly trying to push beneath the surface have a way of pushing back. They are persistent and insistent. They demand to be dealt with—now or later, at a time you choose or at the most inopportune moment. They can manifest themselves in depression or in anxiety problems like panic attacks. Like all the other escapes, work, work, working on other things is only temporary respite from the soul work you need to do.

3. *You engage in potentially addictive behaviors.* We've already discussed how a prime time for susceptibility to addictive behaviors is when you've been through deep hurt. It's tempting to try to drown or anesthetize your pain through the abuse of alcohol, illicit or prescription drugs, overeating, gambling, acting out sexually, or shopping. The temporary relief lets you pretend for a moment that all is well. However, harsh reality sets in soon, inviting you to seek that escape again. Without realizing it, you can find yourself neck-deep in addiction, thinking, "*This* wasn't supposed to happen to me!"

I need to clarify here that I am not talking about taking helpful medication that you take as prescribed by a physician who understands the psychological and physical struggles of people in severe crisis. That's different from *abusing* prescription or illegal drugs.

4. *You prematurely throw yourself into a good cause.* You may be surprised that my list contains a caution about becoming involved in a good cause. Getting involved in something positive, after all, has wonderful healing properties. However, some people almost immediately go on a campaign against the type of people, the type of problem, or the type of system that they believe caused their troubles. Diving into a cause prematurely can be a form of avoidance. Of course, the key word here is *prematurely*.

I won't mention a name, but I have watched with interest the father of a young girl who was abducted, sexually abused, and murdered. He immediately launched multiple media appearances and a campaign against child molesters and murderers. To this day, years later, when he gives a media interview, his face looks almost twisted with anger. I am in no way criticizing his cause. It is well justified, and no one knows that better than he does. However, I wonder if he, like many others, jumped in the fray of that worthy cause before he was ready.

"Doing something" helps to relieve anxiety and gives you a greater feeling of power. All in good time—you will have much to offer to others who have gone through similar experiences or to a system in need of improvement. However, feverishly "doing something" before you deal with your own anger and grief can short-circuit your healing process. First give yourself time to be with yourself and work through your own pain, and then you will be able to help others.

YOU HAVE A CHOICE: AVOIDANCE OR COURAGE

Sometimes you just have to be brave. Staying away from all the things that frighten you may seem to be the best option, but avoidance comes with bad side effects. Let's talk about them.

Avoidance Can Be Deceiving

Allow me to warn you again: avoidance is both deceptive and seductive. You try to avoid the triggering of memories and the scary emotions that come with them. Sometimes it works; that's what makes avoidance so seductive. Avoiding these triggers seems to be fixing the problem.

You feel better when you just stay away from those things that make you nervous. However, the avoidance is "reinforced" by the fact that it gives temporary pain relief. Therefore, because it is followed by something pleasant (relief), avoidance is strengthened as your coping method of choice. Unfortunately, there's a hefty price to pay when you do this.

1. *Your fear spreads.* You avoid a person, a conversation, a place, an activity because you are afraid of how you will react should you encounter it. You try to stay away from anything that reminds you of your bad experience. Yet your fears expand and grow stronger. Here's why.

First, you tend to generalize the fear. The cues that bring on your anxiety and invite avoidance tend to multiply. This is because of a phenomenon psychologists call "classical conditioning." Allow me to illustrate the concept.

Five-year-old Jimmy has to go to the hospital to get his tonsils removed. His doctor wears a white jacket, and the nurses don white uniforms. The hospital is a scary place. The doctor pokes around on the child, the boy gets several shots during his stay, and he has to go into a scary room with great big machines. His throat hurts like crazy after the surgery, and those big needles are really frightening and painful.

The next time Mom says, "We're going to the doctor," meltdown! That doctor makes his throat hurt and gives him shots. Soon afterward, another family member is in the hospital, and Mom takes Jimmy with her to visit. You guessed it. Jimmy balks, not wanting to go through those big doors. Another day, Ms. Hughes and her child visit a butcher shop, and the butcher wears a white jacket. Jimmy begins to scream and hold on to his mommy. The next week, Jimmy even whines when his mother tells him they are going to go to the butcher shop.

Do you see what's happening? All the things the child associates with his pain and fear have acquired the power to upset him. A trip to the doctor is, of course, directly associated with his painful experience, as was the hospital building. Then the anxiety spreads, and the child reacts to anything he associates with his hospital stay—a white uniform, then even a store where he sees a person in white clothing.

So it is with you. You avoid one thing, and another pops up. The second one may not logically be tied to your trauma, but it somehow reminds you of it. Your fear grows in sheer magnitude as the "triggers" expand.

> *Hiding leads nowhere except to more hiding.*
> —MARGARET A. ROBINSON

Another reason your fears can grow is that avoidance leaves the fears untested. Joan might tell herself after a life-threatening accident, "I'll never be able to drive on an interstate highway again." If she doesn't try it, she'll be right. Jason at Virginia Tech could tell himself after the shooting tragedy there, "I just can't go back into a Virginia Tech classroom," and decide to drop out. Right again.

> *If you don't confront them, your fears, anxieties, and losses will finally confront you.*

When you tell yourself that whatever you fear is more powerful than you are and that you'll be all right as long as you stay away from it, your feelings of powerlessness increase. If you never get the courage to face your fears, they win.

2. *Your personal world becomes smaller.* The more components of your life that you slice away, the less of life you have left. You've already taken a hit from forces outside your control. However, if you choose to give in to your fears and don't stand up to them and reclaim your territory, your original losses will be compounded. You'll feel the urge to avoid additional people, places, and activities, and slowly you'll become trapped in a smaller and smaller world.

3. *Your recovery takes longer.* Avoidance delays and complicates the work that has to be done if you are going to move forward. If

you don't confront the reminders, your fears, anxieties, and losses will finally confront you. They insist on being recognized and dealt with. When it comes to your anxieties or to just plain grief, you can't run forever.

I learned that the hard way in the early 1990s on one of my first speaking tours of South Africa. When I met Letitia, I was strangely drawn to her. During my stay in Durban, I managed to spend several hours in the company of this bubbly, musically talented nine-year-old daughter of an Indian pastor. One day Letitia shared with me how lonely she felt when her father went away to the U.S. to preach, how she missed him when she came in from school, and how much she loved her dad. All of a sudden, I couldn't hold back the tears myself. I whispered, "I know what that feels like. My daddy went away too." My heart finished the rest: "And he never came back."

Suddenly I realized one of the reasons I had been so drawn to Letitia. I saw myself in her—the outgoing, musically inclined preacher's kid who was exactly the age I was when my father died of cancer. For the last two weeks of that trip, my tears were never far away.

When I returned from the trip, I asked my mother, "Tell me, how well did I cope after Daddy died?"

"You did great!" she answered reassuringly. I was anything but reassured. Her description let me know the truth I suspected. I had taken care of her, my grieving mother, and I had never really dealt with my own anxieties and grief. Forty-plus years later, I had to do the work I had avoided.

Courage Conquers Fear

As you think about breaking out of the cocoon you have created, everything in you may be screaming, "No! Don't! Stay safe! Stay in a secure, more comfortable place." But just like the butterfly in the cocoon, if you stayed there and didn't go through the struggle to free yourself, you would die. Living trapped is not living.

What is courage? It's definitely not the absence of fear. In fact, if you didn't have fear, you wouldn't need courage. No, courage means acting *in spite of* fear.

Now I can't tell you that the minute you begin to act, all will be well and your anxieties will immediately evaporate. But I can tell you that if you take it in steps, telling yourself the truth about God's provision for you and the ultimate rewards of exercising courageous behavior, gradually you will become more desensitized to the overwhelming emotions. You'll learn to celebrate, not discount, small achievements. Gradually, your way of thinking and acting will become more confident, giving you the strength to tackle more. You'll nudge, then push the boundaries that trauma has created, venturing out farther and farther and doing those things you were afraid you'd never be able to do again.

> *Courage is resistance to fear, mastery of fear—not absence of fear.*
>
> —MARK TWAIN

Grammy-nominated blues artist Bobby Rush knows what it's like to experience tragedy and to have to call on courage.[2] Three of his children died in separate illnesses, and his first wife died of cancer. Later in his life, Bobby and his band were traveling in a van together when they were involved in a serious accident. One band member was killed, and all were seriously injured. Bobby sustained a broken foot, a broken right hand, and a badly injured back and shoulder. This legendary entertainer told me about the courage it took to get back on the stage and perform almost immediately.

"I was very, very hurt. I could hardly move, and I was in a wheelchair. Yet I believed it was my responsibility to encourage and inspire the others who were hurt. Physically, I could not have done this on my own. God had everything to do with it. They lifted me up on the bandstand. I was determined to stand up, though I hadn't been able to stand up on my own since the accident. I was weak and dizzy at first when I stood. But a few seconds after that, something came over me. I felt very little pain on that stage for about twenty or thirty minutes. I just believe spiritually God had me in another place. My father was a preacher, and he taught me, 'When I'm weak, then I'm strong.'"

Bobby Rush had every reason just to rest awhile. But he was determined not to give up. He recognized that the longer he avoided getting back out there and dealing with his situation as it was, the more difficult it would become.

Bottom line is, avoid avoidance! Embrace courage, and act with the confidence that as you move out, little by little, God will empower you and help you. You can do it!

BEGIN NOW TO CHOOSE COURAGE

Facing your memories can be some of your most intense work in your recovery process, and that takes courage. If you have PTSD or if your symptoms are severe, you may want to work with a mental health professional who is skilled and experienced in trauma and grief work. In fact, sometimes it takes courage to acknowledge that you need professional help! This does *not* mean that you are crazy or weak. It doesn't mean you'll need to lie on the couch forever. Rather, seeking help is a sign of commitment—commitment to do whatever it takes to get yourself and your life back. This book can be used as an integral part of your therapy.

However, there's plenty you can do on your own. I'm going to lead you through several steps of preparation and then teach you a practical process you can use to desensitize yourself from the intense anxiety you feel when reminded of your traumatic experiences.

Get Ready to Get Ready

Let's lay a wise foundation before we work on the memory triggers. I want you to know more about how to approach the tasks and what to expect from this work.

1. *Pace yourself.* Don't think that you can or should try to implement all of these suggestions in one sitting, or that you should keep at it constantly so that you can hurry up and get it over with. The mind doesn't work that way.

When you have gone through an experience that is so traumatic that it has literally jarred your nervous system and you have intense, intrusive, and distressing memories, you're going to need to break this process down into smaller steps so that you don't overwhelm yourself.

Sometimes it's difficult to find the "therapeutic window," the hypothetical psychological midpoint between too much and too little exposure and emotional re-experiencing. You have to be willing to tolerate some distress in order to move yourself forward and conquer your fears. (That's where the *courage* comes in). At the same time, you have to monitor yourself and know when it's just too much right now. That's when you take a break and use some of the strategies I'll give you to help you relax and contain your emotions.

2. *Don't be surprised if at first it gets worse.* It goes against common sense to deliberately place yourself in personal distress, yet that's one of the things you must do to conquer your fears. Prior to now, you've probably devoted a significant amount of energy trying to hold those feelings back. Yet unresolved trauma memories

need to be talked about and re-experienced, or else they will probably keep coming back as anxiety or depression symptoms.

> *Never grow a wishbone, daughter, where a backbone ought to be.*
>
> —CLEMENTINE PADDLEFORD

Over time, as you focus on the memories within a safe context and feel the associated emotions, pain and fear will gradually diminish. However, in a more immediate sense, be aware that your symptoms may actually get worse. Distressing feelings and disturbing dreams between work sessions may become a little more intense. That's a normal temporary reaction and not necessarily a bad sign. However, if you find that your symptoms get significantly worse, do ask for professional help to guide you along the way.

OK, take a breath. If you're ready, let's get to work.

Practice Soothing Strategies

"Do I need to dive right in?" you may be asking yourself. No, not yet. Before we start the memory work, let's place into your toolbox a few strategies that you can use to soothe yourself when you start feeling overwhelmed. They'll help you relax and refuel so that you can recommit to courageously facing the difficult emotional tasks. Practice so that you can become adept at these. You'll want to use them when your emotional reactions are so intense that you're tempted to slide back into procrastination, isolation, and total avoidance.

1. *Deep breathing.* Deep breathing is one of my favorite relaxation exercises because it's so easy. You can use it anytime, anywhere, with no special equipment. In only a minute or two, you can reduce your level of built-up stress. (Deep breathing several

times a day is also a great habit when you're not doing memory work.) Do deep breathing before, during, and/or after your trauma-related work session. Here's how.

First, develop an awareness of how shallow your typical breathing is. Stand in front of a mirror, take a deep breath, and watch the movement of your body. Your upper chest will rise, if you're like most people. The goal in deep breathing is to create the relaxation response by getting your breath way down into your diaphragm, into the lower part of your lungs, so that the oxygen can be carried more effectively to the cells in your body. (You don't have to do this each time, just when you're learning.)

Next, sit up straight, and put your hand on your diaphragm. Now you're going to practice deep breathing until when you take that long breath, you see a rise in your diaphragm just below your breasts. In a moment, if your hand is pushed outward by the breath, you'll know you've probably been successful in getting the air into the lower areas of your lungs.

Inhale slowly through your nose so that your diaphragm rises, pushing your hand outward. The key word is "slowly." Don't gulp in the air. Watch to see if your upper chest moves versus if your upper tummy pushes out your hand. I've also found that if you actually distend your tummy, as if you're trying to look fat, the air will go into that area a little more easily.

Hold your breath while you count to five, smiling slightly. You want each of those five counts to be about a second, so you could use the "one thousand one, one thousand two . . ." method. The smile sends a message to your brain and your heart, "All is well."

Exhale slowly through your mouth, making a "shushing" sound. Don't release a blast of air. Take as long as possible to exhale. Keep on releasing air until it's *all* gone.

Breathe normally for a few seconds, then repeat the deep breath at least three or four times. Scan your body to see if and where any tension remains. If you still feel tense, continue with the exercise a little longer.

2. *"Safe place" imagery.* During your memory work, it is very helpful to have a "safe place" to go when you're feeling too anxious. You won't get into your car and travel there; you'll use the vehicle of your imagination.

The scene you identify should be a place you've been in the past where you felt the most relaxed, comfortable, and comforted. A few of the scenes my clients have chosen through the years include a beach, the mountains, a spot in the woods, a field of clover, or in the arms of a person or religious figure perceived as totally safe and supportive.

Identify your special safe place and think about the feeling of peace and comfort you've had there. Now close your eyes and imagine that you are there right now. Use all your senses to soak up the experience:

- Look around you. Note in detail what you see.

- Listen carefully. What sounds do you hear?

- What kinds of things do you smell? (Your sense of smell is among the most powerful of the senses for evoking memories.)

- Notice your taste. Can you taste anything that you associate with this safe place?

- Now reach out and "touch." How would you describe the things you are touching—are they soft, rough, cool, warm, what?

When you deploy multiple senses, you become more emotionally engaged. As a result, this positive imagery has the power to comfort and soothe your emotions when the going gets too rough in your memory work. If you're feeling overwhelmed, you can transport your mind and your emotions to a calm, peaceful location.

In preparation for your desensitization exercises, practice going to your safe place at least three times a day for about a week. You won't even have to take time off from work to take a mini-vacation!

3. *Progressive muscle relaxation.* This relaxation exercise takes a little more time. Basically, you travel from your head to your feet, alternately tensing and relaxing each muscle group. Tensing gives you practice in recognizing the tightness that may have become a habit for you and helps you identify where your body tends to store its tension. When you do the exercise, you'll feel the soreness you already have in those spots that need more attention, though you may have been unaware of it previously.

Find a comfortable place to stretch out, like a recliner, a sofa, or your bed. As you focus on each of the muscle groups I'll name in a minute, tense for five to seven seconds, then relax for twenty to thirty seconds. As you relax, whisper to yourself something like, "Relax . . . let it go."

Now work your way through the four muscle groups below, alternately tensing and relaxing:

a. hands, forearms, biceps;

b. head, face, throat, shoulders;

c. chest, stomach, lower back;

d. thighs, calves, feet.

Note: There are plenty of relaxation tapes available. A soothing voice actually walks you step by step through this process. I also have one available at www.DrBevSmallwood.com.

4. *Encouraging self-talk.* King Solomon said, "The tongue has the power of life and death."[3] King Solomon's wisdom has been borne out by an abundance of psychological research. What you say to yourself has the powerful ability to impact your emotions and your actions. And you don't even have to say it out loud!

When it comes to trauma processing, how you talk to yourself about your work is critical. Think about the impact if you say to yourself things like these:

- "It's no use. I'll never get any better."

- "This stuff is hocus-pocus. I was feeling better before I started it. This is crazy."

- "My future is hopeless."

Now consider telling yourself some more encouraging words like these:

- "The memories bring back strong emotions, but the truth is, I am now safe."

- "If I stay with it, it will eventually get better."

- "I have the courage to face this. It's not going to defeat me."

Right now, before you begin the memory work, practice "listening" to what you say to yourself and breaking negative thought habits by reassuring yourself that with God's help, you can do this.

Courage is rightly esteemed the first of human qualities because, as has been said, it is the quality which guarantees all others.

—WINSTON CHURCHILL

5. *Prayer, inspirational reading, and meditation.* This one is placed last for emphasis, certainly not because of importance. I cannot overstate the importance of drawing on divine strength to empower you to do the work you have to do. Prayer, spiritual and inspirational literature, and meditation can be wonderful tools to prepare you to work, as well as to soothe during a work session and afterward.

If you find comfort in biblical scriptures, there are many that encourage you to be strong, to take courage, to know that God won't forsake you, and to feel confident that you can do everything you need to do with a divine infusion of strength.[4] And there are many more words of encouragement where that came from!

You may have a collection of favorite quotes from other religious literature, from favorite role models, from inspirational speeches, or from other meaningful writings. Or you may want to search the Internet or quote books to find the motivational words of others that you can use when you need a boost of confidence and courage. Create a notebook of words that inspire and encourage you so that they are readily available when you need them.

Facing Your Demons

I think we've done enough "getting ready to get ready"! Now it's time to do the memory work. I'm about to walk you through a process of identifying your unique list of triggers for flashbacks and for the unpleasant feelings you associate with your trauma. Then, step by step, we'll work on learning to tolerate those triggers, gaining control of your emotional reactions, and gradually gaining more freedom and the ability to live your life more normally. First, let me share Barb's story to give you a sense of how the recommendations below might work in real life.

Barb was one tough woman. (By the way, being tough doesn't exempt your psyche from injury.) She was a civilian eighteen-wheeler driver in Iraq, transporting supplies to the troops. Daily, Barb was a part of the convoy that moved through the dust, leaving only a tiny bit of space between her and the next vehicle to prevent suicide bombers from pulling between them. The drivers constantly had to be on the alert for IEDs (improvised explosive devices), which could be found along the roadside in boxes, dead animals, or any number of traps. The sounds of gunfire and bombs were all around. One day Barb's truck was hit with an IED. She escaped physical injury, but the cumulative effects of her psychological injuries resulted in her being sent back to the U.S. (which really ticked her off; nothing had ever "beaten" her before).

When she came to see me at The Hope Center six months after her return, Barb was extremely anxious. She was only sleeping about one hour per night, and panic attacks punctuated her attempts to drive. Because of the panic, she had severely limited her driving, not even visiting the family members she loved.

In her office therapy sessions, we identified her anxiety triggers (e.g., driving in general, cars too close, boxes or animals along the road). I prepared Barb to do the work of desensitizing herself to the triggers by teaching her several relaxation exercises. I explained the rationale for the work, along with the what and why of PTSD.

Then we were ready to begin work. She went through a process of imagining herself encountering various situations, first conquering them in her mind. Gradually the intense pain in her chest and rapid heartbeat would subside as we talked about them one by one and as she completed homework assignments to write about each experience.

When the day came that we were actually going out driving, I got a more vivid sense of the torture Barb was going through when she tried to drive. Not only did she experience extremely high anxiety when we passed a box or dead animal or "anything that could potentially have a bomb in it," she was on the highest alert for all cues on the road that could signal "danger." She assessed each and every vehicle for safety threats—darker windshields, older cars with peeling paint that someone might not mind sacrificing, anyone coming up beside her car, cars coming between her and the vehicle in front of her. She even described the expressions on the faces of drivers of approaching cars. ("That one had a mean face.") When we passed the local university, she pointed out the students walking with book bags, stating that those might have bombs in them. When I challenged her perception of threat with the idea that students logically carry bags, Barb countered with, "Even more opportunity to sneak a bomb in without being suspected." (Mind you, this was not a paranoid woman before her traumatic experiences in Iraq.)

During this and several other driving practice sessions, we talked about each of her fears, using deep breathing to help her stay reasonably calm. I coached Barb to remind herself of the truth about her current environment (such as, "That was then, and this is now. The dangers in Iraq are very different from those in our community. I can do this. I've tackled tough things before").

In her driving sessions with me, as well as her "homework" driving session, Barb took gradually more distant and unfamiliar routes. As time went on, Barb was able to push past the psychological boundaries her traumatic experiences had imposed. She regained her confidence and her independence. Now she frequently drives to visit her kids and grandkids two states away.

You can use a similar process to push past avoidance and conquer your own fears. Implement what you need from the process I'm about to describe until you've "reclaimed your territory" so that you are no longer limited in doing what you want and need to do.

1. *Create your trigger list.* You'll recall that triggers are those things you associate with stressful experiences that have the power

to evoke anxiety or depression. These might be situations you've encountered since the trauma, or they could be things you fear approaching because you know they would be upsetting. Make a list of them.

2. *Rearrange your list into a "ladder," from least distressing to most distressing.* Now put those situations in order, beginning with the ones you'd have the least trouble confronting, all the way up to the one that would feel most overwhelming to you. This ladder will give you a sequence for your practice exercises.

You're going to go from least threatening to most threatening. You'll work with one item until you can think about it, talk about it, and do it without feeling overwhelming nervousness. Then you'll move up the ladder to the next item. I'll show you how to do that momentarily.

3. *Settle down and settle in.* Choose a quiet, comfortable place and use one of the exercises you've practiced to help you relax (e.g., prayer, deep breathing, progressive muscle relaxation, safe place imagery, inspirational reading).

After you've done this and feel reasonably calm, you're ready to begin to focus on the lowest rung on your ladder.

4. *One at a time, focus on each anxiety trigger, conquering it before moving to the next.* You'll begin with the least threatening trigger on your list.

I'm about to describe a desensitization process consisting of several possible steps. For each of the items on your list, use as many of the six elements below that you need to desensitize yourself to that trigger. (The earlier ones may not require all the steps, such as creative expression.)

You're ready to move to the next item when you can tolerate actually being in the presence of that cue without overwhelming anxiety. That doesn't mean you'll have no nervousness at all, but your anxiety will be manageable. When your threat alert has diminished for one rung on your anxiety ladder, it's time to move up to the next one and repeat the process.

OK, here we go. Take the items one at a time, beginning with least threatening, and use some or all of these six desensitization techniques:

- *Think about it.* Mentally review the elements you associate with your trauma—what you saw, what you heard, what you touched or what touched you, and what you smelled.

- *Put your thoughts in writing.* Detail what you learned and observed as you thought about this trigger.

- *Read what you've written out loud.* After you've read it out loud to yourself, enlist the ear of a supportive person—a therapist, friend, or family member—and read it again.

- *Talk about it.* Tell your support person about what this trigger brings back. Continue to discuss it until your anxiety level decreases.

- *Express your feelings about the memories.* Use your imagination to find creative ways to give voice to your feelings and memories, such as drawing, scrapbooking, writing or playing music, writing poetry, doing handcrafts, or creating a visual image of your feelings using paint, chalk, or other media;

- *Expose yourself to the trigger.* When possible, deliberately bring yourself in contact with the anxiety-producing situation. You'll be taking charge of the situation rather than living in fear that you'll accidentally encounter it. It's okay if you need that support person with you again during the exposure. After you're reasonably comfortable, you can take that next mini-step, which is to do the same thing alone.

Don't forget, address these desensitization sessions over time. It may take you several days to complete your work on one trigger. However, don't let too many days elapse between work sessions. It's easy to start avoiding again!

Take Good Care of Yourself

This work can be exhausting. Eat nutritiously, avoiding junk body fuel. Get at least some exercise, such as walking a few minutes each day. When you're doing active memory work, don't take on too much—new projects, others' responsibilities, or frenetic busyness. Get some good rest.

Very importantly, attend to your spiritual health. Stay in close touch with God, who provides stability and strength when you're feeling unstable and weak (not unusual when you're confronting memories). God is not only on your team, He's a great coach as you're making your way through this wilderness.

ROSEMARIE, A TESTAMENT TO COURAGE

In an earlier chapter I told you about speaker and writer Rosemarie Rossetti, Ph.D., who became paralyzed in a freak accident, struck by a falling tree while she and her husband were out bike riding. In an article Rosemarie wrote about two years after her accident, she shared how she confronted her anxieties by going back to the scene of the accident. She gave me permission to share an excerpt from that article, "Having the Courage to Face Your Demons."[5]

Oftentimes we have bad memories tied to specific locations. Perhaps a crisis, dispute, death, injury or illness occurred in a particular place and you have not been able to return to that location due to the bad memories that it provoked. Every time you think of or drive near that site, you become emotional and purposely avoid going back.

That's how it has been for me for the past two years. I have purposely steered clear of the bicycle path in Granville, Ohio. On June 13, 1998, I was crushed by a tree while riding my bicycle on this path and was paralyzed from the waist down.

This past March, a business trip brought me to Granville for the first time since I was injured. I felt an avalanche of emotions flooding over me as I drove by the entrance of the path. I parked my van in the same parking place where I parked two years ago, and I wept.

As I returned home I thought about the sense of accomplishment that I would feel if I could ride that trail again. I had researched and tested many recumbent trikes that I would be able to pedal with my weakened legs and paralyzed feet and ankles. Finally, I found one that met my special needs.

On June 13, 2000 my husband, Mark Leder, and I were off to Granville. This ride was one we both were uneasy about taking. A return to our favorite trail, yet a return to the memories of the worst day of our lives.

As we face our demons, we build courage to stand up to what we fear. Like a magnet that repels, our bad experiences cause us to go in opposite directions to avoid a confrontation. Courage is the power to face your adversities.

It is inevitable that deep emotions will come to the surface as we return to a location where sadness prevailed. A purging of emotional tensions is good for spiritual healing.

Mark and I celebrated our victory over tragedy. We rode to the exact spot where the tree fell on me. We were there, and the tree was gone. It was then that we were able to put many of the missing pieces together.

It is better that we rejoice over our accomplishments following a tragedy than to dwell on self pity. It is as if sometimes we are dealt an unfortunate hand of cards in our game of life. What we must do is to take our misfortune and make the best of it. We have to make some changes ourselves if we want things to change.

MY COMMITMENT TO *COURAGE*

Courage—it's what I need to face these fears that have found their way into my mind and have stolen my confidence. I take courage because I know that I don't have to face my fears alone. I rely on God, who has encouraged me over and over, "Fear not, for I am with you." I open myself to support from friends and loved ones who walk beside me, don't judge me, and support my steps into once-familiar territory that now seems foreign and frightening.

I know that I have courage, for it has served me well in the past. As I look back over my life, I remember facing so many scary things, yet I have lived through them. In fact, when I confronted them head on, they soon lost the power I imagined they wielded. I draw strength from those memories.

Though I don't feel particularly courageous right now, I rest in the knowledge that courage, like adrenaline, flows only when I need it. Therefore, I know that I can do what I need to do, when I need to do it. No longer will I avoid the false monsters that have held me hostage, imprisoning my mind and limiting my life. I resolve to face down my anxieties, step by determined step. I choose courage so that once again I can be free.

10

"They Say Everything Happens for a Reason"

CHOICE #10: POWERLESSNESS OR PURPOSE

We've been on quite a long journey together, and it's not over yet. In this chapter, we're going to talk about learning to live in the power of purpose. If you can get this, really get it, your life will never be the same!

MAKING SENSE OF THE SENSELESS

After a tornado ripped through her home and destroyed all her possessions, Madeline told me, "It feels like my life is a jigsaw puzzle that's been dumped out on the floor, and the top of the box got thrown away. I haven't had a picture to go by or a clue about where to start. I'm not even sure these are the right pieces. Right now, my life just doesn't make sense."

In times like this, when the puzzle pieces are a long way from fitting, you try to make sense of it. One way people do that after something awful has happened is to say, "Well, everything happens for a reason."

The difference between reality and fiction? Fiction has to make sense.

—TOM CLANCY

I understand that the intent of that is to try to make peace with an unwelcome event. However, I want to caution you against searching too long for "the reason it happened." That's quite akin to the "why, why, why?" questions I warned you about in chapter 3. You can get stuck there because "why" is often unanswerable by us mere mortals. Searching for "the reason" is our attempt to make sense of the senseless. It's an attempt to regain some kind of control.

I HAVE BAD NEWS AND GOOD NEWS

When it comes to searching for purpose for life's traumatic events, there is good news and bad news.

First, the bad news. Sometimes there are no inherent and obvious good reasons for horrible happenings. (Hold on, I didn't say that nothing good could *come* from them. We'll discuss that shortly.)

Tragic events often occur for four unfortunate reasons.

Someone Made a Foolish Choice

Josh's father told me, "I'm still struggling to forgive the drunk driver who wheeled head-on into Josh's car, killing him and his girlfriend. Why did it happen? It happened because that man drank about a fifth of alcohol and was stupid enough to get behind the wheel of a car, that's why."

Was it God's will for the driver to operate a vehicle while impaired? No, I think not. But He gave all of us the will to make choices, and that driver made a horrible one. Josh and his girlfriend and all those who loved them paid the price for the man's decision to drink and drive.

You Happened to Be in the Right Place at the Wrong Time

Students sitting in class on a routine Monday morning at Virginia Tech were engaged in learning, preparing for their careers—then the shooting started. Before the rampage was over, thirty-two students and the shooter, Cho Seung-Hui, were dead. Young, promising lives—terminated.

There would be widespread discussions in the media about the perpetrator's mental illness and strange behavior, and there would be a search for how this tragedy could have been averted. Of course, every effort should be made to prevent future occurrences. However, the truth is, these student victims were doing nothing wrong. They were simply in the right place at a very wrong time.

We don't like to consider these things because it feels very scary. It seems so random, and we don't know how to make a plan to avoid events like these.

You Are Subject to Natural Laws

Sometimes things happen simply because of the earth's natural laws. If you accidentally fall off a cliff, no matter how "good" you are, you aren't exempt from being pulled to the ground by gravity. We live on this planet, and we are all subject to the natural laws that govern it.

You Are a Citizen of an Often-Chaotic World

Let's face it. We live in a world in which no one is exempt from such experiences as fierce weather events, accidents, terrorism, fires, illness, crime, and death. Maybe it's just me, but it sure seems like the incidence of those occurrences is on the rise. Or perhaps we hear about them more often.

It would be so much more convenient if God would just draw a circle around us and protect us from all difficult events. However, that would make us spoiled, immature children in adult bodies, people who never develop because we never really have to think, to solve problems, to recognize our limitations, and to depend on Him for strength.

None of us gets a free pass in this life. We're all in this together, and that means that we get to participate in the good, the bad, and the ugly of the human experience. As you well know, the external events in our personal worlds can sometimes be a bummer.

GOD DOESN'T CAUSE IT ALL,
BUT HE CAN USE IT ALL

Does God cause all of these things to happen? Did He decide one day to reach down and zap you to "teach you a lesson"?

Recently a friend of mine was going through some difficult times. I hurt for her when I heard her say in frustration, "I don't know what I did in a former life to tick God off!"

I've even heard horror stories of perhaps well-meaning but misinformed church people who've done dumb things like stating to a fellow member who had lost one son and then another in separate tragic accidents, "You need to search your heart and see what God is trying to show you. You need to find out what sin is there so that you can get rid of it before something else happens." Bunk! (I get so judgmental about judgmental people!)

Yes, God is sovereign, and He has *allowed* these things to occur. He is not caught off guard by them, nor is He stumped. Humans exercise free will, but God is not surprised, and His ultimate plans are not thwarted.

So does God cause tragic events? Not exactly, but He permits them. Do things happen that are not in His perfect will and purpose? Yes. Are some of the things that come into your life bad? You bet.

But, my friend, here is the very good news: absolutely, positively everything that happens to you can be "worked together for good" if you love God and live in your calling and purpose![1]

That is such exciting news! No matter what it feels like, no matter what it looks like—from every single heartache, each disappointment, every tragedy, good can come. And it will come, if you determine afterward to make the choices that strengthen you and prepare you to serve.

It *is* all about choice. It's not what happens *to* you, it's what happens *in* you that counts.

Will you determine, with God's help, to bring good out of the worst situations? As your healing progresses, will you stay open to the experiences that whisper divine messages about how your suffering does not have to be wasted? In the midst of your heartache, will you discover a renewed sense of purpose?

Ironically, your emotional desert is often the most fertile ground to hear or renew a calling to a productive, meaningful, purpose-centered life. You've been tilling and fertilizing that ground as we've worked on the other nine

> *It's not what happens to you, it's what happens in you that counts.*

choices. You've planted good seeds—the seeds of truth and hope. For the rest of your life, it's harvesttime.

It would be the worst of insults if you only experienced the excruciating pain of loss and there was nothing left to show for it. Fortunately, blessings begin to emerge as you go through what looks for the world like a curse.

FINDING THE GIFTS

Adversity does come bearing valuable gifts *if* you choose to receive them. With a divine infusion of strength, insight, and patience, along with your own commitment to make healthy choices, you can receive these gifts.

You Can Learn to Focus on the Things That Matter Most

Funny how we find ourselves correcting our priorities almost instantly when catastrophe strikes. The clutter in your life is suddenly swept away by the enormity of it all. The irritations that seemed so important yesterday feel trivial today. Almost everything but the really big stuff is accurately perceived as small stuff. Tragedy really puts things into perspective.

Your Faith Can Be Strengthened and Your Spiritual Roots Deepened

When you really have no answers and life has brought you to your knees, you are in a wonderful posture to ask for God's help. (Too bad it often takes this to help us understand our deep need for spiritual guidance all the time.) Learning to trust and walk or wait, even when you are clueless about how it will all work out, is a powerful catalyst for maturing and deepening your faith.

You Can Learn the Power of Choice

Adversity is such good training for life. Stuff is going to happen. You are going to encounter the frustration of dealing with many other situations over which you feel powerless. Without your permission, other people will make decisions and take actions that negatively affect your life.

In this book, you have been learning that you are not powerless, even when you are unable to change your circumstances. You can choose to take courageous responsibility for learning from what has happened and for continuing your own journey by making wise choices.

You Can Experience a Loud Wake-Up Call

Sometimes, you look at what's gone wrong, and you can clearly see that it is a consequence of your own actions, your poor judgment, or unhealthy behavior patterns that have insidiously found their way into your life. I am about to give you a tough assignment. Learn to give thanks for the painful warnings that save you from yourself!

Face the truth. In many cases, had you kept traveling the same path, your destruction would have been virtually assured. Be thankful that what you are going through now may have saved you from even greater harm to yourself or others. Negative consequences are often a gift—life's blessed alarm clock!

Adversity Can Give You the Confidence to Weather Future Trials

Unfortunately, confidence and the resilience that come from weathering life's storms are learned by practice. Many of my clients have told me, "After going through this, I can make it through anything."

You Develop a Greater Ability to Reach Out in Genuine Compassion to Others

Something very special happens when you've successfully survived deep and painful struggles. The hardships of others become more emotionally real to you, and your compassion becomes more genuine. No longer do you live in your comfortable little world where, as long as something doesn't directly affect you and those very close to you, it's only an abstract concept.

After being forced to declare bankruptcy, Mike told me, "I used to judge other people a lot when they did things I personally would never, ever do. I was just sure that because I had always lived a pretty wholesome life, 'those things' would just never happen to me. Boy, have I learned! Now not only do I not judge, I feel. When someone apparently has made a big mistake or is going through a tough time, I have no trouble imagining what they might be feeling. I want to let them know I care and that they can come through it."

When you come through a personal catastrophe of any kind, you can emerge with an unprecedented depth of mercy and grace for others. Having "been there," you have a much better sense of what people who are in pain do and don't need to hear—and at the top of the list is usually somebody else's judgment. As never before, your fellow human strugglers can experience your spirit and your touch as nourishing and comforting. Discovering ways to become a channel of healing for others is the ultimate subject of this final chapter.

YOU HAVE A CHOICE: POWERLESSNESS OR PURPOSE

Those benefits of adversity are yours for the taking, but they are by no means guaranteed. Go "left" at the ten forks in the road, and you can sink ever deeply into pathological powerlessness.

Powerlessness Produces a Poor Prognosis

Pathological powerlessness has devastating effects on your life in the long term. I'm not referring to the initial feeling of powerlessness almost everyone has after being blindsided by something they didn't welcome and they didn't choose. That loss of control is almost universal for people who have been struck by the lightning of tragedy.

I'm talking about the ongoing choices you make that may "feel like power" (such as the negative energy of bitterness), but that gradually sap your energy and take away your peace of mind. These negative pathways are emotionally seductive, but deceptive. If you choose to live in powerlessness, giving bitterness, complaints, a sour attitude, and the victim mentality a home in your heart, they'll have to room with depression, chronic pain, and failure. Here's what will happen.

1. *You'll stay a "victim."* In chapter 2, we described the "victim" role as constantly blaming your problems on others, expecting someone else to fix it, ignoring your own responsibility, wallowing in self-pity, and complaining rather than acting. The longer you stay in that role, the more familiar it becomes. You repeat the same mistakes over and over. When I heard the following story, it reminded me of the way "victims" seem never to learn from negative consequences.

A man came into work with both ears bandaged. His boss asked him, "What happened to you?"

The employee explained, "Yesterday while I was ironing my shirt, the phone rang. I accidentally answered the iron instead of the phone."

"I'm sorry," replied his boss, "but what happened to the other ear?"

"They called back!"

When you allow yourself to get caught up in negative cycles in the futile pursuit of power, repeating the same mistakes, you're bound to get burned!

2. *You become disillusioned and cynical.* Ironically, there's a true sense in which disillusionment is a realistic part of your recovery. Before, you probably maintained the *illusion* that something like that would never happen to you and that your world was quite safe. Though you've been working hard on making the wiser ten

choices, you've still had to reach some kind of realistic acceptance of the fact that your life, your environment, and the people in it are not as safe as you had thought. In other words, you've become *dis*illusioned.

However, here I'm referring to an energy-stealing, relationship-breaking type of disillusionment. When faced with the ten choices, if you habitually select the more destructive options, you'll become so disillusioned about people and about the world that you conclude there's no use, nothing will turn out right anyway, and no one can be trusted. That type of cynicism will hinder your willingness to push out into the unknown, reconnect with people and activities that could bring back enjoyment, and take the risks necessary to reclaim "lost territory." Pervasive disillusionment places you in a very powerless position, for it sabotages your will to take action.

3. *You experience spiritual and interpersonal alienation.* A third outcome of chronic powerlessness is detachment and alienation. The habits of blame and revenge live near the root of this problem. These two scoundrels provide a false sense of power. You want to believe that somebody somewhere could and should have stopped what happened. The bitterness that comes from the perpetual projection of blame increasingly separates you from the free flow of communication with God and from relationships with potentially nurturing people.

Think you'll get back power by evening the score? Striking out in revenge neither turns back the clock nor provides lasting satisfaction. Instead, obsessive angry thoughts block positive spiritual energy. Further, they rob you of countless opportunities to see the vision for a more positive future and to open yourself to others who could be a part of it. When your thought life is filled with malice, your spiritual life languishes.

True power comes through love, not hate. It's not easy to love when others don't and life stinks. In my opinion, it's darn near impossible without a divine love transfusion. That life source is available to you from the God who is Love. When you say "yes" to His invitation, He will lovingly guide you on a path of peace with Him and peace with others. He'll give you the real kind of power when you ask.

4. *You neglect positive action.* The fourth outcome of chronic powerlessness is neglecting positive action. This results from the depletion of hope, which is another eventual result of choosing unwisely at each of the ten junctures. Hopelessness steals your motivation because you perceive, "It's not worth it. It's no use." You aren't willing to push past your discomfort to take action.

Not only can you fail to choose positive behavior when you receive catastrophic news, you can become downright foolish. Recently I watched with fascination as one of the morning shows told the story of a man who had received a diagnosis of pancreatic cancer. He was advised that he had only six months to live.

What if this had happened to you? What would you do differently if you had only six months to live? Most of us would develop a laserlike focus on what was most important. We'd become more urgently purposeful—spending more time with those we love and using the time we had left to fulfill our unique assigned calling on this earth. Not this man.

Despite the terminal cancer diagnosis, the man elected not to take the recommended chemo treatments. Instead, he withdrew his life savings and spent it all in fancy hotels all over the world, treating himself to the finest of wines and any luxury he wanted. He stopped paying his mortgage payments and "enjoyed life" to the fullest, depriving himself of nothing.

Six months passed, then a year. At the end of two years, this gentleman started to notice that he wasn't dead! In fact, he was gaining weight and feeling better. He went back to the doctor, and the doctor told him, "There's been a mistake. You never had cancer. You only had pancreatitis."

Relief and rejoicing, right? Nope. He's really mad about it. And he's broke and nine months behind on his mortgage. He plans to sue.

Here's a man who sabotaged himself by responding to a life crisis without wise thought or purposeful action—but still, in the attitude of a classic "victim," it's someone else's fault. Sure, the mistaken diagnosis was unfortunate, but how did he respond to the adversity in his life? He enjoyed the feeling of power—for a season, only for a season.

As I've presented the ten make-or-break choices to you, I've tried to help you see how small negative decisions add up to big ones. Each is unhealthy and destructive in its own way, and the combination of them creates the destructive synergy of powerlessness.

This does not have to be. Not only can you choose to stay out of the ruts that send you deeper into the mire, you can rise above your circumstances and refuse to allow your pain to be wasted. You can make a difference.

Purpose Gives Life Meaning

Throughout this book, we've explored ways to reject the low roads and take the high roads. In so doing, you have the opportunity to discover new ways to honor what you value, to become a living memorial for a person or investment that was lost, and to keep the main things the main things.

God can take your mess and turn it into your message.
—JOEL OSTEEN

Betsy's daughter was killed by a drunk driver. She told me, "I want to be sure that my daughter didn't die in vain. I put together a book about her life. Making that book was a major part of my healing, but I've also been able to share it with other parents who are going through the loss of a child. My sister works at a funeral home, and she also shares it. Also, I speak for MADD [Mothers Against Drunk Driving] at the first-offense DUI classes about six or seven times a year."

As you begin to recover, the "products" of your pain can become the very means by which you can help others heal.

MINING THE LOSSES FOR THE LESSONS

One of the biggest challenges of recovery for most people is finding what to do with those gaping holes left by the losses. For instance, if you've lost a close relationship, how are you going to get that need met within the context of what you have left? If you had a dream that got dashed, will you live disillusioned and broken, or will you allow yourself to dream and plan again? Maybe you had a certain job in which you felt fulfilled, but you are no longer employed in it because of reorganization, a layoff, or illness. What was it about that role that you found most fulfilling?

Embedded in those struggles are the nuggets of wisdom about what's been most important to you. Pinpointing what you've valued most in the past gives you clues about what you'll need to re-create in some form as a part of your new life. As you emerge from your adversity with clearer vision and a more tender heart, you can examine the opportunities that are currently available to you.

You can't bring back what you had in the past. However, with God's help and the support of loving people, you can discover fresh ways to get your needs met within the context of your life as it exists now—not as you fantasized it would be, but as it is. You can apply your talents to make a difference in ways you never dreamed of before your crisis.

How will you demonstrate your newfound understanding of the pain of others? How will you reach out to lend a hand?

What Is Your Purpose in Life?

I ask this question to my seminar audiences when I present programs on this topic. Invariably, people begin talking about the roles they fulfill—being a mother, a nurse, a banker, a judge, a physician. Listen, a role is not your purpose. Roles are only vehicles for fulfilling your calling. Your roles may change, either through uninvited change, normal development, or intentional transition. However, your unique gifts, calling, and purpose are constant and unrelenting.[2]

When the embryo called you was formed, your magnificent genetic combination had within it the DNA for your potential talents, personality characteristics, and motivations, all of which you'd need to accomplish God's unique calling on your life. He knew in advance the many opportunities that would be placed in front of you. Even then, He knew all about this crazy phase of your life, and His divine design took that into account.

The golden threads of your purpose may be detected as you look back over the most meaningful experiences you've had. However, golden thread is often seen best against black velvet. As you emerge into the sunlight from what has felt like deep, penetrating, black darkness, you bring forth new insights and a new sensitivity to others. Your angst and heartache can be transformed into passion—passion for bringing light and comfort to those to whom you are "assigned."

Yes, your life has changed. You aren't working with what you've always had. Yet now you've added new tools. You have a firsthand comprehension of what it's like to "walk through the valley of the shadow of death," as the Bible describes.[3] As you've persistently implemented the ten

> *When life has handed you a slap in the face, purpose is the loving kick in the derriere that gets you up and moving!*

make-or-break choices, you've discovered new parts of yourself, strengths you didn't know you possessed. You are not only surviving, but you're also getting little glimpses of thriving. You don't have pat answers anymore, but you have a caring heart and willing hands. Now, as never before, you're qualified to serve. You can choose to live on purpose.

The Power of Purpose

A strong sense of purpose connects you to something much bigger than you are. As you come to recognize how much you matter, your self-respect is strengthened. Your self-worth is born of the awe and privilege of being a child of a loving God and a member of the worldwide team of folks who are working together to make the world a better place.

A strong sense of purpose is a buffer against stress, a power that keeps you going when you are exhausted. I'll never forget something an adolescent client I'll call Michael told me after returning from a mission trip to Mexico with his church youth group.

"We had to clear the ground to build a school for poverty-stricken Mexican children. We had to work in the blazing sun, chipping and chipping away at the debris and the rock. It was the hardest work I've ever had to do."

Michael continued, "I hated what I was doing. *But I loved why I was doing it!*"

Michael had learned one of the greatest secrets of motivation: a meaningful "why" can take you through almost any difficulty. When life has handed you a slap in the face, purpose is the loving kick in the derriere that gets you up and moving! When you understand that you have important work to do, you don't have the luxury of staying down for the rest of your life.

Whether you want to discover your own purpose for the first time, or whether you are looking for fresh ways to live out what you already know, you're in a wonderful place. You're on the cusp of many productive and joyful adventures. God is about to open doors of destiny and opportunity for service in ways that only you can fulfill.

You can experience a supernatural energy that propels you far beyond your mere human capabilities. One day in an airport, that fact was brought vividly to my awareness.

In an attempt to save time as I hurried between flights, I took the "moving sidewalk." Of course, no self-respecting "hyper" person would ride passively in the right lane; I had to move to the left so that I could walk while the sidewalk was moving.

God arrested my attention in the middle of that busy day. (He has a sneaky way of doing that!) In a flash of insight, I saw the amazing similarity between that moving sidewalk and purpose. I was choosing to put one foot in front of the other; I expended my own energy in the process. But there was something moving under me! It was a power that propelled me at a rate and with an ease that I could not have felt if I had simply been walking in my own strength. Had I gotten tired and stopped walking for a moment, that power would still have been insistently taking me toward my destination.

Then an interesting thing happened. I was so lost in my thoughts about purpose, I didn't notice that I was coming to the end of the sidewalk. You guessed it. My unexpected departure from the device bolted me forward, and I almost took a tumble. And so the metaphor continued. When I get distracted by life and get off purpose, a fall is not far behind!

BEGIN NOW TO CHOOSE PURPOSE

Are you ready to rediscover purpose, to commit yourself to join God in His intent to weave all your struggles and your heartaches into the tapestry of a beautiful, purposeful life? That's where we begin.

Commit to Align Yourself with God's Intent to Bring Good out of a Bad Situation

It's a red-letter day when you make the unshakeable decision to cooperate with God's plan to bring the best out of the worst circumstances. Some of the resultant blessings happen *in* us; other blessings happen *through* us.

The treasures you experience along the way—new insights, fresh courage, the restoration of hope, the acquisition of new skills, unprecedented strength, resilience, and heartfelt compassion for others—these might never have developed in calmer waters. God's work in you after personal trauma is nothing short of miraculous. You cooperate in that work by choosing to follow the psychologically and spiritually sound principles I've shared with you in this book.

You can also become a channel of blessings, allowing the grace you've received during your time of trouble to flow through you to others. As you become whole again, you are able to give from the storehouse of comfort you have received from God and others.

Delores, a cancer survivor, said, "I've learned that there can be good in everything that happens, no matter how tragic. I work in a cancer center now. Today, I spoke to two patients, both as bald as they could be. I relate with them from my own experience with cancer, and I let them know how important it is to keep your faith in God and open yourself to others in the process.

"It's amazing how all the experiences in our lives prepare us for the people we are to reach out to. I just found out today that one of those bald ladies is being cared for by her daughter, who is an alcoholic. I was married to an alcoholic. You see, nothing is wasted. If I can use what I've been through to hold someone's hand and provide love and comfort, no matter what they've done or who they are—that makes my life worthwhile."

Look for Positive Changes in You Since Experiencing This Crisis

To gain some momentum on this trip into destiny, look inside and recognize that despite your struggles, many positive things have begun to happen *in you*. Write in your journal about these things:

- Do you have a clearer perspective, making it possible to differentiate the "small stuff"?

- Have your priorities shifted, giving you a greater awareness of what's really important?

- Has the trouble you've encountered matured you and strengthened your character?

If you've been journaling throughout this journey, and I hope you have, look back on your notes. You really aren't in the same place as when you started, are you? If you haven't been keeping notes, pick a specific time since your trauma that's meaningful and memorable. What changes have taken place in you since that time?

Recognize and give thanks for the Invisible Hand that has been guiding your growth through this process. You're making it. You are here for a reason. We may not ever discover the reason it happened, but I know one thing for sure: if you're still breathing, you are here for a reason.

Recognize That You Have Unique Gifts to Share with Others

No one else on earth has exactly what you have to offer. The triumphs and tragedies of your life have uniquely positioned you to serve at "your post." If you are open to it, God will bring person after person across your path who needs to learn from you and to be comforted and inspired by you.

Sometimes the very things you want with all your heart to reject, the things that embarrass you most, the experiences that have created the most havoc in your life—those become the very doors to the hearts of those you are destined to help. I've found this to be true in my own life.

As a psychologist, I would simply love to be able to say that I always practice what I preach and don't make dumb mistakes. That's a long way from true. I've made plenty of mistakes in my life, and I have the battle scars to prove it. Yet I've found over and over that you don't have to be perfect to be a helper. (Otherwise, there would be no helpers.) We are all "wounded healers," and as we allow ourselves to be God's instruments of healing for others, we ourselves are healed.

Affirm the Fact That You Have Purpose

It's a luxury now if, before the tragedy happened, you had already developed clarity about "what you're here for." Even then, after disappointment and heartache, you may have to do some difficult emotional work in order to get back to your purpose and reestablish new ways to fulfill your mission on the planet.

Never been quite clear about your own personal purpose? When the most intense of your pain has begun to subside, there's no better time to explore that issue. Out of chaos comes order. Everyone who goes through significant loss must eventually answer the question, "What now?"

Listen to how Don Medley, author of *The Book of Luke*, describes his life after the loss of his son and sister: "After my son and sister were killed in the plane crash, I didn't change professions. I was still a lawyer like I've always been. But I became a different kind of lawyer at heart. I became more compassionate. I know, you wouldn't think of lawyers and compassion at the same time. But in my work, I now see that I deal with families who are grieving. If it's a divorce, there's anger, sadness, all those issues you deal with in death. It's the death of a relationship, the death of a marriage. I've been able to help people not get stuck in that anger, deal with things, and move on. I can help them see that it's not a perfect world, but they have important choices about how they're going to respond to the things that happen in their lives. I've also had many opportunities in my personal life to talk with people going through loss.

"I would never have chosen to go through this tragedy. However, I have to say that it's made me a better person. I have a depth of understanding I didn't have before. I remember how much it meant when people extended the hand of love. I think that's what it's all about—to love one another."[4]

As you look at recreating your future, reflect on how you can infuse more meaning into your life through purposeful living. In a moment, I'll ask you some questions that will guide your exploration. For now, just believe and affirm that by discovering and acting on purpose, you'll be energized to continue to implement the healthy side of all the ten make-or-break choices.

Make a Commitment to Make a Difference
Gradually, you're realizing that the Serenity Prayer makes so much sense. You've had to accept the things you cannot change—but you are accountable for changing the things you can. (The problem in the middle of your struggle is not recognizing the difference!) You can't rewrite history; your opportunity now is to create your future. Your calling is to make a difference.

You may live out your purpose by influencing people or systems with respect to the very type of trauma you experienced. Maybe you'll have a role in educating others about prevention, comforting others who are going through the problem, or getting laws changed that impact the target issue. You may be a person who tries to change systems, or your inclination may be to help others one at a time. In any case, your own experience will fuel your passion and add immense credibility to whatever action you choose to take.

I want to share with you some of the lyrics to a song entitled "Make a Difference," which I cowrote with Vasti Jackson.[5] These words reflect my heart's prayer. If you've made the choice for purpose, they will resonate in your heart as well.

> As I begin this day, O Lord,
> In Your presence and Your peace,
> I draw on all You are
> To give me all I need.
> Give me eyes of compassion,
> Listening ears and helping hands.
> I need your courage to face my fears.
> In Your strength, I will stand.
>
> You know me inside and out.
> You know I struggle and I fall.
> But you're always there to lift me up,
> Answering every call.
> Keep me centered in your will,
> Walking in the path that You lead,
> With Your Spirit as my guide,
> I am destined to succeed.

Dear Lord, I know,
Words don't always make Your message clear.
So I want my life to show
Your peace without confusion,
Your truth without illusion,
Give me wisdom to do what's right,
And power to heal the hurt and strife,
O Lord, I pray.
Help me make a difference today.
Lord, help me make a difference today.

Live Each Day as If It's Your Last

Before catastrophe strikes, you tend to think you have all the time in the world. You learn the hard way that time is precious.

My friend, professional speaker Mike Stewart, wrote an article on the occasion of the rededication of St. Mark's Chapel for Children at St. Martin-in-the-Fields Episcopal Church in Atlanta in honor of his son, Mark Robert Stewart. Mark died of cancer at the age of thirty-one. Here's a portion of what Mike wrote:

Five years! A lifetime when measured in terms of black days, hours, and minutes of impossibly excruciating grief that only a parent can know. Or five years that pass as quickly as the kiss of a breeze lingering momentarily upon my cheek when I remember sitting on the edge of Mark's hospice bed holding his hand and brushing his hair back from his forehead and hearing his nurse quietly say, "He's gone."

Mark had been diagnosed with cancer exactly four years and ten months before he died. Never once did I, or anyone else as far as I know, hear him ask, "Why me?" Instead of worrying about himself, he made the conscious choice to focus his energy in a positive way on others. He said to me, 'Dad, we're all living on borrowed time. Most people live dying; they die a little bit every day. I'm going to die living. Every day I will learn something new, do something to help someone else, and make someone laugh.'

As I think about how unselfish Mark was and the wise choices he made in the last, too short years of his life, I strive to follow his example and make wise choices too. Still, I can't help but wish I had had just a little more time with him. Just one more day, please.

Dear Reader, time is short. Make the most of it. None of us knows the number of days that lie ahead of us, or the number that lie ahead of our loved ones, so we need to consciously choose to make the most of each and every one of those days. Just one more day, please. Today, and every day that lies ahead, can be that day for you.[6]

Thank you, Mike . . . and Mark . . . for that precious reminder.

I love what professional speaker Michelle Nichols did to commemorate the fifth anniversary of her son's death.[7] She and her family rented a billboard on a major freeway in Houston. The sign said, "Hug your kids today. We wish we could. In memory of Mark Nichols, 1989–1998."

As a result of the billboard, she and her family were interviewed at Houston's largest television station, giving them the opportunity to share that message of inspiration with millions of others.

You never know how much time you or your loved ones have. Is it possible that in your pain, you're not making the most of the opportunities today with those you love? My friend, squeeze the most out of each day. Don't foolishly diminish the value of any minute or hour. You don't have an unlimited number to spend. Live each day as if it's your last.

Pray, Meditate—Get Quiet, Be Still, Listen

Some of your sense of renewed purpose may seem to come accidentally, though I don't believe for a minute that any of it is an accident! In other words, you can have teachable moments that "just happen" in which an incident occurs or a person shares something with you that sets off all kinds of bells in your spirit. You know that you've just encountered something significant, though you may not yet understand exactly how that applies to you or how that knowledge will play out in your future. Or you may be involved in a project or task, and you think, *Wow! I was born to do this kind of thing!*

However, sometimes the insights don't come without deliberately setting aside time to be still and listen. You are in pursuit of life-changing revelations. You're working on identifying and discovering the privilege of implementing a divine plan that's more wonderful than you could have thought or imagined. You're preparing for your unique contribution to improving the lives of the people with whom you share the planet.

Set aside some time each day to get alone to pray, read, meditate, ponder, write, and search your soul. Don't discount little snippets that come into your consciousness by telling yourself that you are just imagining things, trying too hard, or hearing what you want to hear. Write it down, don't judge it. Just record it. Your cumulative thoughts and writings will begin to form a pattern and provide you with exciting insights about your life and your future.

Ask Yourself Eight Questions

The questions that follow in a moment will help you discover what's most important to you in your core, which is where your purpose resides. You may not be able to do this at one sitting. Take the time that you need to review your life and get back in touch with instructive past experiences.

Don't just give one-word responses. Go into some detail about what your significant experiences have been, how you felt about them, and what about them was most meaningful. Do record all your answers in writing because when you're done, you can search for patterns in your responses.

1. What desires have been consistently present throughout my life?

2. In the past, what have I been doing when I've felt "in the flow" of what I was "meant to do?"

3. What was I doing when I've felt most productive?

4. In the past, what kinds of things have awakened me in the night with a new idea?

5. When do I feel that I'm at my best?

6. What "whys" run throughout my most satisfying experiences, both work and personal?

7. Why have I kept going throughout this ordeal? What has given me the will to persist?

8. What would I hope people would say about me in my eulogy?

Now look at what you've written. What themes do you notice? How would you summarize what you are trying to accomplish when you are at your best, when your talents are fully deployed, and when you are receiving your greatest satisfaction?

I'd like to tell you about my experience in a similar search as an illustration of how you trim down your observations to a statement of purpose. My inspiration came from a Dutchman named Parvis Tavakoly.

I was getting ready to conduct a leadership retreat for a manufacturing company in Texas. They had flown their plant managers in from all over the world for this time of team building and leadership skill development.

The evening before the program was to begin, we gathered for a get-acquainted meal. Prior to sitting down, I was milling about meeting the participants, engaging in that social chitchat typical of such an occasion. I had only been in Parvis's presence long enough for the first two of the customary opening questions (What's your name? Where do you work?) when he looked me in the eye and with his Dutch accent asked, "Tell me, what is your purpose in life?"

I was startled. It wasn't the question I was expecting. Now understand, it wasn't that I didn't know I was called to do the work that I do. But what was my purpose in life? Hmm . . . that was a pretty tough one. I managed to sputter something; I don't remember what. But I admitted to myself that evening that Parvis had asked me a very important question and that I didn't have a ready answer for it. I decided to change that.

I spent the next several months doing just what I'm asking you to do now—praying, observing my reactions in various situations in my life, writing, talking with others about how they saw me. Finally, it crystallized for me.

My purpose in life is *bringing out the best in people.* That purpose is in operation, no matter what role I'm fulfilling. Whether I'm talking with my kids, playing with my grandmunchkins, communicating with a friend, doing one-on-one counseling or coaching, speaking to a convention, presenting an in-house educational program, or writing—my goal is the same. It's to bring out the best in people.

Remember, a role is not your purpose. You will have different roles in different phases of your life. Roles change over time, sometimes voluntarily, sometimes involuntarily. When you understand the constancy of purpose, you realize that no role change can shake the calling that God has on your life. No tragedy or disruption of plans can sabotage purpose. Your purpose is not subject to your circumstances. As the old saying goes, "Bloom where you are planted." Wherever you are right now, that's exactly the right place for the fulfillment of your purpose today.

So again, I ask you, "What is your purpose in life?" If you can't state your purpose yet (remember it took a few months for me to crystallize it), keep thinking, praying, observing, and researching. Continue to record your thoughts and ideas, and refine your statement of purpose as you go along. In the meantime, get busy experimenting with the opportunities for service that are before you.

Connect with Others Who Share Your Values

Positive action is so much easier with support and teamwork. A friend of mine recently told me about his Sunday school class working side by side with tenants in a local government housing project to help them plant a community vegetable garden.

One woman in our community had the creative idea to get together a group of women to crochet outfits for premature babies at the local hospital. Now the group has grown to the point they are making gifts for all babies who are born there.

Many workplaces are recognizing the value of team projects outside work, discovering that sharing worthwhile goals like building a house for Habitat for Humanity translates to improved relationships in the workplace.

If you're not ready for a group project, talk with a friend with whom you feel comfortable. What interests do you share, and what are some ways you could pool your talents to serve someone else?

Opportunities Are All Around You

Armed with your desire and commitment to make a meaningful contribution, open your eyes to the world around you. Don't try to formulate the grand plan. Just look for tiny little ways you can honor your lost loved one or make a difference to someone in your vicinity. You see that tired face of the elderly lady in line at the grocery store? I'll bet a smile and a cordial hello would brighten her day a little. Could you do some behind-the-scenes volunteering at church? Maybe make the coffee or fold bulletins? How about offering to mow the lawn of the neighbor down the street who has cancer? Or maybe you could just give her a phone call or send a card that says, "I'm thinking of you."

It's those baby steps that are in line with your talents, your spiritual gifts, and your motive to serve that get you going. You just can't beat the feeling that comes from knowing you made someone else's load just a little lighter. Helping another person takes your focus off your own pain. Doing something positive for your fellow travelers not only helps them, but it facilitates your own healing.

Uh-uh-uh! Don't you discount that little action, telling yourself that it's nothing or that others do so much more or that it's nothing like you used to be able to do. Celebrate it, because the smallest acts of service are flashing signs that you are getting up again, determined to re-create a useful, fulfilling, and purposeful life.

MY COMMITMENT TO *PURPOSE*

I was placed on this earth for a purpose. God gave me one-of-a-kind talents and abilities embedded uniquely in my DNA, mixed in exactly the right combinations to enable me to accomplish those things that are uniquely mine to do. I've had many experiences in my life that have delighted me, stunned me, distressed me, shaped me, and taught me. I've allowed some events and people to bring out the best in me, and at times I've been at my worst. Sometimes I've succeeded and sometimes I've stumbled. But all of my life experiences have worked together to mature me and to prepare me for the next assignments that are mine to fulfill.

Nothing that has happened or will ever happen can separate me from the love of God and from the calling on my life. As my circumstances change, so may my methods of action change, but my purpose is intact. In fact, the experiences I thought would destroy me have made me stronger, more compassionate, more capable of reaching out to others in a real way. Through it all, I've been equipped as no one else to make a difference as no one else can. I am still living, so I know that I still have work to do on this earth.

I affirm that I have purpose, and I open my spirit to its rediscovery. I commit to daily prayer, meditation, and mindful observation. I open the eyes of my heart to the opportunities in my path today and to creative ideas for service. I relish the joy that comes from knowing that I'm doing what I was created to do. I commit myself to the fulfillment of my purpose.

Conclusion

CHOOSING HOPE—ONE STEP AT A TIME

As our conversation draws to a close in this book, I want you to know that I'm so full of hope for you. I know from my own life and from my work with thousands of people over the years, you can and will make it. As you draw on God's unconditional love and unfailing strength, and as you diligently make the ten choices we've discussed, you're going to rise up and become more than you ever dreamed possible.

I've been thinking about the message I want to leave with you, and I believe that message is *hope*. Hope keeps going, keeps believing, keeps persisting. Hope in your heart trumps even seemingly hopeless circumstances. Hope gives rise to the peaceful assurance that even when your world looks the darkest, God will light a way for you. Make the choice to act on hope now, exploring this pathway or that. Just one step, then another, then another. You may not know where this adventure will take you, but you can rest assured that at every juncture, you'll have what you truly need.

In closing, I want to share with you a story that took place when my daughter, Amy, was just four years old.[1] One evening, she made an observation containing wisdom beyond her years.

Amy and I had let the time slip away on our visit to Ms. Franks, the elderly lady who lived on the hill across the street. We quickly said our good-byes and began the long, winding trek down the driveway. The thick darkness was interrupted only by the distant light of our open garage.

Grasping my hand, Amy exclaimed, "Mommy, Mommy, we can't see!"

Seconds later, she made an exciting discovery. "Oh, look, Mom! We can't see out there—but if we look right down at our feet, we can see how to take the next step."

You may not understand it all, now or ever. You may still be confused about where you go from here. Things may look dark around you. But look! Right there in front of you. God has given you the light you need to take your very next step!

My love and my prayers are with you on your journey.

Notes

Introduction: *The Power of Choice*

1. Romans 8:28.
2. Viktor Frankl, *Man's Search for Meaning* (Boston: Beacon, rep. 2006).
3. See, for example, A. T. Beck, A. J. Rush, B. F. Shaw, G. Emery, *Cognitive Therapy of Depression* (New York: Guilford, 1987) and J. S. Beck, *Cognitive Therapy: Basics and Beyond* (New York: Guilford, 1995).
4. Compiled and arranged by John Cook, *The Book of Positive Quotations* (Minneapolis: Fairview Press, 1993), 523.

Chapter 1: "I'm Fine . . . Really!" *Choice #1: Denial or Reality*

1. John 8:32.
2. S. Lyubomirsky, L. Sousa, R. Dickerhoof, "The Costs and Benefits of Writing, Talking, and Thinking about Life's Triumphs and Defeats," *Journal of Personal and Social Psychology* 90, no. 4 (2006): 692–708.
3. Ibid.
4. R. A. Bryant, L. M. Moulds, R. V. D. Nixon, "Cognitive Behavior Therapy of Acute Stress Disorder: A Four-Year Follow-Up," *Journal of Consulting and Clinical Psychology* 41 (2003): 489–94.

Chapter 2: "Poor Me" *Choice #2: Victimhood or Responsibility*

1. Compiled and arranged by John Cook, *The Book of*

Positive Quotations (Minneapolis: Fairview Press, 1993), 543.

2. Michelle Nichols is a professional speaker and the sales columnist for *BusinessWeek Online*. She may be reached at 877-352-9684 or by e-mail at michelle.nichols@savvyselling. com. Her Web site is www.savvyselling.com.

CHAPTER 3: "I Have a Thousand Questions" *Choice #3: Why or How*

1. Captain Dave Carey is a motivational speaker and author who may be reached at 512-819-9481 or by e-mail at dave @davecarey.com. His Web site is www.davecarey.com.
2. M. Scott Peck, *The Road Less Traveled* (New York: Simon & Schuster, 1979).
3. Dave Carey, *The Ways We Choose: Lessons for Life from a POW's Experience* (Portland: Amica, 2005).

CHAPTER 4: "How Could God Let This Happen?"
Choice #4: Doubt or Faith

1. Rabbi Harold Kushner, *When Bad Things Happen To Good People* (New York: Harper Collins, 1981).
2. Rosemarie Rossetti, Ph. D., is a speaker and the author of *Take Back Your Life!* (Melbourne: Fortuna, 2003). She may be contacted by phone at 614-471-6100, or by e-mail at rosemarie@rosemariespeaks.com. Her Web site is www. rosemariespeaks.com.
3. Esther M. Sternberg, MD, *The Balance Within: The Science Connecting Health and Emotions* (New York: W. H. Freeman, 2001), 170.
4. *The Merriam-Webster Online Dictionary* (Cambridge, Mass.: Merriam-Webster, 2005), http://www.Merriam-Webster.com. By permission.
5. Harold George Koenig, MD, *Is Religion Good for Your*

Health? The Effects of Religion on Physical and Mental Health (New York: Haworth, 1997), 104–109.

6. Ibid.

7. K. Conway, "Coping with Stress of Medical Problems among Black and White Elderly," *International Journal of Aging and Development* 21: 39–48.

8. P. B. Nelson, "Ethnic Differences in Intrinsic/Extrinsic Religious Orientation and Depression in the Elderly," *Archives of Psychiatric Nursing* 3, no. 4 (1989): 199–204.

9. Harold G. Koenig, J. N. Kvale, C. Ferrel, "Religion and Well-Being in Later Life," *The Gerontologist* 28: 18–28.

10. P. D. Roth, "Spiritual Well-Being and Marital Adjustment," *Journal of Psychology and Theology* 16: 153–58.

11. W. T. Martin, "Religiosity and United States Suicide Rates, 1972–1978," *Journal of Clinical Psychology* 40(5): 1166–69.

12. H. G. Koenig, S. M. Ford, L. K. George, D. G. Blazer, K. G. Meador, "Religion and Anxiety Disorder: An Examination and Comparison of Associations in Young, Middle-Aged, and Elderly Adults," *Journal of Anxiety Disorders*, 321–42.

13. H. G. Koenig, L. K. Meador, D. G. Blazer, S. M. Ford, "Religious Practices and Alcoholism in a Southern Adult Population," *Hospital and Community Psychiatry* 45 (1994): 225–37.

14. C. G. Ellison, L. K. George, "Religious Involvement, Social Ties, and Social Support in a Southeastern Community," *Journal for the Scientific Study of Religion* 33 (1994): 46–61.

15. C. G Ellison, D. A. Gay, T. A. Glass, "Does Religious Commitment Contribute to Individual Life Satisfaction?" *Social Forces* 68 (1989): 100–23.

16. C. G. Ellison, et. al., "Religious Involvement, Social Ties, and Social Support in a Southeastern Community," 46–61.

17. J. A. Thorson, F. C. Powell, "Meanings of Death and Intrinsic Religiosity," *Journal of Clinical Psychology* 46 (1990): 379–91.

18. H. G. Koenig, et. al., "Religious Practices and Alcoholism in a Southern Adult Population," *Hospital and Community Psychiatry* 45 (1994): 225–37.

19. L. R. Probst, R. Ostrom, P. Watkins, T. Dean, D. Mashburn, "Comparative Efficacy of Religious and Nonreligious Cognitive-Behavioral Therapy for the Treatment of Clinical Depression in Religious Individuals," *Journal of Consulting and Clinical Psychology* 60 (1992): 94–103.

20. E. L. Idler, S. V. Kasl, "Religion, Disability, Depression, and the Timing of Death," *American Journal of Sociology* 97 (1992): 1052–79.

21. P. Pressman, J. S. Lyons, D. B. Larson, J. S. Strain, "Religious Belief, Depression, and Ambulation Status in Elderly Women with Broken Hips," *American Journal of Psychiatry* 147 (1997): 758–60.

22. J. W. Yates, B .J. Chalmer, P. P. McKegney, "Religion in Patients with Advanced Cancer," *Medical and Pediatric Oncology* 9 (1981): 121–28.

23. D. B. Larson, H. G. Koenig, B. H. Kaplan, R. S. Greenberg, E. Logue, H. A. Tyroler, "The Impact of Religion on Men's Blood Pressure," *Journal of Religion and Health* 28 (1989): 265–78.

24. Y. Friedlander, J. D. Kark, Y. Stein, "Religious Orthodoxy and Myocardial Infarction in Jerusalem: A Case Control Study," *International Journal of Cardiology* 10 (1986): 33–41.

25. H. G. Koenig, "Religion and Medicine IV: Religion, Physical Health, and Clinical Implications," *The International Journal of Psychiatry in Medicine* 31, no. 3 (2001): 321–36.

CHAPTER 5: "Of Course I'm Angry!" *Choice #5: Bitterness or Forgiveness*

1. Ephesians 4:26 (KJV).

2. J. Julkanen, J. R. Ahlstrom, "Hostility, Anger, and Sense of Coherence as Predictors of Health-Related Quality of Life: Results of an ASCOT Sub-Study," *Journal of Psychosomatic Research* 61, no. 1 (2006): 33–39.

3. G. L. Reed, R. D. Enright, "The Effects of Forgiveness Therapy on Depression, Anxiety, and Posttraumatic Stress for Women after Spousal Emotional Abuse," *Journal of Consulting and Clinical Psychology* 74, no. 5 (2006): 920–29.

4. Martin Luther King Jr., *The Strength to Love* (Philadelphia: Fortress, 1963), 51–52.

5. Charles Stanley, *The Gift of Forgiveness* (Nashville: Thomas Nelson, 2002).

6. Matthew 5:7 (KJV).

7. Romans 12:18.

CHAPTER 6: "I Can't Forgive Myself" *Choice #6: Guilt or Self-Forgiveness*

1. Abby Shields, MEd, is a professional speaker who may be reached by phone at (985) 809-1511 or by e-mail at reconnect us@yahoo.com. Abby's Web site is www.abbyshields.com.

2. A. T. Beck, "Cognitive Models of Depression," *Journal of Cognitive Psychotherapy: An International Quarterly* 1 (1987): 5–37.

3. Pauline Rose Clance, *The Imposter Phenomenon: Overcoming the Fear That Haunts Your Success.* Atlanta: Peachtree, 1985).

CHAPTER 7: "Just Stay Away!" *Choice #7: Isolation or Connection*

1. Susan Anderson, *The Journey from Heartbreak to Connection* (New York: Berkeley, 2003).

2. Ecclesiastes 4:9–12.

3. Bernie S. Siegel, MD, *Love, Medicine, and Miracles* (New York: HarperCollins, 1998).

4. M. Franks, M. Stephens, M. A. Parris, K. S. Rook, B. Franklin, A. Keteyian, S. J. Artineas, "Spouses' Provision of Health-Related Support and Control to Patients Participating in Cardiac Rehabilitation," *Journal of Family Psychology* 20, no. 2 (2006): 311–18.

5. Abby Shields, MEd, is a professional speaker who may be reached at (985) 809-1511 or by e-mail at reconnectus @yahoo.com. Abby's Web site is www.abbyshields .com.

6. Michelle Nichols is a professional speaker and the sales columnist for *BusinessWeek Online*. She may be reached at 877-352-9684 or by e-mail at michelle.nichols@savvy-selling.com. Her Web site is www.savvyselling.com.

7. Barbara Glanz, *What Can I Do? Ideas to Help Those Who Have Experienced* Loss (Minneapolis: Augsburg, 2007). Barbara is a professional speaker who may be contacted at 941-312-9169 or by e-mail at bglanz@barbaraglanz .com. Her Web site is www.barbaraglanz.com.

8. R. Kessler, "Levels of Serious Mental Illness in Katrina Survivors Increase; Majority Also Feel Deeper Sense of Meaning," Department of Health Care Policy, Harvard Medical School, 2006. http://www.hcp.med.harvard.edu /news/stories/index.php?id=24.

CHAPTER 8: "My Dreams Have Turned into Nightmares"
Choice #8: Depression or Grief

1. Elisabeth Kübler-Ross, *On Death and Dying* (New York: McMillan, 1969).

2. Therese A. Rando, *Treatment of Complicated Mourning* (Champaign, IL: Research Press, 2993), 33–43.

3. Romans 11:29.

4. Barbara Glanz is a professional speaker who may be contacted at 941-312-9169 or by e-mail at bglanz@ barbara glanz.com. Her Web site is www.barbaraglanz.com.

5. Don Medley, *The Book of Luke* (Nashville: RA Publishing, 2004). Don Medley is an attorney who may be contacted at 601-544-8110.

CHAPTER 9: "I Can't Go There—It'll Start All Over Again"
Choice #9: Avoidance or Courage

1. *Diagnostic and Statistical Manual of Mental Disorders (DSM-IV)* (District of Columbia: American Psychiatric Association, 1994).

2. Bobby Rush's career as a blues legend spans fifty years. Bobby's Web site is www.bobbyrush.net. Booking for Bobby is handled by Frank Beaty, Beaty Four Entertainment, Inc., 702-880-7911.

3. Proverbs 18:21.

4. Joshua 1:6; Isaiah 43:1-3; Philippians 4:13.

5. Rosemarie Rossetti, Ph. D., "Having the Courage to Face Your Demons," 2000, http://www.rosemariespeaks.com. Used with permission.

CHAPTER 10: "They Say Everything Happens for a Reason"
Choice #10: Powerlessness or Purpose

1. Romans 8:28.

2. 2 Corinthians 4:3-4.

3. Psalm 23:4.

4. Don Medley, *The Book of Luke* (Nashville: RA Publishing, 2004).

5. "Make A Difference," © 2006 Beverly Smallwood and Vasti Jackson.

6. Mike Stewart is a professional speaker who may be reached at 770-512-0022 or by e-mail at Mike@StewartSalesDyna mics.com. Mike's Web site is StewartSalesDynamics.com. Article used with permission.
7. Michelle Nichols, interview with author, used by permission.

CONCLUSION: *Choosing Hope—One Step at a Time*
1. This story was first published in Judy Moon Denson and Beverly Smallwood, *KidSpiration: Out of the Mouths of Babes* (Pearl, MS: Quail Ridge, 1997).

About the Author

BEV SMALLWOOD, Ph.D., has been committed to her personal mission of bringing out the best in people throughout her 25-year career as a psychologist. She does this by (1) providing high-involvement "how-to" seminars and inspiring keynotes on resilience, leadership, and teamwork; (2) conducting retreats for individuals recovering from personal disappointment and tragedy; (3) working with individuals, couples, and families who want to rise above difficult circumstances and become their personal best; (4) consulting with organizations that want to attract, energize, and keep the best people; (5) writing articles and books that provide practical wisdom and action ideas; (6) writing motivational songs; and (7) working as a disaster mental health volunteer.

An active member of the National Speakers Association, Bev has worked with numerous professional associations; healthcare organizations; other "helping" organizations, banks, Fortune 500 companies; and city, county, and state governments.

Dr. Bev is also frequently interviewed by television, print, and radio media. She's been featured on CNN, MSNBC, Fox News, *The Mitch Albom Show*, CBS Radio, TalkAmerica, and in the *New York Times*, *USA Weekend*, *Self* Magazine, *Women's Health*, *Cosmopolitan*, and *Entrepreneur*.

Bev received her Ph.D. in Counseling Psychology in 1981 from the University of Southern Mississippi. She's continued to actively contribute to her profession, having been recognized by the Mississippi Psychological Association as "Fellow," for "outstanding, unusual, and sustained contributions to Psychology."

Dr. Bev says, "Writing this book has truly been a labor of love, born of a conviction that God called me to the task. It is my deepest hope that as you put these ideas to work, you will not only rise above the despair, you will rediscover a powerful sense of purpose."

Contact Dr. Bev Smallwood at 601-264-0890 or 877-226-5323. Or, e-mail her at Bev@DrBevSmallwood.com. Her website, www.DrBevSmallwood.com, has plenty of other resources to help you continue your journey.